Decision
Support Systems

Decision
Support Systems

Concepts and Resources
for Managers

Daniel J. Power

Q

QUORUM BOOKS
Westport, Connecticut • London

Library of Congress Cataloging-in-Publication Data

Power, Daniel J.
    Decision support systems : concepts and resources for managers / Daniel J. Power.
      p. cm.
    Includes bibliographical references and index.
    ISBN 1–56720–497–X (alk. paper)
    1. Decision support systems. 2. Decision making. I. Title.
    HD30.213.P69 2002
    658.4′03—dc21   2001048807

British Library Cataloguing in Publication Data is available.

Library of Congress Catalog Card Number: 2001048807
ISBN: 1–56720–497–X

First published in 2002

Quorum Books, 88 Post Road West, Westport, CT 06881
An imprint of Greenwood Publishing Group, Inc.
www.quorumbooks.com

Printed in the United States of America

The paper used in this book complies with the
Permanent Paper Standard issued by the National
Information Standards Organization (Z39.48–1984).

10 9 8 7 6 5 4 3 2 1

Copyright Acknowledgments

The author and publisher gratefully acknowledge permission for use of the following material:

Material from DSSResources.COM used by permission of D. J. Power and C. E. Power.

Microsoft screen shots reprinted by permission from Microsoft Corporation.

Contents

Tables and Figures

TABLES

FIGURES

Preface

Today, at the turn of the 21st century, many managers are using computers, business databases, and models to help make decisions. This is a positive change in behavior, and some evidence indicates the use of computers to support management decision making is entering a new and more sophisticated stage. The novelty of managers using computers is wearing off, and, more importantly, the capabilities of our support systems are beginning to match the expectations of managers. Decision Support Systems (DSS) are now both a business necessity and an opportunity to gain competitive advantage. This book tries to build on these positive changes and provide an updated exploration of computerized decision support systems.

Decision Support Systems: Concepts and Resources for Managers is only one part of an innovative knowledge resource for people interested in learning more about DSS. It is an extension and integration of materials at DSSResources.COM. The idea is to develop a book that is strong on concepts and theory with timely and up-to-date application examples, integrated with Web-based materials.

MISSION, AUDIENCE AND OBJECTIVES

The mission of both the book and DSSResources.COM is to help people increase their knowledge of how to use information technologies and software to improve decision making. The primary target audience is managers interested in investigating innovative Decision Support Systems.

My perspective at DSSResources.COM and in this book is both managerial and technical. In writing the chapters and collecting resources, my overriding concern has been to help people gain capabilities, knowledge, and skills that they can apply as they use and manage information systems and technologies. Some readers can apply the knowledge in this book to help build a DSS. Some readers may want to read additional, specialized books and work as decision support analysts; some may be assigned to DSS project teams; and others may help in managing a DSS or in training DSS users.

The primary focus of this book is helping people develop intellectual capabilities related to the design and development of DSS. The book also explores how DSS can support organization goals and how DSS impact organizations and managers. Throughout the book, DSS are defined broadly as interactive computer-based systems that help people use computer communications, data, documents, knowledge, and models to solve problems and make decisions. DSS are ancillary or auxiliary systems; they are not intended to replace skilled decision makers.

This book examines the design, development, and implementation of systems that support management decision making. The focus is on technology-based systems. After completing *Decision Support Systems: Concepts and Resources for Managers*, readers should:

- Have a more sophisticated understanding of how a DSS can help a company meet its objectives, including gaining a competitive advantage, increasing revenues and profits, decreasing expenses, providing better customer service, and improving decision making;
- Be better informed consumers of DSS and information technology resources, especially for end-user development of DSS applications;
- Know more about the Internet, the World Wide Web, its potential uses to support decision making, and its impact on decision behavior;
- Have more capabilities related to DSS design and development; and,
- Understand that Decision Support Systems are intended to support rather than replace decision makers.

The emphasis throughout the book is on making sense of a rapidly changing computing applications area. Both descriptive and prescriptive ideas are linked to an expanded component-driven DSS framework. The focus is heavily oriented to practice and applications, but, when possible, empirical results and theory are referred to in an attempt to create a more enduring context for the conclusions. Also, every effort has been made to find examples that are current and understandable.

In general, this is an "applications" book more than a "theory" book. It provides enough concrete detail to help people understand their experiences using DSS, and it has suggestions for people involved with DSS projects. Also, the book provides the knowledge and framework needed by people who want a general familiarity with current developments and with "what is possible."

OVERVIEW OF THE CONTENTS

Decision Support Systems: Concepts and Resources for Managers has 12 chapters. Chapter 1, titled "Supporting Business Decision Making," provides a rationale for studying about and understanding DSS and presents an expanded framework for categorizing DSS. Also, the chapter explains the differences between transaction processing systems and DSS.

"Gaining Competitive Advantage with Decision Support Systems" is the focus of Chapter 2. After reviewing some technology trends that provide new opportunities for building DSS, the chapter discusses how DSS can create a competitive advantage. A few classic examples of DSS that provided companies with a competitive advantage are summarized in the chapter.

Understanding business decision making and business decision processes is the key to building an effective DSS. Chapter 3, titled "Analyzing Business Decision Processes," explains fundamental concepts related to business decision making.

Chapter 4, "Designing and Developing Decision Support Systems," is a pivotal chapter that changes the focus of the book to more technical issues. Once the topic of building and buying DSS is raised and discussed in Chapter 4, the next chapter addresses the topic of greatest importance to DSS success, the user interface. In Chapter 5, "Designing and Evaluating DSS User Interfaces," various types of user interfaces are briefly reviewed. The goal is to examine guidelines for DSS user interfaces.

Chapter 6 is titled "Understanding DSS Architecture, Networking, and Security Issues," and it attempts to present a simplified introduction to extremely complex technical topics. The topics in this chapter are important for management-oriented and more technically savvy readers.

Chapters 7 through 11 provide more details and examples related to the categories in the expanded DSS framework. Each chapter provides a survey of what is possible and an introduction to technical issues for making an innovative DSS a reality. Chapter 7 focuses on "Implementing Communications-Driven and Group Decision Support Systems;" Chapter 8 is titled "Building Data and Document-Driven Decision Support Systems;" Chapter 9, "Building Knowledge-Driven DSS and Mining Data," examines two related technologies, management expert systems and data mining. Chapter 10 discusses "Building Model-Driven Decision Support Systems;" Chapter 11, titled "Building Web-Based and Interorganizational Decision Support Systems," examines the latest developments in decision support.

The concluding chapter of *Decision Support Systems: Concepts and Resources for Managers* is titled "Evaluating Decision Support System Projects." After reading the prior chapters, managers and aspiring managers may have some novel or interesting ideas for DSS. So, this chapter reviews and discusses tools and issues associated with evaluating proposed DSS projects. This book also includes a decision support readiness audit and a glossary of key decision support system terms.

Acknowledgments

This book is an evolutionary product of 35 years of research and theory development about Decision Support Systems. In particular, the prior work of Steven Alter, Eric Carlson, Gordon Davis, Vasant Dhar, Paul Gray, George Huber, Peter Keen, Michael S. Scott Morton, Ben Shneiderman, Ralph Sprague, Charles Stabell, Efraim Turban, and Hugh Watson have significantly impacted my thinking about DSS. I want to thank them, but the responsibility for misinterpreting or misunderstanding their perspectives and ideas is mine.

No book is possible without the help, assistance, and encouragement of many people. That is especially the case for *Decision Support Systems: Concepts and Resources for Managers.* My family, especially my wife Carol and my sons Alex, Ben, and Greg, have been an extraordinary help. Alex has been especially involved in the production of the various versions of the book. He has been an outstanding operations manager.

The staff at Greenwood Publishing and Quorum Books have been supportive and encouraging in completing this project. My editor Eric Valentine especially deserves my thanks for his persistence in making this project a reality. I also want to acknowledge the help of Nicole Cournoyer, Marsha Goldstein, and Margery Heffron.

Many students have helped with comments, research on content issues, and proofreading. I want to particularly acknowledge Nikole Hackett, Lucian Strong, Saksatit Svetarundra, Andrea Putman, and John Ting. Lucian brought his enthusiasm and curiosity to the project. Nikole helped with researching some case study examples and contributed some important ideas and materials that influenced my thinking on DSS and competitive advantage. Saksatit read chapters and influenced my thinking on model-driven DSS. Andrea worked on formatting and production of some materials. John worked on proofreading, research tasks, creating some figures, and creating the subject index.

My DSS colleagues who have sent me email and commented on materials at DSSResources.COM also deserve my thanks. I want to especially thank my colleagues in the University of Northern Iowa MIS group, Gary Baker, Shashidar Kaparthi, Rex Karsten, Roberta Roth, and Leslie Wilson. Their encouragement and support for this project has made the effort much easier. Finally, I want to especially thank my colleagues Garrett A. Bozylinsky, Janyl Mukashova, and Gerald F. Smith. Their comments and suggestions about an earlier version of the book were both useful and stimulating.

I also want to thank my contacts at the following vendors who provided me information that has helped in the development of this book: Alphablox, Inc., arcplan, Artemis Intl., Brio, Inc., Business Objects, Inc., Comshare, Inc., DataBeacon, Inc., Decisioneering, Inc., Dimensional Insight, Inc., Expert Choice, Inc., Facet Decision Making, Microstrategy, Inc., Nucleus Research, and Palisade Corp.

Decision Support Systems: Concepts and Resources for Managers is the product of more than five years of effort. Versions of the chapters have been used in a specialized course in DSS for undergraduate MIS majors and in more managerial MIS courses for MBA students and senior undergraduate business majors. My students who have used various drafts of the book deserve special thanks for their patience and goodwill.

Chapter 1

Supporting Business Decision Making

INTRODUCTION

Beginning in the late 1970s, many vendors, practitioners, and academics promoted the development of computer-based Decision Support Systems (DSS). Their actions created high expectations for DSS and generated much optimism about the prospects for improving decision making. Despite the buildup and excitement, the success rate of decision support applications has been unsatisfactory. Although the computing industry has transformed how business transactions and data are processed, managers have frequently been disappointed by attempts to use computers and information technology to support decision making (cf., Drucker, 1998). Recently, because of technological developments, managers have become more enthusiastic about implementing innovative decision support projects. This attitude change is a positive development, but both managers and Management Information Systems (MIS) practitioners need to discuss and review their expectations about Decision Support Systems before beginning new projects.

According to Sprague and Carlson (1982), "DSS comprise a class of information system that draws on transaction processing systems and interacts with the other parts of the overall information system to support the decision-making activities of managers and other knowledge workers in organizations" (p. 9). Decision Support Systems are defined broadly in this book as interactive computer-based systems that help people use computer communications, data, documents, knowledge, and models to solve problems and make decisions. DSS are ancillary or auxiliary systems; they are not intended to replace skilled decision makers.

Decision Support Systems should be considered when two assumptions seem reasonable: first, good information is likely to improve decision making;

and second, managers need and want computerized decision support. Anecdotes and research show that some computer-based DSS can provide managers with analytical capabilities and information that improves decision making.

In pursuing the goal of improving decision making, many different types of computerized DSS have been built to help decision teams and individual decision makers. Some systems provide structured information directly to managers. Other systems can help managers and staff specialists analyze situations using various types of models. Some DSS store knowledge and make it available to managers. Some systems support decision making by small and large groups. Companies even develop DSS to support the decision making of their customers and suppliers.

Today, e-business technologies are transforming business transactions, and similar technologies can transform and improve decision activities. This book discusses how computing, the World-Wide Web, and information technologies can support and improve business and managerial decision making. This chapter begins with a short history of Decision Support and Management Information Systems; and then examines the DSS concept. Based on that analysis, a revised framework for categorizing DSS is proposed and discussed. Finally, the revised DSS framework is linked to the traditional components of a Decision Support System. The last section previews the topics in subsequent chapters.

A BRIEF HISTORY OF DECISION SUPPORT SYSTEMS

Prior to 1965, it was very expensive to build large-scale information systems. At about this time, the development of the IBM System 360 and other more powerful mainframe systems made it more practical and cost-effective to develop Management Information Systems (MIS) in large companies. MIS focused on providing managers with structured, periodic reports. Much of the information was from accounting and transaction systems.

In the late 1960s, a new type of information system became practical—model-oriented DSS or management decision systems. Two DSS pioneers, Peter Keen and Charles Stabell, claim the concept of decision support evolved from "the theoretical studies of organizational decision making done at the Carnegie Institute of Technology during the late 1950s and early '60s and the technical work on interactive computer systems, mainly carried out at the Massachusetts Institute of Technology in the 1960s" (Keen and Scott Morton, 1978, preface).

In 1971, Michael S. Scott Morton's book, *Management Decision Systems: Computer-Based Support for Decision Making,* was published. In 1968–1969 Scott Morton studied how computers and analytical models could help managers make a key decision. He conducted an experiment in which marketing and production managers actually used a Management Decision System (MDS) to coordinate production planning for laundry equipment. Scott Morton's research was a pioneering implementation, definition, and research test of a model-based decision support system.

T.P. Gerrity, Jr. focused on DSS design issues in his 1971 *Sloan Management Review* article, "The Design of Man-Machine Decision Systems: An Application to Portfolio Management." His system was designed to support investment managers in their daily administration of a client's stock portfolio. DSS for portfolio management have become very sophisticated since Gerrity began his research.

In 1974, Gordon Davis, a professor at the University of Minnesota, published his influential text on MIS. He asserted that the MIS concept was "a substantial extension of the concepts of managerial accounting taking into consideration the ideas and techniques of management science and the behavioral theories of management and decision making" (p. 8).

Davis defined a Management Information System as "an integrated, man/machine system for providing information to support the operations, management, and decision-making functions in an organization. The systems utilize computer hardware and software, manual procedures, management and decision models, and a database" (p. 5). His book helped create a broad foundation for DSS research and practice. Management information systems were providing fact-based decision support reports.

By 1975, J. D. C. Little was expanding the frontiers of computer-supported modeling. Little's DSS, called Brandaid, was designed to support product, promotion, pricing, and advertising decisions. Also, Little (1970) in an earlier article identified criteria for designing models and systems to support management decision making. His four criteria included robustness, ease of control, simplicity, and completeness of relevant detail. All four criteria remain relevant in evaluating modern DSS.

Peter G. W. Keen and Michael Scott Morton's DSS textbook (1978) provided a comprehensive behavioral orientation to DSS analysis, design, implementation, evaluation, and development. In 1980, Steven Alter published his MIT doctoral dissertation results in an influential book titled *Decision Support Systems: Current Practice and Continuing Challenge*. Alter's research expanded the framework for our thinking about management DSS. Also, his case studies provided a firm descriptive foundation for identifying DSS.

Bonczek, Holsapple, and Whinston (1981) created a theoretical framework for understanding the issues associated with designing knowledge-oriented DSS. Their book showed how Artificial Intelligence and Expert Systems technologies were relevant to developing DSS. Also, they identified four essential "aspects" or components that seemed common to all DSS:

1. A language system (LS) that specifies all messages a specific DSS can accept;
2. A presentation system (PS) for all messages a DSS can emit;
3. A knowledge system (KS) for all knowledge a DSS has; and
4. A problem-processing system (PPS) that is the "software engine" that tries to recognize and solve problems during the use of a specific DSS.

Ralph Sprague and Eric Carlson's (1982) book *Building Effective Decision Support Systems* was an important milestone. It provided a practical, understandable overview of how organizations could and should build DSS. Although the book probably created some unrealistic expectations, the problems stemmed more from the limits of existing technologies for building DSS than the limits of the concepts Sprague and Carlson presented.

In the mid-1980s, academic researchers developed software to support group decision making (cf., DeSanctis and Gallupe, 1987; Huber, 1984). Since that time, many research studies have examined the impacts and consequences of Group Decision Support Systems (GDSS). Also, a number of companies have commercialized GDSS and groupware.

Executive Information Systems (EIS) evolved from the single-user model-driven decision support systems and improved relational database products. The first EIS used predefined information screens and were maintained by analysts for senior executives. Beginning in about 1990, business intelligence, data warehousing and On-Line Analytical Processing (OLAP) software began broadening the capabilities of DSS (cf., Dhar and Stein, 1997).

In the early 1990s, a shift occurred from mainframe-based data-driven DSS to client/server DSS. Some desktop OLAP tools were introduced at this time. In 1992–1993, some vendors recommended object-oriented technology for building "re-usable" decision support capabilities. Also, some of the first data warehouses were completed. In 1994, many companies started to upgrade their network infrastructures. Database Management System (DBMS) vendors changed their focus from On-Line Transaction Processing (OLTP) and "recognized that decision support was different from OLTP and started implementing real OLAP capabilities into their databases" (Powell, 2001).

In 1995, data warehousing and the World Wide Web began to impact practitioners and academics interested in decision support technologies. Many companies purchased enterprise resource planning (ERP) applications. Independent data marts were popular alternatives to data warehouses.

Corporate intranets were initially developed in the mid-1990s to support information exchange and knowledge management. The primary decision support tools in use in 1996 included ad hoc query and reporting tools and quantitative models.

By 1997, according to Powell, "The data warehouse became the cornerstone of an integrated knowledge environment that provided a higher level of information sharing across an organization, enabling faster and better decision making." In approximately 1998, enterprise performance management and balanced scorecard systems were introduced to update the executive information systems of the 1970s and 1980s.

As the millennium approached, the rush was on by the laggards to introduce new Web-based analytical applications. Also, many vendors upgraded their Web-based analytical applications and business intelligence solutions.

In 2000 and 2001, application service providers (ASPs) began hosting some application software and some of the technical infrastructure for decision support capabilities. Decision support has gone full-circle and returned at least partially to the time-sharing DSS of the late 1970s. More sophisticated decision portals have also been introduced that combine information portals, knowledge management, business intelligence, and communications-driven DSS in an integrated Web environment.

A more detailed history on the origins of OLAP products, written by Nigel Pendse (1999), is available on the Web at URL http://www.olapreport.com/. Pendse traces multidimensional analysis and OLAP to the APL programming language, Express, and Comshare's System W. He claims the first Executive Information System product was Pilot Software's Command Center. Table 1.1 summarizes some major developments in the history of Decision Support Systems.

Evolution of DSS Concepts			
1960s	**1970s**	**1980s**	**1990s**
MIS and Structured Reports	BrandAid	Key Books	Business Intelligence
			Data Warehouses
		GDSS	Data mining
Interactive Systems Research	MDS	EIS	OLAP
		Expert Systems	
Theory Development			Portals

Table 1.1 Evolution of DSS Concepts

Today, a number of academic disciplines provide the substantive foundations for DSS development and research. Database research has contributed tools and research on managing data and documents. Management Science and Operations Research have developed mathematical models for use in model-driven DSS and provided evidence on the advantages of modeling in problem solving. Cognitive Science, especially Behavioral Decision Making research, has provided descriptive and empirical information that has assisted in DSS design and has generated hypotheses for decision support research. Some other important fields related to DSS include artificial intelligence, human-computer interaction, software engineering, and telecommunications. The history of DSS is relatively brief, but the concepts and technologies are still evolving. In fact, the Internet and Web have sped up developments in decision support and have made it hard to keep up with the rapid changes in DSS capabilities.

A CONCEPTUAL PERSPECTIVE

By the late 1970s, a number of companies had developed interactive information systems that used data and models to help managers analyze semistructured problems. These diverse systems were all called DSS. From those early days, it was recognized that DSS could be designed to support decision makers at any level in an organization. DSS could support operations, financial management, and strategic decision making. Over the years, many of the more interesting DSS have been targeted for middle and senior managers. DSS are also often designed for specific types of organizations like hospitals, banks, or insurance companies. These specialized systems are sometimes referred to as vertical market or industry-specific DSS.

DSS are both off-the-shelf, packaged applications and custom designed systems. DSS may support a manager using a single personal computer or a large group of managers in a networked client-server or Web environment. These latter systems are often called enterprise-wide DSS.

Characteristics of DSS

Although the term "Decision Support System" has many connotations, based on Steven Alter's (1980) pioneering research, we can identify the following three major characteristics:

1. DSS are designed specifically to facilitate decision processes,
2. DSS should support rather than automate decision making, and
3. DSS should be able to respond quickly to the changing needs of decision makers.

Clyde Holsapple and Andrew Whinston (1996) identified characteristics one should expect to observe in a DSS (see pages 144–145). Their list is very general and somewhat abstract, but it provides an even broader perspective on the DSS concept. Holsapple and Whinston specify that a DSS must have a body of knowledge, a record-keeping capability that can present knowledge on an ad hoc basis in various customized ways as well as in standardized reports, a capability for selecting a desired subset of stored knowledge for either presentation or for deriving new knowledge, and must be designed to interact directly with a decision maker in such a way that the user has a flexible choice and sequence of knowledge-management activities.

Sprague and Carlson (1982) and others define DSS broadly as interactive computer-based systems that help decision makers use data and models to solve ill-structured, unstructured or semi-structured problems. Bonczek, Holsapple and Whinston (1981) argued that the "system must possess an interactive query facility, with a query language that ... is ... easy to learn and use" (p. 19). Various types of DSS help decision makers use and manipulate very large databases; some help managers apply checklists and rules; others make extensive use of mathematical models.

Many terms are used for specific types of DSS, including "business intelligence," "collaborative systems," "data mining," "data warehousing," "knowledge management," and "on-line analytical processing." Software vendors use these more specialized terms for both descriptive and marketing purposes. What term we use for a system or software package is a secondary concern. Our primary concern should be finding software and systems that meet a manager's decision support needs and provide appropriate management information.

Management Information Needs

Managers and their support staffs need to consider what information and analyses are actually needed to support their management and business activities. Some managers need both detailed transaction data and summarized transaction data. Most managers only want summaries of transactions.

Managers usually want lots of charts and graphs; a few only want tables of numbers. Many managers want information provided routinely or periodically and some want information available on-line and on demand. Managers usually want financial analyses, and some managers want primarily "soft," nonfinancial or qualitative information.

In general, an Information System can provide business transaction information, and it can help managers understand many business operations and performance issues. For example, a computerized system can help managers understand the status of operations, monitor business results, review customer preference data, and investigate competitor actions. In all of these situations, management information and analyses should have a number of characteristics. Information must be both timely and current. These characteristics mean the information is up-to-date and available when managers want it. Also, management information must be accurate, relevant, and complete. Finally, managers want information presented in a format that assists them in making decisions. In general, management information should be summarized and concise, and any support system should have an option for managers to obtain more detailed information.

In summary, DSS must provide current, timely information and analyses that are accurate, relevant, and complete. A specific DSS must present information in an appropriate format that is easy to understand and manipulate. The information presented by a DSS may result from analysis of transaction data, it may be the result of a decision model, or it may have been gathered from external sources. DSS can present internal and external facts, informed opinions, and forecasts to managers. As many others have noted, *managers want the right information, at the right time, in the right format, and at the right cost.* These system requirements seem simple and straightforward, but meeting them remains a challenge.

DSS versus MIS

Is a DSS an MIS? How does a Decision Support System differ from a Management Information System? One can begin drawing distinctions between these two terms by first examining the concepts Management Information System (MIS) and Information System (IS). Many authors have used the term "MIS" to describe a broad, general category of information systems. Also, MIS and IS are used interchangeably to describe a functional department in companies and organizations responsible for managing information systems and technology. A number of computing jobs are grouped together under the heading of MIS or IS professionals. Finally, the term "Management Information Systems" or "MIS" is used to identify an academic major and an area of scholarly inquiry in universities.

In the 1970s, an MIS generated periodic management reports. Today, managers use data-driven DSS to meet their management reporting needs. When the term "Management Information System" is defined narrowly, it refers to a management reporting system that provides periodic, structured, paper-based reports. In contrast, data-driven DSS are intended to be interactive, real-time systems that are responsive to unplanned, as well as planned, information requests and reporting needs. Model-driven DSS are usually focused on modeling a specific decision or a set of related decisions (cf., Power, 1997).

DSS include a wide variety of analytical information systems. DSS provide managers more control of their data, access to analytical tools, and capabilities for consulting and interacting with a distributed group of staff. An enterprise-wide DSS is linked to a large data warehouse and serves many managers within one company. Also, a DSS is defined as an interactive system in a networked environment that helps a targeted group of managers make decisions. The primary focus in the following discussion is on various types of DSS. The term MIS will be used sparingly and will usually refer broadly to an information system that provides managers with on-line access to information.

DECISION SUPPORT VS. TRANSACTION PROCESSING SYSTEMS

Development of Decision Support Systems is one of the rapidly changing frontiers in the application of computers in organizations. One reason we study DSS is to understand how they differ from other systems. We have successfully implemented computer-based Transaction Processing Systems (TPS), but knowledge of building these operational systems is not adequate to create effective DSS. So if DSS are to be successfully designed, developed, and implemented, then both managers and many MIS professionals need a more sophisticated technical and philosophical understanding of DSS.

Technology is creating new decision support capabilities, but much learning and discussion needs to occur to successfully exploit the technological possibilities. DSS differ in many ways from operating systems that process business transactions. For example, a popular system that has been widely implemented is called Enterprise Resource Planning (ERP). ERP is *not* a Decision Support System even though the term suggests that decision making and planning will be improved. In general, ERP is an integrated TPS that facilitates the flow of information between the functional areas of a business. Recently, DSS have been built that help managers analyze data from ERP systems. The implementation of ERP systems has made it much easier to create a enterprise-wide data-driven DSS.

A major difference between TPS and DSS is the general purpose of each type of system. TPS are designed to expedite and automate transaction processing, record keeping, and simple business reporting of transactions. DSS are intended to assist in decision making and decision implementation. Transaction processing is, however, related to the design of DSS because transaction databases often provide data for decision-oriented reporting systems and data warehouses.

Transaction Processing Systems usually provide standard reports on a periodic basis and support the operations of a company. DSS are used on demand when they are needed to support decision making. A manager typically initiates each instance of DSS use, either by using the DSS herself or by asking a staff intermediary to use a DSS. Clerical employees, and some managers, use TPS to support operations. Line managers and support staff are the primary users of DSS. TPS record current information and maintain a database of transaction information. DSS generally use historical internal and external data for analysis. DSS may focus on quantitative analysis and modeling current and future scenarios. TPS emphasize data integrity and consistency; and although both of these qualities are important in every system, the primary emphasis for a DSS is on flexibility and on conducting analyses and retrieving decision-relevant information and knowledge.

One can draw many distinctions between TPS and DSS, but analysts and managers need to stay focused on the phrase "decision support" in the term "Decision Support System." DSS are intended to improve and speed up the processes by which people make and communicate decisions. Thus, the emphasis in building a DSS is on increasing individual and organizational decision-making effectiveness rather than on increasing efficiency in processing operating data.

CATEGORIZING DSS APPLICATIONS AND PRODUCTS

Hundreds of DSS applications are described in professional journals like *Interfaces* (cf., Eom, Lee, Somarajan, and Kim, 1997) and in IS trade publications like *Information Week* (http://www.informationweek.com). Many DSS case studies are also available on the World Wide Web at vendor Web sites and at DSSResources.COM. This section lists some DSS examples and summarizes some relevant frameworks and taxonomies for categorizing DSS.

One of the long-standing conclusions that comes from reading DSS case studies is that what managers, vendors, and consultants call DSS can "take on many different forms and can be used in many different ways" (Alter, 1980, p. 71). DSS certainly vary in many ways. Some DSS focus on data, some on models, and some on communications. DSS also differ in scope: some DSS are intended for one "primary" user and used "stand-alone" for analysis, and others are intended for many users in an organization. Also, DSS differ in terms of who uses a specific system; that is, some DSS are used by actual decision makers, and some are used by intermediaries like marketing analysts or financial analysts. If a computerized system is not a TPS, and if a manager uses it, many observers will be tempted to call the system a DSS.

Some examples show the wide variety of DSS applications. Major airlines use DSS for many tasks including pricing and route selection. Many companies have DSS that aid in corporate planning and forecasting. Specialists often use these DSS that focus on financial and simulation models. DSS can help monitor costs and revenues and track department budgets. Also, investment evaluation and support systems are increasingly common. Frito-Lay has a DSS that aids in pricing, advertising, and promotion. Route salesmen use handheld computers to support decision-making activities.

Many manufacturing companies use Manufacturing Resources Planning (MRP) software. This specific, operational-level DSS supports master production scheduling, purchasing, and material requirements planning. More recent MRP systems support "what-if" analysis and simulation capabilities. DSS support quality improvement and control decisions. Monsanto, FedEx, and most transportation companies use DSS for scheduling trucks, airplanes, and ships. The Coast Guard uses a DSS for procurement decisions. Companies like Wal-Mart have large data warehouses and use data mining software. Business Intelligence and Knowledge Management Systems are increasingly common. On the World Wide Web one can find DSS that help track and manage stock portfolios, choose stocks, plan trips, and suggest gifts. DSS can support distributed-decision activities, using groupware and a corporate intranet. The following paragraphs provide more details on four decision support applications:

Federal Express has business intelligence capabilities for 700 end-users. FedEx created a central, integrated data warehouse hub, which provides Web-based, real-time access to financial and logistical information necessary for planning and decision making. Most access is from browsers over the corporate intranet, along with some standard client/server deployments using Excel spreadsheets.

In 1997, ShopKo developed a "Merchandise Data Warehouse." The main strategy in developing a decision support tool was to allow ShopKo associates to make ad hoc queries and prepare reports. ShopKo extended its DSS capabilities to its store units by using a Web-based DSS.

According to a MicroStrategy case example, the U.S. Air Force developed a decision support application called the Base Closure and Analysis DSS. It provided a common framework for analyzing the impact of various base closure scenarios. The software used a model to evaluate the relative impact of closing each base. Using the DSS, committee members could perform analyses using eight main criteria and 212 subcriteria on which all bases were evaluated. These criteria, specified by the U.S. Department of Defense (DOD), focused on elements that affected operational effectiveness, including such items as alternate airfield availability, weather data, and facility infrastructure capacity.

Also at DOD, during the weeks leading up to and immediately following January 1, 2000, approximately 150 people participated in crisis management activities, 24 hours a day, 7 days a week. An "off-the-shelf" decision support product, GroupSystemsOnLine, was used to communicate information and provide input, discuss solutions, and create reports of recommended action (cf., http://www.groupsystems.com).

Alter's Taxonomy

In 1977, Steven Alter proposed a taxonomy of DSS. The next few paragraphs summarize his taxonomy and discuss some of the key issues for each type of DSS. Alter's taxonomy is based on the degree to which DSS output can directly determine the decision. The taxonomy is related to a spectrum of generic operations that can be performed by DSS. These generic operations extend along a single dimension, ranging from extremely data-oriented to extremely model-oriented. DSS may involve retrieving a single item of information, providing a mechanism for ad hoc data analysis, or providing prespecified aggregations of data in the form of reports or "screens." DSS may also include estimating the consequences of proposed decisions and proposing decisions.

Alter's idea (cf., 1977, 1980) was that a DSS could be categorized in terms of the generic operations it performs, independent of type of problem, functional area, or decision perspective. Alter conducted a field study of 56 DSS that he categorized into seven distinct types. These include:

- **File drawer systems** that provide access to data items. Examples include real-time equipment monitoring, inventory reorder, and monitoring systems. Simple query and reporting tools that access OLTP fall into this category.
- **Data analysis systems** that support the manipulation of data by computerized tools tailored to a specific task and setting or by more general tools and operators. Examples include budget analysis and variance monitoring, and analysis of investment opportunities. Most data warehouse applications would be categorized as data analysis systems.
- **Analysis information systems** that provide access to a series of decision-oriented databases and small models. Examples include sales forecasting based on a marketing database, competitor analyses, and product planning and analysis. OLAP systems fall into this category.
- **Accounting and financial models** that calculate the consequences of possible actions. Examples include estimating profitability of a new product; analysis of operational plans using a goal-seeking capability, break-even analysis, and generating estimates of income statements and balance sheets. These types of models should be used with "What if?" or sensitivity analysis.
- **Representational models** that estimate the consequences of actions on the basis of simulation models that include causal relationships and accounting definitions. Examples include a market response model, risk analysis models, and equipment and production simulations.
- **Optimization models** that provide guidelines for action by generating an optimal solution consistent with a series of constraints. Examples include scheduling systems, resource allocation, and material usage optimization.
- **Suggestion models** that perform the logical processing leading to a specific suggested decision for a fairly structured or well-understood task. Examples include insurance renewal rate calculation, an optimal bond-bidding model, a log-cutting DSS, and credit scoring.

An understandable taxonomy like Steven Alter's helps reduce the confusion for managers who are investigating and discussing DSS. The taxonomy also helps users and developers communicate their experiences with DSS.

Other Taxonomies or Frameworks

Holsapple and Whinston (1996) identified five specialized types of DSS (see pp. 178-195). First, they identified an evolving group of systems they called text-oriented DSS. This type of DSS supports a decision maker by electronically keeping track of textually represented knowledge that could affect decisions. This type of system supports document creation, revision, viewing, searching, and hypertext links. Holsapple and Whinston also discuss database-oriented DSS, spreadsheet-oriented DSS, solver-oriented DSS, and rule-oriented DSS. A solver is a general algorithm that can be customized to solve a specific instance of a more general class of problems. These last four types of DSS match up well with Alter's categories.

Donovan and Madnick (1977) classified DSS as either institutional or ad hoc DSS. Institutional DSS support decisions that are recurring. Institutional DSS are often integrated in business decision processes. An ad hoc DSS supports problems that are not anticipated and that are not necessarily expected to reoccur. Ad hoc DSS are often used for special analytical studies in companies. Hackathorn and Keen (1981) identified DSS in three distinct yet interrelated categories: Personal DSS, Group DSS and Organizational DSS. These three categories identify differences in who the intended users are for a particular DSS. Many DSS are designed for a particular problem in a particular company, but some DSS are generic DSS generators or "ready-made" DSS for particular applications like budgeting (cf., Turban and Aronson, 1998). Golden, Hevner, and Power (1986) identified decision insight systems as a particular category of model-oriented DSS that uses decision analysis tools to help decision makers structure decision situations and gain insight about possible solutions. All of the above categories provide adjectives to help describe a specific DSS or decision support product.

AN EXPANDED DECISION SUPPORT SYSTEM FRAMEWORK

The terms "frameworks," "taxonomies," "conceptual models," and "typologies" are often used interchangeably. Each can be used to help classify objects and to show how mutually exclusive types of things are related. The idea is to create a set of labels that help people organize and categorize information. Sprague and Watson (1996) argue typologies, frameworks, or conceptual models are "often crucial to the understanding of a new or complex subject." A good set of categories should show the parts of a topic and explain how the parts interrelate. "Framework" seems like the broadest and most general term to use for a classification system. This section provides a framework or scheme for categorizing the large number of computerized systems that support decision making.

A broader framework than Alter's is needed today because DSS are much more diverse than when he conducted his research and proposed his taxonomy. His seven categories are still relevant for identifying some, but not all, types of DSS. To keep the number of categories in a new framework manageable, one should simplify Alter's 1980 taxonomy (p. 73) into three types of DSS: data-driven, model-driven, and knowledge-driven DSS. One can and should continue to categorize DSS in terms of intended users, purpose, and enabling technology. The following expanded DSS framework helps categorize the most common DSS currently in use (cf., Power, 2001). Some DSS are hybrid systems driven by more than one major DSS component or subsystem. The framework focuses on one major dimension with five categories and three secondary dimensions. The term "driven" is used as a common or shared descriptive adjective in the expanded framework. "Driven" refers to the tool or component that is providing the dominant functionality in the Decision Support System.

Data-Driven DSS

The first category of DSS, data-driven DSS, emphasizes analysis of large amounts of structured data. These systems include file drawer and management reporting systems, data warehousing and analytical systems, Executive Information Systems, and Spatial DSS (SDSS). EIS are targeted to senior managers, and SDSS display spatial data for decision support. Business Intelligence (BI) systems are also examples of data-driven DSS. A data-driven DSS provides access to and manipulation of large databases of structured data and, especially, a time-series of internal company and external data. Simple file systems accessed by query and retrieval tools provide the most elementary level of functionality, including aggregation and simple calculations. Data warehouse systems that allow the manipulation of data by computerized tools tailored to a specific task and setting or by more general tools and operators provide additional functionality. Data-driven DSS with On-Line Analytical Processing provide the highest level of functionality and decision support that is linked to analysis of large collections of historical data (cf., Dhar and Stein, 1997).

Model-Driven DSS

A second category, model-driven DSS, includes systems that use accounting and financial models, representational models, and optimization models. Model-driven DSS emphasize access to and manipulation of a model. Simple statistical and analytical tools provide the most elementary level of functionality. Some OLAP systems that allow complex analysis of data may be classified as hybrid DSS systems providing modeling, data retrieval, and data summarization functionality. Model-driven DSS use data and parameters provided by decision makers to aid them in analyzing a situation, but they are not usually data intensive. Very large databases are usually not needed for model-driven DSS, but data for a specific analysis may need to be extracted from a large database.

Knowledge-Driven DSS

The terminology for this category of DSS is still evolving. Currently, the best term seems to be "knowledge-driven" DSS. Sometimes it seems equally appropriate to use Alter's term "Suggestion DSS" or the narrower term "Management Expert System." Knowledge-driven DSS suggest or recommend actions to managers. They use business rules and knowledge bases. These DSS are person-computer systems with specialized problem-solving expertise. The "expertise" consists of knowledge about a particular domain, understanding of problems within that domain, and "skill" at solving some of these problems. A related concept is "data mining." This term refers to a class of analytical applications that search for hidden patterns in a database. Data mining is the process of sifting through large amounts of data to produce data content relationships. Tools used for building these systems are also called Intelligent Decision Support methods (cf., Dhar and Stein, 1997). Data mining tools can be used to create hybrid data-driven and knowledge-driven DSS.

Document-Driven DSS

A new type of DSS, a document-driven DSS, is evolving to help managers gather, retrieve, classify and manage unstructured documents, including Web pages. A document-driven DSS integrates a variety of storage and processing technologies to provide complete document retrieval and analysis. The Web provides access to large document databases including databases of hypertext documents, images, sounds, and video. Examples of documents that would be accessed by a document-driven DSS are policies and procedures, product specifications, catalogs, and corporate historical documents, including minutes of meetings, corporate records, and important correspondence. A search engine is a powerful decision-aiding tool associated with a document-driven DSS (cf., Fedorowicz, 1993). Some authors call this type of system a Knowledge Management System.

Communications-Driven and Group DSS

Group Decision Support Systems (GDSS) and groupware came first, but now a broader category of communications-driven DSS can be identified. This type of DSS includes communication, collaboration, and decision support technologies that do not fit within those DSS types identified by Alter. Therefore, communications-driven DSS need to be identified as a specific category of DSS. It seems appropriate to call these systems communications-driven DSS even though many people are more familiar with the term GDSS. A GDSS is best viewed as a hybrid DSS that emphasizes both the use of communications technologies and decision process models. A GDSS is an interactive computer-based system intended to facilitate the solution of problems by decision makers working together as a group. Groupware supports electronic communication, scheduling, document sharing, and other group productivity and decision support activities. A number of technologies and capabilities are included in this category in the framework – GDSS, decision rooms, two-way interactive video, white boards, bulletin boards, chat and e-mail systems.

Interorganizational or Intraorganizational DSS

A relatively new category of DSS made possible by new technologies and the rapid growth of the public Internet is interorganizational DSS. These DSS serve a company's customers or suppliers. The public Internet is creating communication links for many types of interorganizational systems, including DSS. An interorganizational DSS provides stakeholders with access to a company's intranet and authority or privileges to use specific DSS capabilities. Companies can make a data-driven DSS available to suppliers or a model-driven DSS available to customers to design a product or choose a product. Most DSS are intraorganizational DSS that are designed for use by individuals in a company as "stand-alone DSS" or for use by a group of managers in a company as a group or enterprise-wide DSS. The prefix "intra" means the DSS is used within a specific organization; "inter" means the DSS is used more widely.

Function-Specific or General Purpose DSS

Many DSS are designed to support specific business functions or types of businesses and industries. We can call such DSS function-specific or industry-specific DSS. A function-specific DSS, like a budgeting system, may be purchased from a vendor or customized in-house using a more general-purpose development package. Vendor developed or "off-the-shelf" DSS support functional areas of a business like marketing or finance; some DSS products are designed to support decision tasks in a specific industry, such as a crew-scheduling DSS for an airline. A task-specific DSS has an important purpose in solving a routine or recurring decision task. Function or task-specific DSS can be further classified and understood in terms of the dominant DSS component, that is, as a model-driven, data-driven or knowledge-driven DSS. A function or task-specific DSS holds and derives knowledge relevant for a decision about some function that an organization performs (e.g., a marketing or a production function). DSS can be categorized by purpose: function-specific DSS help a person or group accomplish a specific decision task; general-purpose DSS software helps support broad tasks like project management, decision analysis, or business planning. Some general-purpose DSS actually help create task-specific DSS. Such systems have been called DSS generators.

Web-Based DSS

All of the above types of DSS can be implemented using Web technologies. When the enabling technology used to build a DSS is the Internet and Web, it seems appropriate to call the system a Web-based DSS. A Web-based DSS is a computerized system that delivers decision support information or decision support tools to a manager or decision support analyst using a "thin-client" Web browser like Netscape Navigator or Internet Explorer (Power, 2000). The computer server hosting the DSS application is linked to the user's computer by a network with the TCP/IP protocol. In many companies, a Web-based DSS is synonymous with an intranet or enterprise-wide DSS. A company intranet supports a large group of managers using Web browsers in a networked environment. Managers often have Web access to a data warehouse as part of an Information System architecture. Today, Web technologies are powerful tools for creating DSS and especially interorganizational DSS that support the decision making of customers and suppliers. Web or Internet technologies are the leading edge for building DSS, but some DSS will continue to be built using mainframe and client/server-enabling technologies.

Column one of Table 1.2 lists five broad categories of Decision Support Systems that differ in terms of the dominant decision support component, including communications-driven DSS, data-driven DSS, document-driven DSS, knowledge-driven DSS and model-driven DSS. Subsequent chapters explain these DSS categories in more detail and identify development and implementation issues. The expanded DSS framework also categorizes DSS by user groups—intraorganizational and interorganizational. The new category called interorganizational DSS helps one focus on the broadening of the DSS user group to include external stakeholders.

Dominant DSS Component	User Groups: Internal, External	Purpose: General, Specific	Enabling Technology
Communications **Communications-driven DSS**	Internal teams, now expanding	Conduct a meeting Bulletin board Help users collaborate	Web or Client/Server
Database **Data-driven DSS**	Managers, staff, now suppliers	Query a Data Warehouse	Main Frame, Client/Server, Web
Document base **Document-driven DSS**	Specialists and user group is expanding	Search Web pages Find documents	Web
Knowledge base **Knowledge-driven DSS**	Internal users, now customers	Management advice Choose products	Client/Server, Web
Models **Model-driven DSS**	Managers and staff, now customers	Crew scheduling Decision analysis	Stand-alone PC

Table 1.2   An Expanded DSS Framework

From a different perspective, DSS can be categorized by the purpose of the DSS. Many DSS have a narrow, focused, and specific purpose rather than a general purpose. Finally, DSS can be categorized by the basic enabling technology. The Web is an important new development arena for DSS, so it is crucial to examine and understand Web-based DSS. One can use the dominant DSS component, user group, purpose, and enabling technology to categorize a specific system. For example, a manager may want to build a model-driven, interorganizational, product design, Web-based DSS to support a business decision process. Another manager may want to build a data-driven, Web-based DSS to support senior executives in business operations monitoring and control.

BUILDING DECISION SUPPORT SYSTEMS

Traditionally, IS academics and practitioners have discussed building DSS in terms of four major components: 1) the user interface, 2) the database, 3) the models and analytical tools, and 4) the DSS architecture and network (cf., Sprague and Carlson, 1982). This traditional list of components remains useful because it identifies similarities and differences between categories or types of DSS, and it can help managers and analysts build new DSS. The expanded DSS framework is based on the different emphases placed on DSS components when a specific system is actually constructed (see Figure 1.1).

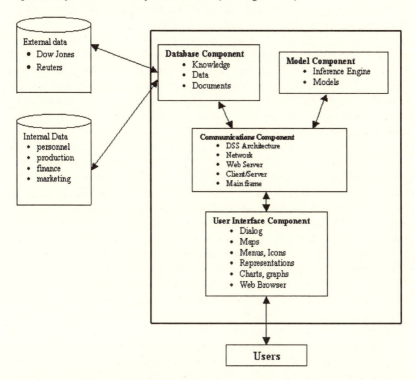

Figure 1.1 Traditional DSS Components

Data-driven, document-driven and knowledge-driven DSS need specialized database components. A model-driven DSS may use a simple flat-file database with fewer than 1,000 records, but the model component is very important and it provides the functionality. Experience, and some empirical evidence, indicates that design and implementation issues vary for data-driven, document-driven, model-driven and knowledge-driven DSS. Multiparticipant systems like group and interorganizational DSS also create complex implementation issues. For instance, when implementing a data-driven DSS, a designer should be especially concerned about the user's interest in applying the DSS in unanticipated or novel situations.

In creating an accounting or financial simulation model, a developer should attempt to verify that the initial input estimates for the model are thoughtful and reasonable. In developing a representational or optimization model, an analyst should be concerned about possible misunderstandings of what the model means and how it can or cannot be used (cf., Alter, 1980). Networking issues create challenges for many types of DSS, but especially for communications-driven systems with many participants, so-called multiparticipant systems. Today, architecture and networking issues are increasingly important in building DSS.

DSS should be built or implemented using an appropriate process. Many small, specialized model-driven DSS are built quickly. Large, enterprise-wide DSS are built using sophisticated tools and systematic and structured systems analysis and development approaches. Communications-driven and GDSS are usually purchased as "off-the-shelf" software and then implemented in a company. Creating enterprise-wide DSS environments remains an iterative and evolutionary task. As an enterprise-wide DSS grows, it inevitably becomes a major part of the overall information systems infrastructure of an organization. Despite the significant differences created by the specific task and scope of a DSS, all DSS have similar technical components and share a common purpose—supporting decision making.

A data-driven DSS database is often a collection of current and historical structured data from a number of sources that have been organized for easy access and analysis. The above framework expands the database component to include unstructured documents in document-driven DSS and "knowledge" in the form of rules in knowledge-driven DSS. Large databases of structured data in enterprise-wide DSS are often called data warehouses or data marts. Data-driven DSS usually use data that has been extracted from all relevant internal and external databases. Managing information often means managing a database. Supporting management decision making means that computerized tools are used to make sense of the structured data or documents in a database.

Mathematical and analytical models are the major component of a model-driven DSS. DSS models should be used and manipulated directly by managers and staff specialists. Each model-driven DSS has a specific set of purposes, and hence, different models are needed and used. Choosing appropriate models is a key design issue. Also, the software used for creating specific models needs to manage needed data and the user interface. In model-driven DSS the values of key variables or parameters are changed to reflect potential changes in supply, production, the economy, sales, the marketplace, costs, and/or other environmental and internal factors. Information from the models is then analyzed and evaluated by the decision-maker. Knowledge-driven DSS use special models, an inference engine, for processing rules or identifying relationships in data.

The communications component refers to how hardware is organized, how software and data are distributed in the system, and how components of the system are integrated and connected. A major issue today is whether DSS should be available, using a Web browser, on a company intranet and also available on the global Internet. Both managers and MIS staff need to develop an understanding of the technical issues and the security issues related to DSS architectures, networks, and the Internet. Networking and communications technology is the key driver of communications-driven DSS.

Managers and DSS analysts also need to emphasize the user interface component. In many ways it is the most important component of any DSS. The tools for building the user interface are sometimes termed DSS generators, query and reporting tools, and front-end development packages. Much of the DSS design and development effort should focus on building the user interface. It is important to remember that the screens and displays in the user interface heavily influence how a manager perceives a DSS and whether it is used. What one sees is the DSS.

CONCLUSIONS AND COMMENTARY

The rapid growth of the World Wide Web has created enormous opportunities for making more organizational information available to decision makers. Web architectures permit IS professionals to centralize and control information and yet easily distribute it in a timely manner to managers who need it. Also, the internal intranet is providing many opportunities for delivering information from data warehouses, models, and other tools to the desktop. Web-based DSS permit and encourage further analysis and collaboration. The technologies and software associated with DSS continue to change rapidly, and development tools are overlapping for some applications. In general, managers and IS staff need to recognize that the overall technological and social context of DSS and business management is changing.

The managers who are, and will be, using company intranets and the Internet are more technologically sophisticated than the managers of the past. They will have high expectations for DSS, but in many ways they will be much better customers of computerized decision support. Managers need broad knowledge of the managerial and technical issues associated with the various categories of DSS. MIS professionals need this same general knowledge, and they need specific skills in analysis, design and development of DSS.

The DSS design and development environment is changing as rapidly as the software tools and in as positive a direction. Web technologies will facilitate improved DSS tools at managers' desktops. The Web does not, however, solve all problems. In 1974, Gordon Davis wrote, "The application of computer technology and MIS concepts has produced some spectacular successes and also some rather expensive failures." Both successes and failures will continue to occur. Failures occur in leading edge application areas and for what turn out to be overly ambitious projects. A shortage of DSS professionals is also slowing development in some areas and increasing failures of innovative systems. Managers need to recognize that resistance to change and insufficient user involvement contributes to DSS project failure in some situations. Also, managers need to resolve political issues associated with building novel DSS and with providing greater access to management information. For example, senior managers need to address questions like: How should data be shared and how much data should be shared? Should all managers be required to use a DSS and support systems like e-mail?

Managers and MIS practitioners need to consider at least six major issues associated with building, implementing and using DSS. First, managers and MIS practitioners must determine what business and decision processes should be computerized. And in some situations one needs to ask what part of a process should be supported. It is also necessary to evaluate what ad hoc or on-demand information retrieval and analysis is needed. In many companies this broad purpose issue needs to be reexamined. Chapters 2 and 3 address this major issue. Second, one must ask what data should be captured in processes and how should it be stored and integrated? Continuing to rely on existing decision processes may limit the information that can be provided to decision makers. Chapter 4 discusses DSS design and development issues.

Third, one needs to ask how data should be processed and presented to support decision making. Chapter 5 emphasizes user interface design issues. Fourth, and perhaps the major issue, is whether current DSS are creating results that are "decision-impelling"? (based on Davis, 1974, p. 6). Chapters 7 to 11 review the possibilities for building innovative "decision-impelling" DSS.

Fifth, one needs to ask what information technology should be used for building DSS. Chapter 6 reviews DSS architecture and networking issues. Managers need some technical familiarity and sophistication to evaluate the wide-ranging set of technologies that are available for DSS applications. Sixth and finally, one must always ask why a project sponsor wants a proposed DSS. Understanding the various categories of DSS that can be built begins the task of rationally answering some of the above questions. Subsequent chapters provide more elaboration and some details of the expanded framework and on decision support technologies.

DSS are not a panacea for improving business decisions. Most people acknowledge that managers need "good" information to manage effectively, but a DSS is not always the solution for providing "good" information. A DSS can provide a competitive advantage and a company may need computerized decision support to remain competitive, but decision support capabilities are limited by the data that can be obtained, the cost of obtaining, processing, and storing the information, the cost of retrieval and distribution, the value of the information to the user, and the capability of managers to accept and act on the information. Our capabilities for supporting decision making have increased, but we still have very real technical, social, interpersonal, and political problems that must be overcome when we build a specific DSS (cf., Davis, 1974). Chapter 12 specifically discusses the evaluation of proposed DSS projects.

Chapter 2

Gaining Competitive Advantage with Decision Support Systems

INTRODUCTION

During the past 50 years, managers and MIS professionals have created many important transaction-oriented Strategic Information Systems (Callon, 1996; Neumann, 1994). These systems have significantly improved the processing of business transactions and created business advantages. In some organizations, the search for strategic opportunities remains focused on enhancing business transaction processing. This focus on business operations is too narrow. Although transaction processing can involve managerial decision-making, redesigning transaction processing systems (TPS) creates advantages that are very different from the advantages that can result from building a novel DSS. A Decision Support System meets different needs and serves different purposes than TPS. Managers need to recognize that innovative strategic decision support applications can provide substantial opportunities for targeting sales efforts, improving strategic control and improving profits. Information technology advances are creating new DSS capabilities that can and should be used to build innovative, specific DSS that yield competitive advantage for an organization.

Today, many companies have fragmented and isolated decision support capabilities that are hard to use and hard to access. For example, a data mart may have been built for analyzing customer data, a project management system may exist for tracking large-scale projects, or Excel analyses may be routinely used in a business decision process. Also, managers are experiencing information overload and are having difficulty finding the right information when it is needed.

You may be asking: Can a new or upgraded DSS really provide a competitive advantage to a company? A DSS can be a strategic information system, and a specific DSS can create a competitive advantage. Managers need to know when and why DSS are competitive weapons.

Evidence indicates managers can now use sophisticated data-driven and document-driven DSS to obtain information that was buried for many years in filing cabinets or archived on computer tapes. Model-driven DSS can reduce waste in production operations and improve inventory management. Knowledge-driven DSS can analyze cash register transaction data and help managers find relationships in consumer buying behavior that increase sales and inventory turnover. Communications-driven DSS can support teams working all over the world. Interorganizational DSS can support a company's suppliers and customers. Also, by reducing stock-outs and inventory carrying costs an interorganizational DSS can increase the number of happy customers. A Decision Web Portal can provide access to information from different systems, synchronize relevant and personalized information, support collaboration, and extend decision support to partners, customers and suppliers.

This chapter provides examples of how various types of DSS can enhance and improve managerial decision-making processes and, in some cases, provide an organization with a competitive advantage. It emphasizes understanding technology trends, gaining a competitive advantage, discussing how DSS can provide a competitive advantage, examples of Strategic DSS, characteristics of Strategic DSS, identifying opportunities and Information Systems Planning, and finally, DSS risks and benefits.

TECHNOLOGY TRENDS

Computers have become indispensable tools in companies, government offices, and in most other organizations. For many managers, computers are recognized and accepted as necessary productivity tools. Despite the general and widespread acceptance of computers and their important role in organizations, the business computing revolution is far from complete. If anything, the pace of technology change is speeding up, not slowing down, and the expectations for computers and information systems in companies continues to expand and grow (cf., Power and Kaparthi, 1998). So, what are the trends associated with information technology that may have a major impact on the design and development of DSS? In my opinion:

1. Network technologies are very important and mission-critical in most companies. Computing and network technologies have become more integrated and more powerful. The speed and capacity of networks is increasing. Bandwidth expansion can support interactive video and real-time decision support any where in the world. Access to fast network connections is becoming widespread and less costly. An open architectural view of networking and computing is dominating IS/IT thinking and the development of DSS. Decision support applications are and will be needed 7 days a week and 24 hours a day in many companies; if the network is down, decisions won't be made.

2. Open source software may impact some DSS development tools. With access to source code programmers can read, redistribute, and modify the software;

advocates of open source software feel the software will evolve faster (cf., www.opensource.org). For example, Linux is becoming an important operating system for Web servers in corporations. Major vendors like IBM and Oracle are supporting some open source software like Linux and the Apache Web server. This trend is negatively impacting the use of proprietary UNIX and Microsoft Windows software as the corporate server environments of choice.

3. Visualization technologies are more powerful than at any time in the past. New software helps users visualize almost anything they can imagine in a realistic, manipulatable format. Visualization tools can help pilots simulate flights and help managers "try" new products.

4. The World Wide Web is expanding and it is forcing major changes in business transaction processing. But the Web is much more than a means of transferring order entry tasks to customers. The Web supports e-business including internal and external global communications, decision making, and collaboration for managers. Also, the Web can help managers gather, manage, share, and use information.

5. The World Wide Web is facilitating new models of business cooperation, including extranets, interorganizational DSS and shared computing resources. For example, interorganizational and supply-chain decision support applications can be outsourced and hosted by application service providers.

6. Handheld computing is gaining greater acceptance, and the use of pocket PCs by managers and other employees will increase. Wireless Web devices are expected to outnumber wired devices in the next few years. Pocket PCs support distributed data collection for data-driven DSS, expanded communications-driven DSS and distributed decision making. Mobile computing systems extend the reach of an enterprise-wide DSS.

7. Large data storage systems and multiprocessing computers have removed the constraints on what can be stored and how much data can be stored. Data storage is faster and it is easier to organize and backup data of all types. Web site logs, customer documents and data from transactions can be kept forever in a form that can be sorted, analyzed and processed.

This list of trends is incomplete and dated even as it is written. Seizing opportunities to build innovative DSS involves continuously monitoring technology trends and having the courage to "think outside of the box." This phrase is already trite, but the need to innovate remains if a company is to gain a competitive advantage from building a DSS.

GAINING COMPETITIVE ADVANTAGE

A DSS creates a competitive advantage if three criteria are met. First, once the DSS is implemented, it must be used, and it must become a major or significant strength or capability of the organization. Second, the DSS must be unique and proprietary to the organization. Third, the advantage provided by the DSS must be sustainable for at least three years. Even with rapid technology change, a three-year payback is a realistic target. Managers who are searching for strategic investments in information technology need to keep these three criteria in mind. In general, a competitive advantage means an organization does something important much better than its competitors.

The widespread use of computer technology has changed the way companies do business. Information technology has altered relationships between companies and their suppliers, customers, and rivals. Porter and Millar (1985) discuss two specific ways that information technology can affect competition: by altering industry structures, and by supporting cost and/or differentiation strategies. A common approach used to identify opportunities to change the structure and profitability of an industry is to examine five competitive forces and the business value chain. Michael Porter (1979) argued that the power of buyers, the power of suppliers, the threat of new entrants, the threat of substitute products, and the rivalry among existing competitors determines the profitability of an industry. How a company uses information technology can affect each of the five competitive forces and can create the need and opportunity for change. For example, information technology has altered the bargaining relationships between companies and their suppliers, channels, and buyers. Information systems can cross company boundaries and support supply chains. These inter-organizational systems have become common, and, in some instances, they have changed the boundaries of the participating industries. DSS can reduce the power of buyers and suppliers. DSS can erect new barriers that reduce the threat of entrants, help differentiate products and services, and reduce the threat from substitutes. Also, DSS can help managers reduce the cost of rivalry actions and, in some cases, lessen the need for competitive actions and reactions.

Some firms have no competitive advantage. Firms can achieve a competitive advantage by making strategic changes, and firms can lose a competitive advantage when competitors make strategic changes. Information systems and information technologies are changing rapidly and are viewed by many managers as "strategic weapons" for gaining competitive advantage. These systems are also known as Strategic Information Systems (SIS).

SIS are systems designed to change goals, products, services, or environmental relationships of organizations. Some authors argue that any information system that helps an organization compete is an SIS (cf., Neumann, 1994). Both definitions should guide managers in their search for ways to use information technology to support decision making. DSS that create changes in products, services, or relationships are especially important for gaining an advantage over competitors.

Strategic Impact Grid

Information systems and information technology play different roles in different industry settings. McFarlan, McKenney, and Pyburn (1983) proposed a four-quadrant strategic impact model of the strategic relevance of information systems and information technologies (IS/IT) (see Table 2.1). Firms in the *Factory* quadrant are dependent on cost-effective, reliable IS/IT operational support for internal operations. Firms with mainframe legacy systems, including some direct mail processing companies and some banks, fall in this category. IS/IT development emphasizes maintenance and program improvements. Smooth functioning of computerized systems is vital to daily operations. New decision support applications in data warehousing, On-Line Analytical Processing (OLAP) and GDSS are potentially useful, but are not a priority and are not fundamental to the ability of a firm in this quadrant to compete.

	Low impact of new IS/IT applications	High impact of new IS/IT applications
High strategic impact of existing IS/IT	**Factory**	**Strategic**
Low strategic impact of existing IS/IT	**Support**	**Turnaround**

Table 2.1 Categories of Strategic Relevance

In the *Strategic* quadrant, information systems and information technologies are essential for executing current strategies and operations for firms. For example, e-businesses like Amazon.com and Ameritrade, Inc. are dependent on Internet and database technologies to operate. Information systems are critical to the survival and competitive position of the firm. In this quadrant, novel decision support applications will be crucial to future competitive success.

In the *Support* quadrant, information technology resources are important for applications like accounting and payroll, but firms are not dependent on technology. Examples of industries with firms in this category include job shop manufacturing, restaurants, and funeral services. Firms in this quadrant that develop innovative DSS are unlikely to gain competitive advantage.

In the *Turnaround* quadrant, managers who want to use information systems and especially DSS to improve the competitive position of a firm will encounter special challenges. Firms in this quadrant are usually trying to revitalize operations through new Transaction Processing Systems (TPS). These firms have not previously depended on IS/IT, and yet new applications will likely impact their survival. Firms in this quadrant are laggards and can come from many industries. Some indicators that a firm is in this quadrant include the enabling technologies in use, the applications that are being implemented, and the attitudes of the IS/IT staff. If most of the attention is on implementing "new" TPS, then the firm is probably in the turnaround quadrant.

The strategic impact grid can help managers analyze a firm's current information systems position. Firms in the *Strategic* quadrant are in the best position to gain advantage from building novel DSS. Multibusiness corporations can also use the grid to compare several business units or divisions.

HOW CAN DSS PROVIDE A COMPETITIVE ADVANTAGE?

Evans and Wurster (1997) argued in a recent *Harvard Business Review* article that the world is in the midst of a fundamental shift in the economics of information. They argue that major changes will occur in the structure of entire industries and in the ways companies compete. The change that they believe is so important is the widespread adoption of Internet technologies, which they see as supporting new behaviors that are reaching critical mass. They claim millions of people are communicating at home and at work in an explosion of connectivity that threatens to undermine the established value chains for businesses in many sectors of the economy.

Internet technologies have also opened wide the doors for innovative Web-based DSS. Interorganizational DSS can improve linkages with customers and suppliers. In some situations, communications-driven DSS can remove time and location barriers. DSS can help a firm operate 7 days a week, 24 hours a day and without regard to an employee's or a customer's location. In some cases, DSS can help integrate a firm's operations. An interorganizational, Web-based DSS can create linkages to customers and suppliers that are difficult to challenge or overcome.

DSS can potentially help a firm create a cost advantage by providing many benefits, including improving personal efficiency and reducing staff needs, expediting problem solving, and increasing organizational control. Managers who want to create a cost advantage should search for situations where decision processes seem slow or tedious and where problems reoccur or solutions are delayed or unsatisfactory. In some cases, DSS can reduce costs where decision makers have high turnover and training is slow and cumbersome, and in situations where activities, departments, and projects are poorly controlled.

Also, DSS can create a major cost advantage by increasing efficiency or eliminating value-chain activities. For example, a bank or mortgage loan firm may reduce costs by using a new DSS to consolidate the number of steps and minimize the number of staff hours needed to approve loans. Technology breakthroughs can sometimes continue to lower process costs, and rivals who imitate an innovative DSS may nullify or remove any advantage.

Potentially, DSS can create a differentiation advantage. Providing a DSS to customers can differentiate a product and possibly provide a new service. Differentiation increases profitability when the price premium charged is greater than any added costs associated with achieving the differentiation. Successful differentiation means a firm can charge a premium price, and/or sell more units, and/or increase buyer loyalty for service or repeat purchases. In some situations, competitors can rapidly imitate the differentiation, and then all competitors incur increased costs for implementing the DSS.

Finally, DSS can be used to help a company better focus on a specific customer segment and hence gain an advantage in meeting that segment's needs. MIS and DSS can help track customers, and DSS can make it easier to serve a specialized customer group with special services. Some customers won't pay a premium for targeted service, or larger competitors may also target specialized niches using their own DSS.

WHAT COMPANIES HAVE GAINED AN ADVANTAGE WITH DSS?

A major problem in answering this question is that firms want to maintain any advantage they gain, and hence, they are, and should be, reluctant to release many details about a decision support system that provides them a competitive advantage. Also, DSS that provide an advantage at one point in time may seem dated or ordinary after only a few years. An advantage from information technology can be fleeting and short-term (cf., Feeny and Ives, 1990).

In a retrospective research study, Kettinger, Grover, Guha and Segars (1994) identified 30 companies that had gained an advantage from Information Systems. Some of the systems were DSS, but most were TPS. Based on their study, the following companies developed DSS that provided a significant sustainable advantage: Air Products & Chemicals, Inc. developed a vehicle scheduling system; Cigna Corp. implemented a risk assessment system; Digital Equipment Corp. built an expert configurator; IBM created a marketing management system; and Owens-Corning built a materials selection system.

Many of the above DSS have probably been enhanced or redeveloped since they were initially implemented. Having the best technology at one point in time and "innovating first" do not guarantee continued success. Today many consulting firms and software vendors focus on gaining competitive advantage from a data warehouse or a business intelligence system, and that can happen. Many DSS projects do not, however, deliver such results, and cannot create a competitive advantage.

If a company is trying to develop a DSS that provides a competitive advantage, managers and DSS analysts should ask about the uniqueness of the project, IS/IT capabilities, and impacts on costs, customer and supplier relations, and managerial effectiveness. Based on examining specific examples of DSS, managers need to continually invest in a strategic DSS to maintain any advantage. Also, managers should keep the DSS proprietary and secret to maintain an advantage. The above examples and those in the next section demonstrate that some innovative decision support systems can provide a sustainable competitive advantage.

SOME EXAMPLES OF STRATEGIC DSS

The following examples at Frito-Lay, L.L. Bean, Lockheed-Georgia, Mrs. Field's Cookies, and Wal-Mart should clarify how DSS can provide a competitive advantage. These examples are "classics" that have been widely reported in business case studies and the popular press.

Frito-Lay

In the late 1980s, Frito-Lay (www.fritolay.com/home.html) managers felt that they needed to redesign the sales process into a more decentralized organization where route sales people were given decision-making authority on promotions and product mix (cf., Applegate, 1994). The development of a handheld computer enabled this strategic transition to occur. Route sales people collected data on every sales transaction for every customer on a route. Ten thousand Frito-Lay salespeople use handheld computers to track Frito-Lay products. These notebook size computers produce a vast quantity of data that flows into the data center at Frito-Lay headquarters in Texas. This data is used in a data-driven DSS. This technology automated a cumbersome process and improved the quality of data that was already being collected. The technology also provides data to support decentralized decision making while maintaining centralized control systems.

L.L. Bean

In the spring of 1989, L.L. Bean (www.llbean.com) hired consultants to design a system that would provide better allocation of resources in telemarketing. Managers decided to have an Economic Optimization Model (EOM) built in-house (cf., Quinn, Andrews, and Parsons, 1991).

The EOM system required a shift in focus for the company from a traditional service-level criterion, such as 14 calls per agent per hour, to a method that would optimize economic efficiencies. This model-driven DSS examined variables such as the number of telephone lines to carry incoming traffic, the number of agents, and the queue capacity or the number of wait positions for sales agents. Then, through various mathematical modeling tools, the system generated specific resource amounts L.L. Bean should deploy to be most economically advantageous. The system takes into account many variables. For example, installation and maintenance costs of telephone lines, labor costs of sales agents including their training, costs associated with being on hold with the 800-service provider, and the cost of permanently lost orders. This new profitability based model continues to add resources until the marginal cost of additional resources exceeds the return on that investment. EOM also scheduled the resources based on fluctuations in activity. When one group of operators became overwhelmed, the next shift of operators would be starting, and then as things were becoming slow, one group of operators would soon be leaving.

From a $40,000 capital investment in the system, the company estimated a profit gain of $9.2 million to $10 million for 1989. Sales call volumes were up 6.5 percent over the previous year. Managers, who attributed the majority of the gains to the new EOM system, benefited from an integrated planner that could evaluate "what if" scenarios. Most importantly, L.L. Bean's reputation with customers improved. Other benefits included decreased customer wait times, improved morale of employees, and reduced lost order penalties. The EOM provided L.L. Bean a competitive advantage.

Lockheed-Georgia

In 1975, Robert B. Ormsby, president of Lockheed-Georgia, a subsidiary of cargo aircraft producer Lockheed Corporation, was interested in the development of an on-line reporting system that could provide top executives with concise, timely, relevant information that could be shared within the organization to aid with decision making. In the fall of 1978, development began for a Management Information and Decision Support (MIDS) system (cf., Houdeshel and Watson, 1987).

The intended benefits of MIDS were improved communications, an evolving understanding of information requirements by the organization, and cost reductions in the generation of reports and presentation materials. MIDS helped managers identify areas that require attention; thus enabling improved decision making. Information has become more timely, since it is updated as events occur, and accuracy is improved through the verification of all information before it is made available.

After 12 years of successful operation, in 1990, MIDS required a hardware update. At this time, managers reviewed both hardware and software and decided to purchase a commercial Executive Information System (EIS) called Commander EIS from Comshare (www.comshare.com) instead of developing another in-house system. MIDS II, as it became known, resembled the look and feel of the previous system. Lockheed requested that Comshare provide the ability to operate the system through a keyboard in addition to mouse and touch screen, and they wanted the ability of the old MIDS system to monitor use of the system. Lockheed also requested that these changes be done not only to their version, but also to all Commander EIS packages, thus enabling easier upgrades. MIDS II rolled out in 1992 with faster response times, easier navigation, better links to outside resources, and lower maintenance costs.

Mrs. Field's Cookies

Mrs. Field's Inc. (www.mrsfields.com) developed a management information system in the early 1980s to provide uniformity in store management while supporting the objective of rapid expansion. The information system was designed to serve two purposes for the company. The first was control and the other was better management decision making for store managers. What evolved from these needs was a strategic information system that was designed to enable each store to operate in a manner similar to the way Debbi Field ran the original Palo Alto store. Her husband, Randy Field, did this by creating a software system that put decision-making support and operating data on a store-level computer. The software gave the store manager time to do "those tasks that people uniquely do." The system was justified on the basis of potential payback, its ability to generate new sales, and the strategic importance in acquiring competitive advantage (cf., Applegate and Pearlson, 1994).

A DSS was developed that automated routine activities and responded to exceptions by prompting the store manager for input. Eventually, these exceptions were structured and the system responded automatically to many situations. On a more sophisticated level, the system tracked financial performance of each store, provided comprehensive scheduling of operations, including marketing support, tracked hourly sales goals, and even assisted with candidate interview selection. Each store's Tandy PC accessed the corporate management system. Many applications were menu-driven, such as day planning, time clocks, store accounting, inventory management, interviewing schedules, skill testing, and e-mail. After entering basic workday characteristics, the system would run a mathematical model to compute the day's schedule of events, including how many cookies to bake of each type, when to mix and cook them, and projected sales per hour. Store sales were periodically entered into the system, and then revised projections and recommendations were requested. Using sales and inventory information, the system prepared and generated supply orders. Corporate headquarters was able to learn quickly when a store was not meeting expectations, and managers could respond.

Wal-Mart

In the early 1990s, Wal-Mart (www.walmart.com) implemented a number of Strategic DSS including Retail Link and a Sales data warehouse. Wal-Mart collects sales data from its stores in its data warehouse. Retail Link consolidated data into useful reports, and distributes it to suppliers with weekly forecasting information. In addition to forecasting information, suppliers get electronic order forms that help ensure there is an adequate supply of the items that Wal-Mart needs. This system used electronic data interchange (EDI) and satellite technologies to create a competitive advantage that other retailers like KMart have tried to imitate. The result of Retail Link has been reduced inventory in stores, more inventory of the right products at the right time and place, improved revenues for both supplier and retailer, and better partner relationships with suppliers. Retail Link is an example of an interorganizational DSS.

Wal-Mart also developed a large data warehouse to support decision making by Wal-Mart's merchandise buyers. In 1997, Wal-Mart increased the size and information analysis capabilities of its data warehouse. In a press release, Randy Mott, senior vice president and chief information officer for Wal-Mart, said "Our business strategy depends on detailed data at every level." Mott explained "Every cost, every line item is carefully analyzed, enabling better merchandising decisions to be made on a daily basis. It is the foundation for maintaining Wal-Mart's competitive edge and its continuing success in providing everyday low prices and superior customer satisfaction."

In 1998, Wal-Mart and Warner-Lambert began using the Internet to communicate interactively about sales forecasts. They reduced the time a product is in the supply chain by two and a half weeks. That translates into millions of dollars in reduced inventory. Today Wal-Mart is using Web technologies to support collaborative decision making in its supply chain.

IDENTIFYING OPPORTUNITIES AND INFORMATION SYSTEMS PLANNING

How can a manager identify opportunities to create DSS that can provide a competitive advantage? To determine if it is possible to gain advantage from DSS, a manager needs to use a creative search process to identify problems and needs. A cursory review of articles indicates there are many planning processes and analysis frameworks that might help (cf., Neumann, 1994). The Information Systems planning process should provide a systematic method of searching for and evaluating opportunities. IS planning must be linked to business strategic planning, and the process should be ongoing and open-ended. Managers need to collect competitive intelligence, fund DSS research and development projects, conduct brainstorming sessions, and follow hunches and intuition. Managers need to look at business decision processes and their decision tasks from an outsider's perspective. Hiring a consultant who is perhaps a bit unorthodox or is willing to question assumptions may also help.

The Decision Support Readiness Audit in Appendix I can help assess a company's readiness for developing and using innovative and potentially strategic DSS. Both IS and line managers should complete the audit and any discrepancies should be examined. Completing an audit can be part of an IS planning process.

Information systems planning needs to examine the technical infrastructure to determine what is currently possible and examine enhancements that would facilitate or enable new capabilities. IS planning should involve broad consultation and both problem-oriented and opportunistic search. DSS do not always solve specific problems; rather DSS may create new capabilities. Evaluating DSS opportunities is sometimes difficult because of problems with assessing costs and benefits. In some situations the analysis will be directed to a "build versus buy" decision because industry-specific packages are available. This type of DSS may be needed, but it probably will not provide a competitive advantage.

DSS projects have various levels of risk associated with them. When DSS projects have ambiguous objectives and low structure, the projects have higher levels of risk because the costs and scope of work of the project are hard to define. Also, because the objectives of the project are ambiguous, it can be difficult to assess the return on the investment. DSS projects with a higher degree of structure and more clearly defined objectives generally are lower risk. More detailed planning is possible for projects with specific objectives. The project scope in terms of the number of users served and the size of databases developed also impacts the risk of the assessed projects. Small DSS projects, in terms of scope or dollar expenditures, tend to be of lower risk than large projects. Finally, the sophistication of the technology and the experience of the developers using the technology influences the overall project risk. The ultimate decision to invest in a DSS project should not be based solely on project risk. Sometimes, the DSS project that is most likely to result in a competitive advantage is the riskiest project (cf., Applegate et al., 1996).

If managers want to develop effective IS plans and evaluate DSS projects, it is important that they attend IS, industry, and vendor conferences. Also, to gain knowledge and search for opportunities, managers and MIS staff should use the World Wide Web to search for DSS information and visit DSS vendor Web sites. The DSSResources.COM Web site provides a knowledge resource about many aspects of DSS.

DSSResources.COM (Decision Support Systems Resources) is a Web-based knowledge repository. The mission of the site is to help people who are interested in learning how to use information technologies and software to improve business and organizational decision making. The target audience is MIS professionals, MIS students, managers interested in DSS, and academics teaching MIS/DSS. The site is needed because decision support technology is changing and evolving very rapidly. MIS managers, business managers, and academics face a difficult challenge trying to stay abreast of those changes and to make good, informed decisions about building and maintaining DSS for organizations.

People are challenged by too much information and by too many sources of information. Much of the information about DSS is hard to find or "noisy." The DSSResources.COM Web site is an integrated source of information relevant to DSS and it is a "living" hypertext document. The ongoing challenge is to have the site reflect the state of the art in DSS research and practice. DSS Resources changed its URL to DSSResources.COM on September 29, 1999.

DSS BENEFITS, LIMITATIONS, AND RISKS

Development and implementation of DSS has risks. Gaining any advantage may require a large financial investment. Competitors' responses to the innovation may result in a heated race to gain or regain lost market share or provide the new capability. The competitive race can evolve into one of technology one-upmanship rather than one of better meeting customer needs. Sometimes the development of a strategic information system can shift power away from a specific company or an entire industry (cf., Porter and Millar, 1985). Technology risks include picking the wrong vendor, using a new technology too early in the technology life cycle, or using a technology that soon becomes obsolete. The inability to predict human behaviors and reactions, and the basic human instinct to resist change makes people the greatest risk when building new systems. No matter how wonderful a proposed DSS, if people resist the change, then the new system will fail. To gain an advantage a new DSS must work as planned and a company's stakeholders must perceive its strategic significance for the firm.

All categories and types of DSS focus on improving the effectiveness of decision-makers rather than on increasing the efficiency of data storage and retrieval. Managers should routinely ask how a proposed computerized DSS would do this. In what ways do any type of computerized support system increase managerial effectiveness? The following are common individual and organizational benefits of DSS cited by Alter (1980), Turban (1995), Udo and Guimaraes (1994), and others:

1. *Improve individual productivity.* One of the ways to help people become more effective decision makers is to help them become more efficient in manipulating data. At a minimum, a new DSS should allow a person either to perform the same task in less time or perform the same task more thoroughly in the same length of time. The result of automating the clerical component of decision-related tasks is often to improve consistency and accuracy and to allow people to spend more of their time on the substantive rather than clerical aspects of their jobs.

2. *Improve decision quality and speed up problem solving.* A data-driven DSS can provide faster turnaround in retrieving decision-relevant information; can improve consistency and accuracy in decision making; and it may provide

better ways of viewing or solving problems. Users of data-driven DSS can often obtain answers to ad hoc or nonroutine questions quickly. Decision makers can consider more alternatives. Knowledge-driven DSS may reduce the variability in the application of guidelines and policies. Model-driven DSS can help managers conduct "what if" analyses and modify their assumptions and scenarios in financial planning. Communications-driven DSS can reduce the length of management feedback loops and the need to revise analyses. Problems seem to get resolved faster. Also, some managers perceive that DSS provides an "impartial" source of information that encourages "fact-based" decision making. This perception expedites problem solving.

3. *Improve interpersonal communications.* DSS provide users with "tools of persuasion" to help them support an action based on analysis or show that "a good job" has been done. Many types of DSS can provide managers in an organization with a vocabulary and a process for decision making and discussion.

4. *Improve decision making skills.* Frequently, learning occurs as a by-product of the initial and ongoing use of a DSS. Two types of learning seem to occur: learning of new concepts and the development of a better factual understanding of the business and decision-making environment. Some DSS serve as de facto training tools for new employees. Some knowledge-driven DSS reduce the expertise needed by an employee to perform satisfactorily and help newcomers gain expertise. Knowledge-driven DSS may also preserve expertise that might be lost through the resignation or retirement of an acknowledged expert.

5. *Increase organizational control.* Some data-driven DSS provide summary data for purposes of overall organizational control. Summary data can be monitored, retained, and analyzed. Managers need to be very careful about how decision-related information is collected and then used for organizational control purposes. If employees feel threatened or spied upon when they are using a DSS, negative behaviors may occur. Trying to gain increased control of employee decision behavior can be counterproductive.

Other benefits cited for DSS include: extending a decision maker's ability to process information and analyze it; helping a decision maker deal with complex, large-scale problems that would otherwise involve time-consuming data analysis; shortening or decreasing the amount of time needed to make a decision; improving the reliability and enforcing the structure of a decision process; encouraging exploration and discovery by the decision maker in less structured or more novel decision situations related to the domain or scope of the DSS; helping decision makers restructure or reconceptualize a problem space or decision context; confirming assumptions or generating new "facts" to support one's reasoning or decision; and, as mentioned previously, creating a competitive or strategic advantage for an organization.

DSS definitely can have positive benefits for some managers and organizations, but they can also create negative outcomes in situations. For example, some DSS development efforts can lead to power struggles over who should have access to data. Also, managers may have personal motives for advocating development of a DSS. A DSS can increase the "visibility" of its sponsor and have positive rewards if it is successful. Some IS staff support DSS implementations so they can experiment with new technology or expand staff rather than because they believe in the proposed DSS. Isolating and identifying hidden agendas is difficult, but DSS proponents in IS and management must attempt to examine them. The successful development and use of DSS requires that people accept the DSS and are motivated to help make the project a success. Hidden agendas can hurt the motivation of all the people involved in a DSS development project.

DSS have limitations: A DSS is structured for a specific purpose and the data and models limit how it can be used; DSS have a "domain" of use; DSS often need to be integrated into decision processes; DSS can not support decision makers unless a decision maker chooses to use the system and incorporates the analyses into "off line" thinking and analysis; DSS have technology limitations. Finally, DSS are a form of behavioral engineering, and many managers resist such interventions.

Some DSS development opportunities are better than others. The key task for managers is understanding new technology and being able to develop only those systems that create positive business results, while rejecting those that use "technology for the sake of technology." Using IS/IT to gain competitive advantage definitely has risks.

RESISTANCE TO USING DECISION SUPPORT SYSTEMS

Since DSS often have positive benefits, why do some managers resist using them? Let's examine seven possible explanations for management resistance to using DSS that are cited in the literature. First, managers may have insufficient computer training. Because managers are receiving more computer training, and new managers are quite sophisticated in their use of computer software, the magnitude of this problem seems to be decreasing. Second, some managers argue that using a DSS will diminish their status and force them to do a secretary's work. Using a DSS is not the job of a secretary or personal assistant. Today, companies cannot afford to pay an assistant to help a manager use a computer to do their job. This concern about status is counterproductive and raises business costs.

Third, using a DSS may not fit a manager's problem-solving style, which is sometimes intuitive rather than analytical. While this may be true, managers should use both analysis and intuition in solving problems. Fourth, using a DSS does not fit with the manager's work habits of verbal and nonverbal problem solving in face-to-face meetings. DSS should not and cannot replace all face-to-face meetings. Communications-driven DSS are an adjunct to traditional meetings, and other DSS can often be used in a face-to-face meeting. Fifth, DSS models, interfaces, and systems are usually poorly designed. Poor design is a problem, but not an inherent problem. Managers need to be involved in building DSS, and more resources need to be focused on DSS design and development. Sixth, some managers argue that building and using a DSS is expensive and time-consuming. Using a DSS does not need to be time-consuming or tedious or difficult. DSS can actually save managers time and speed up decision processes.

Seventh, information overload is a major problem for people, managers already receive too much information, and many DSS increase the overload. Although this can be a problem, DSS can help managers organize and use information. DSS can actually reduce and manage the information load of a user.

Many of the seven reasons cited above for not using DSS are excuses and rationalizations rather than meaningful objections. To gain competitive advantage, project champions and DSS developers need to overcome the problems caused by managers who resist the use of DSS.

Finally, companies must determine whom they want a proposed DSS to support and what result they want from the new DSS. For example, an interorganizational DSS should offer customers value. Value can be improved service, new products, lower product or service costs, or customization. Often these benefits come from an increase in short-term costs to the DSS provider, but this is better than allowing a competitor to lead in technology innovation and jeopardize an organization's market share in the long term.

CONCLUSIONS AND COMMENTARY

Companies must continually improve information technologies if they are to gain and maintain competitive advantage. Companies that invest significant time and money to achieve an advantage want a system that has sustainability. When competitors can quickly respond with similar or better systems, the result is a higher cost of doing business for all companies involved. To create sustainability, an organization can preempt its competitors by being first to innovate. This creates surprise, competitive respect, and time advantages. Alternatively, sustainability may be achieved through competitor intimidation. Creating a system that is large, complex, or risky can intimidate potential duplicators. Sustainability can, however, only be maintained through continual development and enhancement of a strategic system.

Today, many senior managers are trying to transform their companies into e-businesses. An electronic business infrastructure includes web-based TPS and DSS. If managers are trying to develop web-based strategic DSS, they should ask how improved decision support might affect company costs, customer and supplier relations and managerial effectiveness. Managers should also attempt to assess how a strategic DSS may impact competitors. Also, managers should try to determine if the impact of a contemplated DSS will have any adverse effects. Gaining a competitive advantage is only one of the potential benefits of an innovative DSS. The search for advantage should not blind managers to other benefits that a proposed DSS may provide managers and a company. Some very useful DSS do not provide a significant competitive advantage.

Chapter 3

Analyzing Business Decision Processes

INTRODUCTION

Let's examine some generalizations about decision-making behavior and business decision processes that affect building and using Decision Support Systems (DSS). At a fundamental level, both managers and DSS analysts need to acknowledge that decision making is the most important part of a manager's job. Managers take actions on behalf of an organization and stakeholders. They allocate resources and negotiate agreements. They monitor performance and correct deviations from plans. Managers are evaluated on their ability to make effective decisions. The effectiveness of business decisions is evaluated by many stakeholders, but especially by managers in the managerial hierarchy and by stockholders.

Most of us would agree with the above generalizations, but we need to refine our understanding of business decision making to build successful DSS. Let's begin by asking: What steps do managers follow in making a specific decision? When does a decision process begin and end? How do we identify who is involved in making a specific decision? Managers who want to improve their decisions need to be sensitive to the answers to these questions. DSS designers also need to ask and answer these questions. DSS design should begin with an understanding of an existing decision process. This chapter examines managerial decisions; evaluates decision-making context and decision-making processes; discusses what is "good" decision making; and examines redesigning decision processes.

MANAGERIAL DECISIONS

Managers do not make all of their decisions as part of a deliberate, coherent, and continuous decision-making process (cf., Mintzberg, 1973). Instead, brevity, variety, and fragmented activities characterize the manager's typical workday.

Also, despite its importance, managers do much more than make decisions. They also serve in roles as a figurehead, leader, entrepreneur, negotiator, and liaison to stakeholders.

For managers, decision making is a dynamic process. It is complex and at times ambiguous. Decision makers encounter problems when searching for information, and they must work with delayed feedback of results, uncertainty, ambiguity, and, in some cases, conflict during decision making (cf., Janis and Mann, 1977). In many situations, managers seem to engage in an informal causal analysis in an attempt to favorably influence decision outcomes.

The scope of organizational and managerial decision making is very broad. Decisions are made by individuals at all levels in an organization and by a wide variety of groups in an organization. Robert Anthony (1965) classified decisions in four categories associated with organization levels (see Figure 3.1).

Figure 3.1 Categories of Organizational Decisions

Analysts need to determine if a proposed DSS is intended for use in:

Strategic Planning — decisions related to allocating resources; capital budgeting; controlling organizational performance; developing annual and long-range plans; establishing broad policies; evaluating investment or merger proposals.

Management Control — decisions related to acquisition and use of resources by operating units; buyer and supplier behavior; introduction of new products; R&D project expenditures.

Operational Control — decisions related to the effectiveness of organizational actions; monitoring product/service quality; assessing product/service needs.

Operational Performance — day-to-day decisions made in functional units to implement strategic decisions; functional tactics; and operational activities.

Both managers and DSS analysts need to analyze decision support needs and distinguish among them in terms of who participates, the type of decision, and other factors discussed in later sections. From an analyst's perspective a "decision" is the result of a choice point in an ongoing process of evaluating alternatives to select one or some combination of alternatives that will attain a desired end. DSS often do much more than support a specific "decision".

Decision making and problem solving are intertwined concepts. The type of problem or decision situation has an impact on the type of approach that should be taken to resolve the problem. Problems may be structured, semistructured or unstructured. According to Simon (1965), structured problems can be described in numbers, or can be specified in terms of numerical objectives. In structured problems, specific computational techniques may be available to find an optimal solution. In unstructured decision situations, objectives are hard to quantify and identify, and it is usually not possible to develop a model of the situation. Unstructured situations require managers to use more creativity and subjective judgment to find a solution. Unstructured situations can be supported by computerized systems, but the support focuses more on information presentation, summary, and support analyses and collaboration rather than on finding an optimal solution. The system must be a "support system" that promotes high quality subjective judgment and creativity. Figure 3.2 shows what decision situations are suitable for computerized decision support.

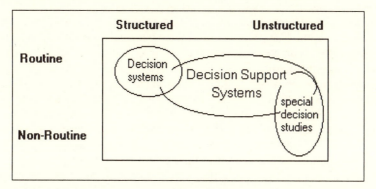

Figure 3.2 Matching Decision Support to Decision Situations

Managers encounter three types of decisions: selection from a list of alternatives, including yes/no decisions; evaluation of alternatives using criteria and decision rules; and design and construction of a custom solution. DSS can potentially support all three of these choice situations. Each decision situation can also be categorized as routine and recurring decisions or as nonroutine or infrequent. Examples of routine decisions that can be automated and programmed with a decision system include placing an order to replenish inventory, sending delinquency notices, or routing packages. Nonroutine decisions that can benefit from decision support include deciding on a new supplier for a part, disciplining an employee who is constantly late for work, or creating a budget.

Managers should not treat routine decisions as if they were nonroutine. If a decision is "generic" and routine, valuable time and resources should not be expended each time the decision occurs as would be required with a nonroutine, nonrecurring decision. Routine decision situations should be analyzed and "programmed" as much as is possible and they should be supported in most situations by technology. The potential rewards from improving routine, recurring decisions are usually very large.

What situations are less likely to benefit from computerized decision aids and decision support? One situation that comes rapidly to mind is one of limited consequence, e.g. low return, and few positive or negative consequences, such as assigning parking spaces. Another is a situation where political factors outweigh or gain ascendancy over facts and analysis. In general, computerized decision aids support rational decision behavior that uses analytical decision processes. Where a decision situation does not require, expect, encourage, or need analysis and intended rationality, using any computer support system will be unnecessary and may lead to manipulation or distortion of outcomes. Rather than dwell on when DSS analysts should avoid suggesting DSS, it seems more important to help analysts identify "good situations" for building such systems.

Computerized decision support should be considered when managers are in decision situations characterized by one or more of the following factors: complexity, uncertainty, multiple groups with a stake in the decision outcome (multiple stakeholders), a large amount of information (especially company data), and/or rapid change in information. Complex decision situations with many variables, complex causal relationships, and an available historical database can sometimes be modeled. These are complex situations, and models can simplify such decision situations, aid in understanding them, and help test alternatives. Computerized models, especially visual models, can be very useful in these situations. The model is a representation of the actual situation, and analyses performed using the model can help the decision maker(s) anticipate consequences of alternatives. Sometimes, a software model can actually recommend optimal choices to a decision maker. In many cases, knowing what DSS tools are available is an important factor in choosing appropriate situations to support. General characteristics like complexity and uncertainty may provide cues to appropriate situations but an understanding of the technologies and their limitations is equally important.

In some unstructured, nonroutine situations, models are sometimes constructed and DSS may be used as part of a special decision study by a decision support analyst. These situations do not justify a large investment in creating a user interface so that managers can directly interact with models or data. Some other names for special decision studies include a quantitative analysis, a simulation study, and a management analysis. DSS analysts and managers need to recognize that every situation that could benefit from using a database or a quantitative model is not a candidate for building a DSS.

Data-driven DSS seem most appropriate where managers need frequent access to conduct ad hoc analyses of large data sets. Model-driven DSS are appropriate in recurring decision situations that are semistructured and where a quantitative model or models can inform or support analyses and choices. Knowledge-driven DSS are appropriate where a narrow domain of expertise can be defined, where one or more experts can be identified, or where knowledge can be codified to help a less expert decision maker. A document-driven DSS should be built when a very large set of documents has been, is or will be created that needs to be filtered, sorted, searched, and analyzed. A communications-driven DSS is most appropriate where two or more people need to be involved in an ad hoc or ongoing decision process, who either cannot meet or find it costly to meet, but want to use technology tools to communicate, collaborate, evaluate, and support decision analysis or evaluation.

Finally, risk and uncertainty characterize many decision situations. Managers in these situations need to assess risks, and in some cases, they need to assess the financial consequences of acting in an uncertain or risky situation. Computerized tools can help elicit and apply risk information in a decision situation. Computerized support systems can also help deal with large amounts of information and rapidly changing information.

DECISION-MAKING CONTEXT

Understanding the context of managerial decision making is important in building DSS. The decision-making context defines both the potential for and the limits to decision support. We need to consider the whole decision cycle and process and all of the varied decision activities of managers and their staff.

The importance of managerial decision making and the types of decisions made vary at different levels in the managerial hierarchy. At the lowest level, supervisors assign tasks, monitor and control operations, and make a variety of short-term decisions. At the managerial control level, decisions are more complex and more information is used to make decisions. At the strategic or senior management level, managerial decisions focus on issues of corporate performance, macro allocations of resources, major personnel choices, and strategic directions on products and markets.

All of the managers in an organization are drawing conclusions from information and making choices from identified alternatives. Some managerial decisions need computerized support more than others. Some decision activities are also easier to support than are others.

Alexis and Wilson (1967) discuss five major elements of a decision situation: goals, relevant alternatives, process of ranking alternatives, decision environment, and decision makers. DSS analysts should first examine the goals to be achieved in the situation, who sets the goals, and when and how are they revised. In some situations, analysts can examine relevant alternatives and how they are identified. An alternative is relevant if it is feasible, can be implemented, and solves an existing problem. Decision situations usually have a process of ranking alternatives from most to least desirable. This process may be subjective or objective. Analysts should determine how alternatives are currently ordered. DSS analysts should especially examine the decision environment and the decision makers in evaluating the advisability of computerizing a decision process. Both the decision environment and the decision makers are important in understanding the decision-making context.

Decision Environment

Various aspects of the decision makers' environment can affect the final decision. Robert Duncan (1974) characterized the decision environment as consisting of two categories—internal and external. The factors in the internal environment that influence decisions include: 1) people, and their goals, experiences, capabilities, and commitment; 2) functional units, including the technological characteristics, independence, interdependence, and conflict among units; and 3) organization factors, including goals and objectives, processes and procedures, and the nature of the product or service. The factors in the external environment that affect decisions include customers, suppliers, competitors, sociopolitical issues, and technological issues. Some DSS help managers assess the above factors, but it is more important to consider them when designing and building a DSS.

Decision Makers

Sometimes we can identify a single individual who is responsible for making a specific decision, but this is not always the situation. What is often more important is determining the scope of the decision (scope refers to who and what the decision will affect). Scope often determines what level of management should be responsible for making the decision. In general, the broader the scope of the decision, the higher the level of management involvement in the decision-making process. Analysts need to identify and evaluate the individual or group who will actually make the choice. Not all decision makers are alike. Some people are weak decision makers who want others to make decisions for them. Others take credit for the good ideas of their colleagues or subordinates. Still other managers accept little help, isolate themselves, and are extremely self-reliant. Finally, some managers make a decision based on how it will make them look, rather than on facts or values.

Pritsker and Sigal (1983) characterize decision makers with respect to how they would use a decision support system if one were available. A *hands-off* DSS user reads reports but doesn't directly use the DSS. A *requester* decision maker has an intermediary, like a decision support analyst, use a DSS. The requester frames the questions, interprets the results, and then makes the decisions. The third type of decision maker is a *hands-on* DSS user. The hands-on user has direct on-line access to the DSS. Finally, a *renaissance* decision maker is a hands-on user, feels comfortable talking about database systems and modeling, can use intermediaries when appropriate, and can build his or her own models and small DSS. The target audiences for DSS are hands-on and renaissance decision makers.

Managers, including hands-on and renaissance decision makers, have a number of limitations that can be compensated for by using information technology. For example, they sometimes use simplistic strategies to search for information. Managers request excessive information or fail to organize and use the information they request.

In general, people are influenced by how information is presented to them; managers, like most people, are also susceptible to social pressure, and they have a desire to avoid cognitive dissonance (Janis and Mann, 1977). This means that once a person has committed to a decision, there is less concern about objectivity. People bias new information to support the already made decision. Sadly, some managers routinely make decisions first and then look for information to support or "bolster" their decision. Comparing and evaluating alternatives is sometimes more haphazard than orderly. Risk preferences are usually not discussed explicitly in decision making. Some managers are generally overconfident or have an illusion of control in situations governed primarily by chance. Also, comparing and evaluating alternatives for many managers is a combination of judgments, political bargaining, and limited analysis.

Managers have cognitive limitations; they receive incomplete and imperfect information, and they experience time and cost constraints in decision situations. Decision makers also often find themselves confronted by too much information, time pressure, and distractions. Janis and Mann (1977) note that when the degree of complexity of an issue exceeds the limits of a person's cognitive abilities, there is a marked decrease in the adequacy of human information processing that is a direct effect of information overload and ensuing fatigue. Decisions may also be affected adversely by personal concerns and agendas. Computerized decision aids can help overcome some of these factors that constrain and limit the overall quality of organizational decision making. DSS can also be used in negative ways to develop rationalizations and bolster previously made decisions. This type of use of a DSS will negate any benefits of computerized decision support and may actually reduce the effectiveness of decision making in an organization.

DECISION-MAKING PROCESSES

How do individuals and groups make decisions? What steps should be completed? A sequential model of decision making can help analyze how decisions are being made and how they should be made (cf., Mintzberg, Raisinghani, and Theoret, 1976).

Simon (1965) identifies three stages in a sequential decision-making process: 1) intelligence—finding occasions for making a decision; 2) design—finding, inventing, developing, and analyzing alternative courses of action; and 3) choice—selecting a course of action. A fourth stage, called implementation, is also often discussed, even though Simon considers implementation as a separate decision process of intelligence, design, and choice. A major decision is made prior to implementation; implementation then involves many supporting actions and, hence, choices. Managing these stages and how they interact can be a major challenge in complex, rapidly changing, and ambiguous or uncertain decision situations. Each of the above stages is part of a business decision process, and each stage can be supported by a variety of DSS. Let's begin discussing how to identify decision-making processes by briefly reviewing the concept of a system and then reviewing some specific examples.

What Is a System?

The term "system" is used in many technology-related concepts including DSS and Transaction Processing System (TPS)—both are computing or information systems. Managers and MIS specialists use the concept of a system frequently and yet it is hard for most of us to define and understand the concept.

A system is an interrelated set of components including people, activities, technology, and procedures that are designed or intended to achieve a predefined purpose. A system receives input from its environment, and the various subsystems or components of the system interact to produce outputs. Systems are defined in terms of their components. System components are surrounded by an imaginary boundary that separates a specific system from its environment. A system designer identifies both inputs from the environment as well as the outputs from the system. Systems also have feedback mechanisms to provide a means of controlling the operation of the system. Feedback is an output from a system that later reenters the system as an input.

Let's examine a simple conceptual specification of a decision process and a system. The initial input into the process and system is a bank customer requesting a loan. The customer makes a request to a bank officer. The bank officer collects information from the customer and enters that information into a computerized form. A loan approval model is built into a computerized decision aid. Some people identify the computerized model as the actual decision support system. The banker uses the result from the computerized loan approval model to finalize the decision to approve or deny the loan. In some cases the loan information will need to be shared with a loan committee, possibly using a group support system. The actual decision is then communicated to the customer either face-to-face or by a formal letter that may be generated by a computerized decision aid. Feedback comes from the customer.

This decision process, and the overall conceptual system, may include various DSS. The bank's TPS would be updated when the loan was made and the funds distributed. The loan is the primary business transaction. Evaluating the loan report is the purpose of the decision process. DSS can support evaluating loan requests, or a DSS can help analyze lending activity at the bank or predict lending activity and interest rates.

In a DSS, the primary focus is often on the computerized components of the system. This is a narrow perspective for defining the components of a system; it is often helpful to define the DSS boundary to include a broader decision process that may involve people performing noncomputerized tasks as well as more routine data gathering tasks. The users of the computerized tools are also part of the broader system. Finally, note that the actual communication or transmission of decisions may not occur using computerized systems. This step in a decision process needs to be considered in the design of the DSS, and it should be included within the boundary of the system.

One needs to define and understand DSS on both a conceptual level and a concrete, technical level. Both managers and DSS analysts need to understand what they are trying to accomplish. The specific purpose of a proposed DSS and its components needs to be defined early in the design and development process.

IBM Credit Corporation Example

According to Hammer and Champy (1993, pp. 36–39), IBM Credit Corporation, a wholly owned subsidiary of IBM, had a business process that evaluated customer's requests for financing that included the following five steps:

Step 1. A salesperson called in a request for financing, which was recorded on paper by one of 14 clerical staff members "sitting around a conference room table in Old Greenwich, Connecticut." This step initiated the process.

Step 2. Someone physically walked the paper request to the credit department, where a specialist entered the request into a computer and checked the credit status of the customer. The result was written on the credit report. Then, the paper-based credit report was delivered to the business practices department.

Step 3. The business practices department used a different computer system to modify a standard loan agreement according to any special requests made by the customer. The document was attached to the original request and delivered to the pricer.

Step 4. The pricer keyed all the information into a PC spreadsheet and determined the appropriate interest rate. This figure was written onto the other forms and delivered to the clerical group.

Step 5. The clerical group converted all paper documents into a quote letter and delivered it to the sales representative using FedEx.

The entire process took six days on average, although it sometimes took as long as two weeks. Some people would say a model-driven DSS is needed to support Step 4, but the entire process can be redesigned and automated. What would you do? Can you redesign the process and then recommend appropriate DSS for each step? Would a communications-driven DSS help?

To redesign the process, two senior managers at IBM Credit took a financing request and walked it themselves through all five steps, asking personnel at each step "to put aside whatever they were doing" and process the request as they normally would. They learned the actual work took 90 minutes. The problem was in the structure of the process and the lack of integrated computer support. IBM Credit developed a new computerized system for a deal structurer who handled all of the steps. In the redesigned process, one person, termed a "deal structurer," completes all of the above steps. A simple DSS helps find information, evaluate the request, and prepare the quote. Difficult decisions could be referred to a small group of specialists. The new DSS and process resulted in a 90 percent reduction in cycle time and an enormous improvement in productivity. Turnaround on credit approvals was cut from seven days to approximately 4 hours. One could look at this example as reengineering a transaction processing system, but that view neglects the importance of the decision making activities embedded in the business process.

A General Decision Process Model

A sequential, decision process model (see Figure 3.3) provides a broad view for understanding the above decision processes. Decision making is more than deciding. Each of the steps in the decision process is important; each step can cause errors and each can potentially be supported by some type of computerized decision aid.

The next few paragraphs review the seven steps in a general decision process model: 1. Define the problem. 2. Decide who should decide. 3. Collect information. 4. Identify and evaluate alternatives. 5. Decide. 6. Implement. 7. Follow-up Assessment.

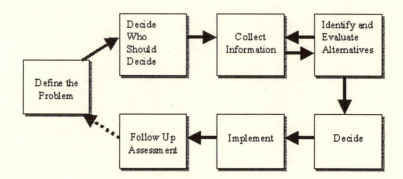

Figure 3.3 A General Decision Process Model

Define the Problem

Many managers feel that a well-defined problem is much easier to solve and that problem definition reduces the chances of having a good answer to the wrong problem. When the wrong problem is defined, it is impossible to make a successful decision. Optimists see problems as opportunities. Pessimists see too many problems. How a problem is "framed" and defined influences how it is solved and the type of decision support, if any, that is used. So what is a problem? A narrow definition of a problem requires that at least the following three conditions be met to label a discrepancy as a problem: First, using a standard, managers have measured how well the company is doing. Second, there is a deviation from a standard, i.e. the company is not achieving the desired result. Third, a manager recognizes the deviation and wants to find a solution.

The above conditions are simple enough to list, but recognizing problems can be difficult. The complexity of today's organizations makes it hard in many cases to identify "real" problems and causes and to get beyond problem symptoms. A number of tools and actions can assist in problem identification, including a good information system, well thought-out standards, and clear and regular communication with key people in an organization. An annual plan that summarizes progress and establishes specific plans for the next year, awareness of new developments in technology, and regular contact and interaction with managers in other organizations also helps managers in identifying decision problems.

Decide Who Should Decide

In decision situations, an individual makes some decisions with available information. An individual manager makes other decisions after consulting with colleagues to gather information and opinions. Finally, some decisions should be made by groups using a participative decision-making process. Vroom and Yetton (1973) developed a decision tree to help managers decide who should decide in a given decision situation. Their criteria for choosing an autocratic, consultative, or group decision process included: need for acceptance of the decision; adequacy of available information; subordinate acceptance of organizational goals; and likelihood of conflict among subordinates about a preferred solution.

Collect Information

Once a problem is defined, one can proceed to determine the factors that affect the problem and the information needed about viable alternatives. Without information, decision making is by hunch and intuition. On the other hand, too much time can be spent gathering data. Formal search and data gathering has a cost in terms of both money and time. The additional costs of data collection need to be weighed against the benefits of additional data. MIS and DSS can provide information for decision making, but a cost is incurred in development and use of the system.

Identify and Evaluate Alternatives

The most creative part of decision making is the identification of alternatives and the determination of which ones should receive serious consideration and analysis. Brainstorming to generate ideas is useful in many situations. A long list of ideas with many poor ideas and one or two good ones is more useful than a short list of old ideas. A large quantity of ideas is more likely to lead to some high quality ideas than focusing on one or a few readily available ones. Early in the brainstorming process, the objective is quantity of ideas. How good, unique, or impractical an idea may be is of very little concern in brainstorming. A commonly used group brainstorming and idea evaluation tool is the Nominal Group Technique (NGT). NGT emphasizes silent idea generation, idea sharing, and rating or ranking of alternatives (see Delbecq, Van de Ven and Gustafson, 1975). Some GDSS have tools based on NGT. Also using explicit decision criteria can help one evaluate alternatives.

Decide

To make a decision is to commit to a course of action or inaction. In some situations, a decision *must* be made—it is required or demanded by circumstances, customers, or stockholders. Decisions are then sometimes made with less information than one would like and with some feasible alternatives not evaluated or even considered. DSS are not usually as helpful in these "crisis" decision situations. In other situations, there is more time for collecting information and evaluating alternatives.

In decision situations with ample time to collect information and evaluate alternatives, the decision is not forced and the result may be a more thoughtful decision or in a worst case a delayed and postponed decision. Indecision is a failure to take action when it should be taken. "I need more information" is a common reason cited by people for not deciding. Indecision or decisions made with great anguish is often a characteristic of an ineffective manager. DSS can potentially reduce procrastination and indecision by helping structure the decision situation and gather information. DSS can also help weight and structure decision criteria on "soft" criteria, like company impact or reaction of competitors.

Implement

A decision or choice among alternatives is the culmination of one specific decision process. The decision process may have been long and convoluted or rapid and simple. But for any problem and set of alternatives, made with or without a decision aid, once a decision is made, something usually happens. What happens is implementation of the "decision". Decisions often trigger actions and information technology can focus and direct those actions and complete a broader process of action and change. DSS can help communicate decisions, monitor plans and actions, and track performance.

Follow-up and Assessment

Measuring and evaluating the consequences of a decision that has been implemented calls for the decision maker to accept responsibility for the decision. During follow-up, new problems may or may not be discovered. In some cases, minor adjustments and corrective actions are necessary. Because situations do not remain the same for very long, managers are often dealing with problems that grew out of the solutions chosen to previous problems. So the decision loop or cycle is complete—definition of a problem leading to assessment of the decision that was implemented leads to consciousness of new problems. DSS can help in monitoring, follow-up, and assessment.

"GOOD" DECISION MAKING

Good decisions are the ones that resolve the problem identified. Not all decisions will have this intended outcome. No manager always makes the right decision. Factors that are unforeseeable, or over which the decision maker has no control, ensure that some wrong decisions will be made.

Defining Success

According to Trull (1966), the success of a decision is a function of its quality and of how it is implemented. Decision quality is judged by a decision's compatibility with existing constraints, its timeliness, and its incorporation of the optimal amount of information. A successful implementation of a decision results when managers avoid conflict of interest, make sure the decision is understood by those who must carry it out, and perceive that the rewards of successful implementation are worth the risks of implementing the decision. Decision success is a measure of whether objectives sought when making a decision have been partially or completely attained.

The distinction between effectiveness of decision making and efficiency in decision making helps DSS analysts understand the impact of DSS on decision behavior. Keen and Scott Morton (1978) present the following explanations of these important concepts: "Effectiveness in decision making requires us to address the process of identifying what should be done. Effective decision making requires consideration of the criteria influencing the decision. ... Efficiency in decision making addresses the means for performing a given defined task in order to achieve outputs as well as possible, relative to some predefined performance criteria."

Increasing efficiency typically takes the form of minimizing time, cost, or effort to complete an activity. Effectiveness focuses on what activities should occur. A focus on effectiveness requires decision makers to adapt and learn and to make a responsive adjustment to changes in the environment for and within which they make decisions (after Bennett 1983, p. 2).

Impediments

There are some known impediments to "good" decisions over which a manager does have some control. Some examples include tradition and bias, lack of knowledge, and improper use of decision aids.

Tradition and Status Quo Bias Impediment

"We have always done it that way." The finality and implied end of discussion suggested by this statement means that tradition is at work. Approaching alternatives with prejudice means that an otherwise good alternative is not given serious consideration because of bias. Tradition and status quo bias reflect fear of change and fear of failure. Comfort with the known and confidence in what has worked before are understandable. But when tradition and bias prevent brainstorming for new ideas, consideration of off-the-wall ideas, making mistakes, and experimenting with new ideas, they are impediments to good decision making. This impediment can hinder the implementation of a novel DSS, and a computerized DSS can do little to reduce this impediment. Managers need to be conscious of this problem and work to overcome it with others who perceive a need for change.

Lack of Knowledge Impediment

Having the right information at the right time is important in many decision situations. It is also important that managers understand the information they receive. In nonroutine decision situations an absence of information and knowledge can be a major impediment to effective decision making. In more routine and recurring decision situations this problem can be overcome. A wide variety of DSS can be built to overcome that impediment. DSS can provide information and knowledge and facilitate understanding in many decision situations.

Improper Use of Decision Aids Impediment

It is discouraging to realize that some of the decision aids and DSS that have been created and implemented in organizations actually hindered "good" and successful decision making. DSS can provide a false sense of confidence that information is complete or that data is accurate. To avoid this problem, it is important that DSS analysts conduct an assessment of situations that results in complete and accurate information. These attributes of information are not guaranteed because the data is in a DSS or because a model is used. DSS need to be designed to positively impact decision behavior for an individual or for a group. Also in Decision Support Systems it is hard to support qualitative issues; so managers are rewarded for placing the greatest emphasis on numbers and quantified attributes. DSS usually neglect political issues, and DSS users may not explicitly consider their personal values and use their general knowledge and common sense while using a DSS. For all these reasons, DSS can be an impediment to good decision making in some situations.

To reduce the likelihood of these problems and to create effective DSS, Herbert Simon (1965) argued that we need to understand the thought process that computerized decision aids will support. Our understanding of decision behavior and thought processes remains incomplete and we need to be especially cautious in assessing when and how a DSS will be used prior to its design and implementation.

REDESIGNING DECISION PROCESSES

Hammer and Champy (1993) defined business process reengineering as the fundamental rethinking and redesign of business processes to achieve dramatic improvements in critical, contemporary measures of performance, such as cost, quality, service, and speed. In some situations reengineering has succeeded, but many failures have also occurred. Managers do not need to focus only on grand efforts to reengineer corporations; what is often needed is redesigned business decision processes that better use information technologies and DSS.

Business Process Reengineering

In a now classic *Harvard Business Review* article, Michael Hammer (1990) asserted that companies rarely achieve radical performance improvements when they invest in information technology. Most companies use computers to speed up, not break away from, business processes and rules that are decades, if not centuries, out of date. Hammer argued the power of computers can be released by "reengineering" work. Managers can use computers and DSS to achieve the important business goals of increasing speed, quality, and flexibility, while lowering business costs. Redesigned decision processes and new DSS can help achieve all of these goals.

In general, a business process is a group of activities, including decision activities, which create value for a customer. Let's briefly examine the process of fulfilling a customer order. Order fulfillment is a process that consists primarily of transaction processing activities, from order entry, picking products from inventory, dealing with back orders, shipping products, and dealing with returns. A number of decisions are made during the process, but they are primarily routine and recurring. What is often ignored are the control decisions about product quality or employee performance that are also made periodically with data from the order fulfillment process. If one reengineers this business process, the goal is most likely a dramatic improvement in results. Hammer argues that dramatic improvement means a quantum leap in performance, a tenfold increase in productivity, or an 80 percent reduction in cycle time. These may be overly ambitious and impossible goals in the context of the order fulfillment process. Rather than accepting the status quo, improving the control decisions with a new DSS may actually be a more practical means of improving process performance, productivity or reducing cycle time.

Business process reengineering (BPR) has other consequences. According to Hammer and others, BPR typically creates an organization with a particular set of characteristics:

1. Processes are simple instead of complex.
2. People perform a broad range of tasks.
3. People become empowered to make decisions, rather than controlled.
4. The emphasis is a team and not an individual.
5. Organizational structure shifts to a flat structure.
6. Key figures are professionals, rather than managers.
7. The new focus is on the end-to-end business process.
8. The basis for performance measurement shifts from activity to result.
9. Managers serve as coaches, facilitators, and decision makers for exceptions.
10. A single point of contact is created for interacting with customers.

These consequences of business process reengineering are often desirable results, and many of them can be realized by more modest efforts to redesign business decision processes. Many of the above characteristics are attitudes, rather than new processes or structures that managers need to develop. Redesigning rather than reengineering Business Decision Processes is a viable alternative and DSS can be part of either strategy for improving work processes.

Redesigning Business Decision Processes

Managers can be logical and even intentionally rational in their decision making and yet still make the wrong decision. Also, there are not always, even after the fact, objectively "right" decisions. The following tips for redesigning decision processes and developing a new DSS should help insure that the decision maker who uses a DSS will benefit from using it.

Begin by clearly defining the business process. Determine if a DSS can help gather, organize, analyze, and/or retrieve information as part of the business process.

Use DSS to manage time pressure in a business process. The greater the time pressure to make a decision, the worse a manager's decision is likely to be. Therefore, a DSS should help a manager obtain enough information to make a high-quality decision in both high and low time pressure situations. A DSS should help managers analyze information thoroughly, help get other people involved, and help explore available options. A business process analysis should look for these opportunities.

Have the DSS manage the steps in a decision process when possible. A DSS should help decision makers and groups act to make timely decisions and to communicate them. In general, if managers delay making a decision past some vague critical point, a decision may lose some or all of its effectiveness. If possible, a DSS should provide information to help assess the urgency of a decision situation. Managers need to consider factors such as competitors' actions, how long the opportunity will last, how reversible the decision is, and the amount of risk involved. A DSS should help a manager deal with ambiguity. A DSS should help a manager conduct appropriate analyses, but it should not promote excessive analysis.

A DSS should enhance a decision maker's confidence. Confident decision makers deal more effectively with opportunities and risks. Managers need to use their decision-making skills to make the right decision and then use persuasion skills to sell the decision. A DSS should not be designed to help managers rationalize decisions, but rather to make more intentionally rational decisions. Analyzing goals and values is an important part of decision making, and DSS should not diminish the importance of values and the importance of assuming responsibility for the decisions that are made.

DSS should encourage creativity. Solutions are not clearly identified in all decision situations. DSS should not impose too much structure in situations that are unstructured or ambiguous. DSS can support creation of custom solutions.

To develop an effective DSS of any type, managers and analysts must focus on the interface between the decision maker and the computer. A new DSS will have an impact on the business process, related decision processes, and the behavior of the decision makers. The actual impact is primarily a function of the DSS user interface. DSS can only increase efficiency and effectiveness of decision making if the user interface is accepted and responsive to user needs. The interface must be responsive, rather than efficient, because what will help managers most may not be the "most efficient." A DSS must first be used in order to have any positive results.

CONCLUSIONS AND COMMENTARY

Making "good" decisions is *not* an easy task for individual managers or for groups of managers. DSS can aid in routine and nonroutine decision making but DSS do not make decision making any easier or less important. People do have significant limitations that hinder their success as decision makers. Despite those limitations, many managers make and have made successful decisions of major significance and importance without using a DSS. So, the issue in evaluating the need for a DSS must be whether DSS can improve the frequency of successful decisions in an organization. This outcome is possible, but at a cost, and simply providing more information for decision makers is the wrong approach. The trade-offs in evaluating proposed DSS are evaluated in more detail in Chapter 12.

Decision makers can benefit from better, timelier information that is presented in a relevant, unbiased way. Understandable analyses and graphical displays are generally better than complex displays and long, complex tables of numbers. Poor or excessive information presentation in a DSS may result in information overload or biased decision making. Both types of negative results will result in bad decisions or inaction when a decision is needed.

DSS analysts need to be cautious in their DSS design activities, and they need to avoid reinforcing the limitations of decision makers in a DSS design.

DSS should enhance the process of decision making and reduce the negative consequences of human information processing limitations. These positive results arise from a sophisticated understanding of decision-making concepts and behavior. DSS analysts need to use their knowledge of managerial decision making when designing and evaluating DSS.

Some managers have very real concerns about developing computerized decision support that must be addressed. For example, George Vickers, a manager turned sociologist, wrote in 1967, "I fear the alluring possibilities of automating decision processes, first, because the decisions which lend themselves to be so treated are decisions about the best means to reach given ends, where the criteria by which means are judged best are given, like the 'ends,' at the outset. I believe that no important decisions are of this type and that those which appear to be so usually conceal more important questions which ought to be dealt with first. I fear that automation will further bury these essential issues. Intractable problems are usually solved by being re-stated; their 'facts' are found to be irrelevant. Vast, vested interests resist such re-statements; and I fear that automation will make these vaster still. Most of all, I fear the possibilities of automated decision making, because I believe that the criteria which determine decisions are only evolved by the process of decision itself and that this process, so tedious and necessarily half-conscious, will be further jeopardized by the appearance of the new technique and the new mystique, with its panache of certainty" (Vickers, 1967, pp. 144–145). Vickers's concerns remain relevant today and his "fears" should be a cautionary cry to managers and to DSS analysts.

Chapter 4

Designing and Developing Decision Support Systems

INTRODUCTION

In the Decision Support Systems (DSS) literature, experts prescribe a variety of approaches or methodologies for designing and developing DSS. Everyone does not, however, agree on what methodology works best for building different types of DSS. If managers and DSS analysts understand the various methods, they can make more informed and better choices when building or buying a specific DSS.

In general, what is called a "decision-oriented approach" seems best for Decision Support Systems projects. After reviewing design and development issues, decision-oriented diagnosis, and feasibility studies, this chapter reviews three alternative approaches for developing a DSS. Because the scope of DSS is expanding, and because development tools are changing rapidly, the perceived advantages of the three alternative development approaches have become somewhat controversial. For example, a highly structured life-cycle development approach has recently become popular with some consultants for developing enterprise-wide DSS. The advantages and disadvantages of each development approach are discussed. The final sections of this chapter discuss outsourcing DSS, project management, and the various participants on a DSS design and development team.

OVERVIEW OF DESIGN AND DEVELOPMENT ISSUES

How does one plan and implement a new DSS? What does it mean to design a DSS? How does one develop a DSS? Who develops a new DSS? When should a company build a DSS and when should a company buy a DSS package? Both managers and Management Information Systems (MIS) professionals need to explore these questions. A company does not receive any advantage from a great idea for a DSS until the new system is built and successfully implemented.

Many Information Systems (IS) professionals develop, modify, and customize software to support decision making. They work in diverse business and organization settings and in specialized DSS software companies. DSS software vendors sell a wide array of products and provide DSS development services. For example, Comshare (www.comshare.com) and Cognos (www.cognos.com) both market business intelligence and management planning and control products.

Design and development is an important topic because DSS serve many different functions and are quite diverse in terms of the software used for their development. Choosing an appropriate approach or methodology for building DSS has been a popular and controversial topic in the Information Systems (IS) literature. Many consulting firms focus on using what they claim is the most effective development methodology. We can define a methodology as an organized set of practices and procedures used by developers. Despite many differences in methodologies and terminology, the prescriptions in the IS literature have generally followed three different conceptual paths.

One group of MIS and DSS experts develop their recommendations for building DSS in the context of the traditional systems analysis and design literature (cf., Thierauff, 1982). A second group has prescribed and explained an iterative, prototyping, or "quick-hit" approach for designing and developing DSS (cf., Sprague and Carlson, 1982). Some authors refer to both types of approaches without explaining clearly the advantages and disadvantages or contingencies favoring a specific approach or some combination of approaches. A third approach to building DSS, called end-user development, is to let managers develop their own personal DSS. In general, the DSS prescriptive literature on design and development is based on personal experiences, case studies, the general IS development literature, and a wide variety of DSS "war stories" from developers. Very little empirical research has been conducted on design and development methodologies.

Because of design and development problems, some highly innovative and potentially useful DSS have been failures. The problem often is that the DSS are designed and developed from the perspective of the programmer and developer rather than from that of the manager and user. Sequences of commands or icons may be obvious to the programmer, but may be totally unknown and puzzling to the DSS user. From a prescriptive standpoint, effective DSS need to be user-oriented. The key issue is what design and development process and which procedures can increase the likelihood that a usable and effective DSS will be created and built.

Building DSS is often very expensive. So, it is important to investigate alternative design and development approaches. We want to choose an approach that increases the chances the DSS will be used and will accomplish its purpose. We need to remember DSS are designed and developed to help people make better and more effective decisions than they could without computerized assistance. Building any type of DSS is difficult because people vary so much in terms of their personalities, their knowledge, their ability, their preferences, the jobs they hold, and the decisions they need to make. Also, DSS must often meet a diverse set of requirements. This wide variety of differing requirements has led to the design and development of a wide variety of DSS capabilities and systems.

The following discussion separates out the diagnostic design and feasibility portion of an overall systems development process. The phrase systems development life cycle (SDLC) is the most commonly encountered term used to describe the steps in a traditional systems development methodology. SDLC is also sometimes known as the applications development life cycle approach and involves three steps: (1) initiation and diagnosis, (2) acquisition (build or buy), and (3) introduction of the new system.

As mentioned above, the two commonly prescribed alternatives to the SDLC development approach are a prototyping approach and end-user development of DSS. In both of these approaches, a portion of the DSS is quickly constructed, then tested, improved, and expanded. Prototyping is similar to a related approach called rapid application development (RAD).

DECISION-ORIENTED DIAGNOSIS

Increasing decision-making effectiveness through changes in how decisions are made should be the major objective for any DSS project (cf., Stabell 1983). Stabell proposes a decision-oriented design approach for DSS. He argues that predesign description and diagnosis of decision making is the key to securing a decision-oriented approach to DSS development.

The diagnosis of current decision making and the specification of changes in decision processes are the activities that provide the key input to the design of the DSS. Diagnosis is the identification of problems or opportunities for improvement in current decision behavior. Diagnosis involves determining how decisions are currently made, specifying how decisions should be made, and understanding why decisions are not made as they should be. A specification of changes in decision processes involves choosing what specific improvements in decision behavior are to be achieved. These statements of improvements provide the objectives for the DSS development.

According to Stabell, diagnosis of problems in a decision process involves completing the following three activities:

1. Collecting data on current decision-making using techniques such as interviews, observations, questionnaires, and historical records;
2. Establishing a coherent description of the current decision process; and
3. Specifying a norm for how decisions should be made.

These activities are interdependent and provide feedback for the DSS analyst. In many DSS development projects it is not feasible to perform a full-scale diagnosis of decision making. A shortened study is often necessary due to cost considerations, limited access to managers, or other organizational constraints. As a consequence, DSS analysts should develop the ability to produce a diagnosis after only limited analysis of a decision situation.

A related diagnostic activity is conducting a Decision Process Audit. In general, it can be very useful to audit operational and managerial decision processes. An audit can be a first step in identifying opportunities to redesign business processes and include new decision aids and DSS in business processes. In some situations an audit can suggest changes in decision technologies that can improve performance and reduce costs. When an audit is completed, the central questions should be how can we do better and what changes should have the highest priority. Table 4.1 identifies five steps in a Decision Process Audit.

	Decision Process Audit Plan
Step 1.	Define the decisions, decision processes and related business processes that will be audited. Define the authority of the auditor, purpose of the audit, scope of the audit, timing of the audit, and resources required to perform the audit. Identify a primary contact.
Step 2.	Examine the formal design of the process. Diagram the process using Data Flow Diagrams and specify participants, data, criteria, etc.
Step 3.	Examine the actual use of the decision process. Observe the process. Interview decision makers and collect data. Is the process implemented and used as intended?
Step 4.	Assess performance of the actual decision process. What works? Can cycle time be reduced? Are decisions appropriate? Timely? Cost effective? Is the process producing value in meeting business objectives? If not, why?
Step 5.	Reporting and recommendations. Summarize steps 1-4 in a written report. Discuss what is working well and what needs to be improved. Develop recommendations for improving the process. Hold an exit meeting with decision makers.

Table 4.1 A Decision Process Audit Plan

Creating a Data Flow Diagram (DFD) is an important step in a Decision Process Audit. A DFD graphically depicts a business process and the flow of data through the process. To create the DFD, the DSS analyst decomposes the process that is being investigated into small steps, actions or events. The steps may occur sequentially or in parallel. A DFD is particularly useful for enhancing communication between a DSS analyst and managers.

An audit should also focus on identifying what is assumed by decision makers in a decision situation and on what is defined by decision makers as the range of available remedial actions. Identifying assumptions and actions is especially appropriate if building a model-driven DSS is a possibility. Assessing the performance of the actual decision process is an important task in the audit. One needs to determine what tasks are effective. Can cycle time be reduced? Are decisions appropriate? Timely? and Cost effective?

Some processes like business planning need improved data access and analysis to increase business intelligence. Rockart (1979) identified an approach for defining decision-making data needs that is appropriate for data-driven DSS and especially Executive Information Systems (EIS). Rockart's Critical Success Factors (CSF) Design Method focuses on individual managers and on each manager's current hard and soft information needs. A CSF analysis can be beneficial in identifying "the limited number of areas in which results, if they are satisfactory, will insure successful competitive performance for the organization." If organizational goals were to be attained, then these key areas of activity—usually three to six factors—would need careful and consistent attention from management.

Good diagnosis is difficult, but DSS diagnosis involves skills that can be developed and sharpened. Both managers and MIS staff need to work on completing the diagnosis task. Does diagnosis always provide sufficient information for specifying a DSS? In most cases, the diagnosis does provide sufficient information for specifying several alternative designs. DSS design usually involves a number of difficult trade-offs. The first trade-off is whether the DSS should support both the existing process and a prescribed new process. There is also a trade-off in the extent of the capabilities of the DSS and the scope of the process the DSS is designed to support. In most cases, the initial version of a DSS focuses on either extensive capabilities for a narrow scope process or on a few capabilities for a broad scope process.

PREPARE A FEASIBILITY STUDY

Diagnosis of decision making should be followed by additional initiation and diagnostic activities and preparation of a feasibility study of the technical and economic prospects related to developing a DSS. This study should occur prior to actually committing resources to developing a proposed DSS. What should be included in a DSS feasibility study? This is a common question. An outline for an extensive feasibility study report is included in Table 4.2. The outline has 15 sections on topics like DSS scope and target users, anticipated DSS impacts, benefits, risks and mitigating factors. Shorter, less comprehensive studies and reports are usually prepared for small scope DSS projects.

A Decision Support System feasibility study examines a proposed project's consequences and impacts. A feasibility study is summarized in a formal report or document. The study addresses issues including the project's benefits, costs, effectiveness, alternatives considered, analysis of alternatives, opinions of potential users, and other factors. This feasibility analysis is a way of exploring the factors and risks affecting the potential for successful development and implementation of a DSS. Large-scale information systems development efforts typically include a feasibility study as a major checkpoint providing critical information about whether it is possible to develop a system, given the project's goals and constraints. This report should be framed to offer important information about the range of issues likely to affect success and therefore should be considered in decisions about whether and how to move forward with a DSS development effort.

I.   **EXECUTIVE SUMMARY**
      A.   Key Business Needs
      B.   Issues
      C.   Solutions
      D.   Benefits and Costs
      E.   Critical Success Factors
      F.   Project Management

II.   **INTRODUCTION**
      A.   Background and Definitions
      B.   Key Questions
           1. Site Readiness: To what extent is the company ready for and
              interested in implementing a new Decision Support System? See
              Appendix II.
           2. Technical Feasibility: Is it possible to develop or adapt software to
              perform the proposed types of analyses.
           3. Financial Feasibility: What are the projected costs of implementing
              the DSS, and do potential benefits justify these costs?
      C.   Feasibility Study Approach

III. **BACKGROUND NEEDS AND ASSESSMENT**
      A.   Goals
      B.   Constraints
      C.   Related Projects
      D.   Business Decision Support Needs
      E.   Decision Support Diagnosis

IV.   **OBJECTIVES**

V.   **DSS SCOPE AND TARGET USERS**
      A.   Scope and Decision Process Definition
      B.   Scope Recommendation
      C.   Scope Issues

VI.   **ANTICIPATED DSS IMPACTS**

VII. **PROPOSED SOLUTION**
      A.   System Integration Issues
      B.   Major Functions Provided
      C.   Technology Tools/Infrastructure Used
      D.   New Organizational Structure and Processes

VIII. **MAJOR ALTERNATIVES**
IX.   **CONFORMITY WITH CURRENT IS/IT PLAN**
X.   **PROJECT MANAGEMENT AND ORGANIZATION ISSUES**
XI.   **ESTIMATED TIME FRAME AND WORKPLAN**
XII. **INCREMENTAL COSTS AND BENEFITS**
XIII. **RISKS AND MITIGATING FACTORS**
XIV. **DRAFT CONCEPTUAL DESIGN**

Table 4.2 DSS Feasibility Study Outline

After completing a feasibility study, a decision is often made between purchasing an application package and in-house development. In general, packaged DSS applications are quite versatile and are usually less expensive to implement than in-house development. Packaged solutions are also often faster to implement. In addition, a packaged DSS may reduce political problems if a DSS project fails. The problems associated with purchasing a packaged DSS should not however be ignored. A package may not "fit" the needs that have been identified, and competitors can also purchase a package. Using a packaged application is less likely to create a competitive advantage. Customizing a packaged application can sometimes overcome these problems and limitations.

CHOOSE A DEVELOPMENT APPROACH

As noted in the overview, three approaches to DSS development are discussed in the IS and DSS literature and are used by practitioners. The approaches or methodologies have been called by a variety of names. Essentially, we begin by focusing on decisions and decision processes in the decision-oriented design steps; then, a project manager or an end-user implements a more or less structured development methodology.

Figure 4.1 shows a recommended process hierarchy for DSS design and development. The process begins with a decision-oriented diagnosis and feasibility analysis and then moves to in-house or outsourced development of the proposed DSS using one of three development approaches. Let's examine these alternative approaches.

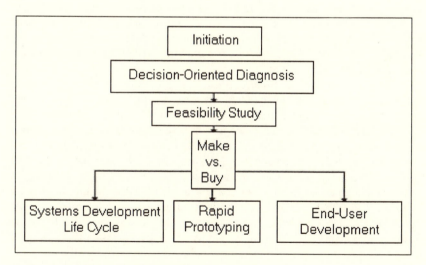

Figure 4.1 A DSS Design and Development Hierarchy

Systems Development Life Cycle Approach

The systems development life cycle (SDLC) approach is based on a series of formal steps, including these seven steps:

1. Confirm user requirements;
2. Systems analysis;
3. System design;
4. Programming;
5. Testing;
6. Implementation; and
7. Use and Evaluation.

Although different versions of SDLC vary in the precise number of steps and in the detailed definitions of those steps, those listed above illustrate the approach. Decision-oriented design begins to address user requirements, but, in SDLC, user requirements need to be defined in great detail.

This formal SDLC approach is sometimes called the "waterfall" model because of the sequential flow from one step to another. Each formal step concludes with preparation of a written progress report that must be reviewed and approved. Reviewers include both prospective users of the system and developers. For example, in Step 5, prospective users verify that the documented functions and capabilities and the user interface meet their needs. Developers verify that the system's internal interfaces are consistently defined and meet all technical requirements.

When the SDLC approach was first formalized in the mid-1970s, it provided structure and discipline to system developers. It was soon adopted widely for developing large-scale TPS. SDLC is especially common when a formal contractual relationship exists between the developers of an application system and its eventual users because it provides written evidence that can be used to arbitrate any disputes.

The development of a large, shared, enterprise-wide DSS is often an undertaking of great complexity. Organizational decision processes are complex, and computerizing systems to support them can increase that complexity. Using a methodology like SDLC provides one way in which business organizations can systematically approach the development of an enterprise-wide DSS.

When the SDLC approach is used, then project plans must be carefully prepared. When developing requirements, it is best to start by determining the needs of all potential users. Then, analysts should identify the outputs that would fulfill those needs. Technical requirements should follow logical requirements, and constraints must be identified for all DSS system components. These requirements must be documented carefully and reviewed by the targeted users.

Several alternatives may exist for meeting the needs identified during the requirements and design steps. Each of these alternatives should be carefully reviewed and the best one chosen. Another choice to be made concerns the "make or buy" decision. If in-house development is not chosen, a request-for-proposal (RFP) may be required. During the design stage, technical processes must be managed, people and procedures prepared, and an installation plan developed.

In many situations a full-scale SDLC approach is too rigid for building DSS, especially those DSS whose requirements are changing rapidly. User requirements, agreed upon at the first stage of the process, are rigidly specified with SDLC. Any significant change restarts the entire development cycle, as subsequent requirements documents are based on the agreed-upon user needs. Changes are therefore often expensive; in fact, SDLC limits change in a DSS rather than accommodating it.

Rapid Prototyping

All of the different versions of rapid prototyping accommodate and even encourage changes in the requirements of a proposed Decision Support System. A typical prototyping methodology usually includes five steps:

1. Identify user requirements.
2. Develop and test a first iteration DSS prototype.
3. Create the next iteration DSS prototype.
4. Test the DSS prototype and return to step 3 if needed.
5. Pilot testing, phased or full-scale implementation.

The prototyping development approach evolved in response to perceived deficiencies and limitations of the SDLC approach. In a prototyping development approach, DSS analysts sit down with potential users and develop requirements. These requirements are specified in general terms and should evolve from the decision-oriented diagnosis and design. The analyst then develops a prototype of a system that appears to meet the requirements. DSS analysts use tools such as Database Management Systems and DSS application generators that support rapid development. Analysts focus on capabilities rather than on resolving problems. A prototype may not resolve how to access a real database, what "help" screens are needed, or define other capabilities that require extensive development time. The prototype is something that users can try out, react to, comment on, and eventually approve with confidence that it meets their needs. Missing features are added later, once users are satisfied with the way the prototype works. Rapid Application Development (RAD) specifies incremental development with constant feedback from potential users. The objective of RAD is to keep projects focused on delivering value and to keep clear and open lines of communication. In most situations, oral and written communication is not adequate for specification of computer systems. RAD overcomes the limitations of language by minimizing the time between concept and actual prototype implementation.

Once approved, a prototype can be expanded in the development environment, or the prototype can be used as a specification for a DSS, developed in a language like Java, C, or C++. When a prototype is reprogrammed, the prototype serves as a detailed specification that is turned into an operational system. The best prototype development approach is to have the actual prototype evolve directly into the finished product. In this approach the prototype is attached to a database and features are added to it, but it remains written in the high-level tools originally used for prototype development.

Compared with the SDLC approach, prototyping seems to improve user-developer communication. It introduces deliberate flexibility and responsiveness into the development process. Change is no longer something to be avoided; it is built into the process and encouraged. The system that is developed is more likely to meet user needs than is a system developed through SDLC.

Prototyping can extend the development schedule if it is improperly used. Managers and developers are often tempted to "tinker" with a DSS and make changes that do not really improve the usability of the finished product. If managers and developers want to build a useful system and meet project deadlines, then they must manage and control systems development efforts.

End-User DSS Development

End-user development of DSS puts the responsibility for building and maintaining a DSS on the manager who builds it. Powerful end-user software is available to managers, and many managers have the ability—and feel the need—to develop their own desktop DSS. Managers frequently use spreadsheets, like Microsoft Excel and Lotus 1-2-3, as DSS development tools. Using a spreadsheet package, they can analyze an issue like the impact of different budget options. Following the analysis, managers select the alternative that best meets their department's needs. Also, managers can develop tools to help them conduct market analyses and make projections and forecasts at their desktop.

The major advantage of encouraging end-user DSS development is that the person who wants computer support will be involved in creating it. The manager/builder controls the situation and the solution that is developed. End-user DSS development can also sometimes result in faster development and cost savings.

End-user DSS development of complex DSS is much less desirable. Managers are paid to manage, *not* to develop DSS. At some point DSS specialists can do the work much better and much faster. Also, managers are not trained to test systems, create documentation, provide for back-up and data security, and design sophisticated user interfaces. DSS analysts should help managers develop more complex end-user Decision Support projects. DSS analysts can help the manager build, document, and test the application. Managers need to emphasize the content of the DSS and not become overly involved with extensive DSS development projects.

End-user DSS development is a controversial topic. IS staffs have many concerns including:

1.   End-users may select an inappropriate software product or hardware platform as a development environment.

2. The end-user may have limited expertise in the use of the product, and the IT group may have limited resources to support end-user development.
3. Errors during end-user DSS development are frequent. Even experienced developers can make errors, and end-users are likely to overlook the need for checking formulas and auditing the DSS they have developed.
4. Unnecessary databases are sometimes developed by end-users for their DSS. Redundant databases can contain outdated and inaccurate data.
5. A major quality issue involves testing and limited documentation. End-users often perform only limited testing of DSS they develop, and they have limited experience in documenting applications.
6. End-user databases may be poorly constructed and difficult to maintain.
7. End-users rarely follow a systematic development process. Some needs and requirements may be overlooked.
8. An end-user developer may leave a company; the DSS then becomes difficult to support.
9. An end-user-developed application may not work when many concurrent users are trying to access its capabilities.

If an organization's MIS group gets actively involved in supporting end-user DSS development, many of the above problems can be minimized, reduced, or eliminated. Packages used for end-user development can be standardized; end-users can be trained in the use of selected packages; support staff can act as consultants and reviewers; a central databases can be maintained for use with end-user applications; and documentation can be encouraged by MIS staff.

One approach is to create an information center. An information center can provide support for end-users and the director of the information center may be able to manage end-user computing. Services that an information center might provide include: software training; user support, including answering specific development questions; installation assistance and advice about new systems; and setting standards for documentation, software application, and distribution of applications. Choosing either SDLC or a prototyping development approach requires selection of a project manager. Let us now examine DSS project management issues.

DSS PROJECT MANAGEMENT

Moving from an informal exploration of a suggestion or desire for a DSS to a formal project is an important step. An executive sponsor should push to have a project manager assigned to the project. The initial tasks of the project manager include diagnosis, a feasibility study, and a definition of the objectives and scope of the proposed project. Once these steps are done, the executive sponsor needs to choose to continue the project or postpone any further work on it. Depending upon the scope of the DSS project, an executive sponsor may be able to directly fund the project, or funding may be budgeted as part of business and information systems planning. The larger the scope of the proposed project, the more important it is to solicit widespread agreement and sponsorship of it. The objectives of a large-scope DSS project must be strategically motivated, should have strong executive support, and must meet a business need. Large-scope projects may benefit from having co-project managers: a business and a technical manager. If co-managers are designated, clear authority and responsibility guidelines should be established.

Once a project is approved, then a methodology and project plan needs to be developed and a project team should be assembled. If the project will be outsourced, then a process needs to be developed for creating a request for proposals and then evaluating the proposals submitted. If the development will occur in-house, development tools and technical issues need to be resolved. (The feasibility analysis should have determined if the project could be completed in-house.)

User requirements need to be specified in some detail. For large projects, the DSS architecture must be specified and any changes or additions to the Information Systems and Information Technology (IS/IT) infrastructure must be planned. Once these crucial preliminaries are completed, then systems design or prototyping can occur. The project tasks will not be completed in a simple, linear sequence, and the project manager must actively manage the project. Whenever possible, the project manager and, in some cases, a co-project manager from the business area most affected should consult and work with other potential users. The project manager must keep the executive sponsor informed. If problems are occurring or might occur, the sponsor needs to be alerted.

The project manager should identify tasks that must be completed, resources that are needed, and project deliverables. Deliverables are especially important for monitoring the progress of the project. Milestones or important project events are also often identified to help nontechnical managers monitor a project. The Chief Information Officer (CIO) of a firm and one or more business managers usually monitor the progress of a large-scope or high-visibility DSS project. Managers expect results from DSS projects. Understanding and meeting the expectations of managers who will use a DSS is the most important and most difficult part of a DSS project manager's job.

The project manager defines project plans and manages the daily activities associated with the project. She also coordinates project resources, the project budget, status reporting, changes in requirements and tasks, relations with vendors, and relations with sponsors, skeptics, and MIS staff. A DSS project manager may come from information systems or from a functional department and needs strong technical skills, outstanding people skills, assertiveness, and knowledge of the business.

Outsourcing

Outsourcing involves contracting with outside consultants, software houses, or service bureaus to perform systems analysis, programming, or other DSS development activities. The outsourcer should be evaluated as a long-term asset and as a source of ongoing value to the company. Time and resources need to be dedicated to managing the relationship and maximizing its value. The customer needs a project manager to manage the outsourcing relationship. The intent should be to keep the relationship for as long as it brings value to the customer. Over time, new technology alliances may be required as technology and organizations change. Therefore, a customer should strive for long-term relationships and work to align the outsourcer's motivation with company goals by developing appropriate incentives and penalties.

Outsourcing DSS projects has a number of risks. First, a company relinquishes control of an important capability to an outside organization. Second, contracts for DSS services may be long term and may lock a company into a particular service provider. Finally, a reliance on external sources for new systems development can lead to low technical knowledge among in-house MIS staff.

Some of the benefits of outsourcing include potentially lower cost development, access to expertise about new technologies, and "freeing up" company resources for other projects. The high risks, however, often lead to in-house DSS development rather than to outsourcing. When does outsourcing seem to work? Outsourcing can be successful when a company needs to turn around DSS activities quickly and when a company's MIS staff seems unable to build innovative DSS in-house. In some companies this situation exists today for Web-based DSS.

DSS PROJECT PARTICIPANTS

A complex DSS, built using either an SDLC or a prototyping approach, requires a team approach to development. Once the system is developed, a group may also need to maintain the system. Some large-scale DSS are built with teams of two or three people, or with a larger group of ten or more. Members of DSS teams are drawn from many areas in an organization, including the IS group.

Any DSS development project requires a mix of complementary skills. Usually, one does not find all of the needed skills in one person. So, in most situations, it is necessary to assemble the right mix of contributors for a DSS project team. The key DSS development roles identified by Sprague (1980), O'Neil et al. (1997), and others are listed below in order of increasing technical expertise. Figure 4.2 summarizes the various roles. A given individual may be assigned more than one role.

Project Manager. This is a business or technical manager who can organize and manage the resources needed to complete the DSS project.

Executive Sponsor or Project Champion. This is a senior manager who has access to other senior executives and has the influence to help resolve major resource and political problems. The sponsor is occasionally actively involved in the development tasks.

Potential DSS User(s). This is a person who makes decisions that a proposed DSS will support. Users are often nontechnical people in functional areas of a business such as marketing and finance.

DSS Analyst. This is the MIS specialist who acts as an intermediary or liaison between users and DSS developers. A DSS analyst may make the decisions about the software tools to use, the hardware platforms to use, the models and/or databases to incorporate into the DSS, and how they will be integrated with each other. This is generally a person with a great deal of experience who understands both the business problem and the available technologies. A DSS analyst often works gathering requirements, analyzing solutions, writing specifications, maintaining product information as well as assisting in training and documentation support. A DSS analyst often works with users to define and document system requirements for Decision Support Systems. A DSS analyst may help redesign business processes to better use a computerized Decision Support System. This person sometimes also assumes the role of project manager.

Technical Support Staff. A number of MIS professionals are involved as technical support staff including data warehouse architects, network specialists, application architects, operations researchers, and developers. A data modeler and data quality analyst are often involved in building data-driven DSS. The data quality analyst is concerned with data integration, metadata, and data scrubbing. A database administrator is an integral part of a development team for a data-driven DSS project. Data administrators, systems administrators, and networking specialists are often consulted on DSS projects and may join a development team for some projects.

DSS Toolsmith. This is a specialist with the tools and technologies that will be used in the construction of the DSS and the packages that will be combined to create the DSS. He or she is an expert on these tools and packages, and their effective use. This is the person who creates underlying capabilities and integrates existing packages into one overall system and carries out custom programming that contributes directly to DSS functionality. His or her responsibility begins with the packages that will comprise part of the DSS and ends with completion of a specific DSS.

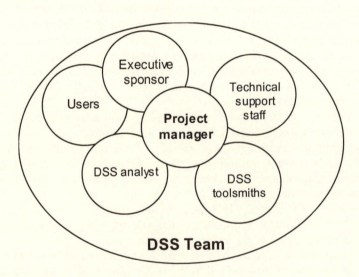

Figure 4.2 Participants on a DSS Development Team

The composition of a DSS team may change over the development cycle, so the project manager and DSS builder need to provide direction and motivation for the DSS team. Also, the executive sponsor needs to maintain an active commitment to the project. Losing a project sponsor can harm and even doom a DSS project.

CONCLUSIONS AND COMMENTARY

In 1985 Jack Hogue and Hugh Watson surveyed managers in organizations with DSS. Each participant was an active DSS user. Two-thirds of the organizations had built their DSS using an evolutionary, prototyping approach and the remaining organizations had used more of an SDLC approach. It appeared that if the DSS supported managers throughout the company, or if it required company-wide data, then the SDLC approach was used. The evolutionary approach was used for smaller-scale systems where a DSS development tool was available. Nine of the eighteen companies used DSS generators to develop their systems. This finding is probably descriptive of current practice.

When managers could specify information requirements in advance, then the SDLC approach was more likely to be used. Hogue and Watson also found that when IS specialists developed the DSS, then SDLC steps were more likely to be followed. Senior managers reported they were most involved in the idea, information requirements, and acceptance steps associated with building a DSS. Middle managers reported they were somewhat involved in all of the steps involved in building the DSS they were using. When prototyping and evolutionary design was used, managers reported more involvement in the design and development process. The IS group was usually involved in building the DSS, but staff from an IS department were rarely in a leadership role. Potential users of the DSS usually assumed the leadership role.

The DSS design and development approach that is used for a new DSS project should depend on the amount of data needed and its sources, the number of planned users, any models and analytical tools used, and the amount of anticipated use. Many small, specialized DSS are built quickly using end-user development or rapid prototyping. Large, enterprise-wide DSS are built using sophisticated tools and systematic and structured systems analysis and development approaches. Creating enterprise-wide DSS environments remains a complex and evolutionary task. An enterprise-wide DSS inevitably becomes a major part of a company's overall information systems infrastructure. Despite the significant development differences created by the scope and purpose of a DSS, all DSS have similar technical components and share a common purpose—supporting decision making.

A number of authors suggest that the perceived usefulness and the perceived ease of use of an IS or DSS is a major determinant of its use. MIS managers can influence both the perceived usefulness and the perceived ease of use of a new system by using a participative development process. MIS staff need to establish a meaningful "social exchange" with potential users, and DSS developers must be responsive to user requests, questions, and needs.

More research is needed on the effectiveness of approaches for designing and developing DSS. But in general, MIS professionals should use a decision-oriented design process and then use either a rapid prototyping or SDLC process. End-user DSS can be satisfactory and inexpensive, and MIS staff should collaborate to support such development rather than discourage it when it seems appropriate. Rapid prototyping is useful in building many types of DSS, but SDLC has a role in developing complex, networked, enterprise-wide, data-driven DSS. DSS analysts and managers need to be familiar with all of the approaches for building DSS.

One can state some generalizations about Design and Development of DSS. First, when a project idea is proposed, the focus should be on description and diagnosis of decision making and an analysis of the decision and the processes involved.   This approach is called decision-oriented diagnosis (cf., Stabell, 1983).

Second, following diagnosis, one should conduct a feasibility study and, in many situations, prepare a feasibility report. Third, if the project seems feasible, then managers and IS staff need to decide to build or buy the proposed DSS. In many situations, a solution will be customized for the DSS.

Fourth, in general, model-driven and knowledge-driven DSS are built using rapid prototyping. Data-driven and document-driven DSS are built using rapid prototyping or an SDLC approach depending on the complexity and scale of the system. Communications-driven DSS are usually purchased and installed on company computers.

Finally, managers need to develop a comprehensive understanding of how to design and develop various types of DSS. Ultimately, senior managers are responsible for ensuring that DSS projects support business goals and provide benefits to an organization. The appropriateness of the design and development process coupled with activities to train users in the operation of a new DSS determine if business goals will be met and if benefits will be realized.

Chapter 5

Designing and Evaluating DSS User Interfaces

INTRODUCTION

An effective user interface is one of the most critical components of any type of Decision Support System, but it is especially important for systems that will be used directly by managers. In the DSS literature, the user interface is sometimes called the dialogue component. Why is the user interface or dialogue component of a DSS so important? Research indicates that the easier it is to use a DSS, the greater the chance that managers will actually use the system. The user interface is what managers see and use when they work with a DSS.

Does the design of a user interface for a Decision Support System differ from the user interface for any other computerized system? What guidelines can improve DSS user interfaces? Managers should be the primary users of DSS, so a user interface should help managers interact with the system. When a user interface is complex or difficult to use, a staff person may need to assist a manager in using a DSS. A complex, difficult to use interface increases the operating costs of a specific DSS and probably limits its use. Can this negative outcome be avoided? If so, how? This chapter presents the basics of user interface design and the technologies that are used to create effective user interfaces. The focus of this chapter is on how display screens should look and how a DSS user interface should function. The chapter examines one specific design approach, a number of issues associated with building a DSS user interface, interface design elements, guidelines for user interface design, and factors that influence user interface success.

The general goal of user interface design is to develop screen layouts and interfaces that are intuitive, easy to use, and visually attractive (cf., Galitz, 1985). Both the intended users of a DSS and DSS analysts need to participate actively in designing and evaluating DSS user interfaces.

USER INTERFACES: AN OVERVIEW

Many DSS users have limited computing expertise. Most of these users do *not* want to learn a command language interface like Structured Query Language (SQL) that may be used by an decision support analyst or by a more technically oriented manager. According to Bennett (1986), for a nontechnical user, the design of an appropriate DSS user interface is the most important determinant of the success of a decision support implementation. So what is a user interface?

A user interface is what managers see and use when they interact with a DSS. More specifically, a user interface is the set of menus, icons, commands, graphical display formats, and/or other representations that are provided by a software program to allow a user to communicate with and use the program. A graphical user interface (abbreviated GUI which is pronounced "goo ee") provides a user a more or less "picture-oriented" way to interact with computing technology. GUIs remain controversial. Many people argue a GUI is the most user-friendly interface for a DSS. Some people disagree strongly with this conclusion. "User-friendly" is an evaluative term for one's subjective impression of a computerized system's user interface. It indicates that users judge the interface as easy to learn, understand, and use.

Also, a user interface refers to the hardware and software that create communication and interaction between a DSS user and the computer. The user interface includes responses and involves an exchange of graphic, acoustic, tactile, or other signs. User interface research is a subset of a field called human-computer interaction (HCI). HCI focuses on the study of people, computer technology, and the way each influences the other.

An effective user interface is important because the data and graphics displayed on a computer workstation screen provide a context for human interaction and cues for desired actions by a user. The user formulates a response to the context provided by the user interface and takes an action. Data then passes back to the computer through the interface.

A well-designed user interface can increase human processing speed, reduce errors, increase productivity, and create a sense of user control. The quality of a DSS interface, from the user's perspective, depends upon what the user sees or senses, what the user must know to understand what is seen or sensed, and what actions the user can and, in some cases, must take to obtain desired results.

To create a well-designed user interface, MIS professionals should work closely with potential users, try various design solutions, and provide users appropriate control over the functions of the system. This approach is often called User Centered Design (cf., Gulliksen, Lantz, and Boivie, 1999). Both groups of design participants need to be familiar with the following important issues and topics related to building and evaluating a user interface:

1. *User interface style* – Is the style or combination of styles appropriate? What styles are used in the user interface?
2. *Screen design and layout* – What design approach should be used? Is the design easy to understand and attractive? Is the design symmetric and balanced?
3. *Use of colors, lines and graphics* – Are colors used appropriately? Do graphics improve the design or distract the user?

4. *Information density* – Is too much information presented on a screen? Can users control the information density?
5. *Use of icons and symbols* – Are icons understandable?
6. *Choice of input and output devices* – Do devices fit the task?
7. *The Human-Software interaction sequence* – Is the interaction developed by the software logical and intuitive? Do people respond predictably to the interaction sequence?

Managers and DSS analysts should focus on these seven design issues when they evaluate a DSS prototype or the proposed screens for a DSS. A systematic evaluation of a DSS user interface can substantially improve its usefulness and increase how much it will be used. Let's examine some of these issues in more detail.

USER INTERFACE STYLES

The user interface determines how information is entered and displayed. The interface also determines the ease and simplicity of learning and using the system. There are four general structures or interface styles that can be used to control interactions with computerized information systems. These styles are: 1) command-line interfaces; 2) menu interfaces; 3) point-and-click graphical interfaces; and 4) question-and-answer interfaces. Each style can be used in creating DSS user interfaces. The styles can often be combined usefully in a single application or set of related applications (see Galitz [1985]; Shneiderman [1992]; and Turban [1995]). When building a user interface, a designer should try to provide multiple ways to perform the same task. For example, a design may include a command-line interface, pull-down menus for commands, and keyboard command equivalents. Many input devices, including keyboard, mouse, touch pad, and voice inputs, can be used to manipulate these four general interface styles.

Command-line Interfaces

Command-line interfaces are the oldest form of computer control. They originated when each command to a program was entered on a punched card. A command-driven interface still dominates some operating systems, including MS-DOS, UNIX, and Linux. In a DSS with a command-language style interface, a user enters a command such as "run" or "plot." Many commands are composed of a verb-noun combination (for example "plot sales"). Command-line interfaces require a user to enter a command telling the system what to do next. It is the user's responsibility to know what commands are available and how to phrase those commands with their parameters. Such interfaces can be quite powerful, giving their users detailed control over system operation, but there is a significant cost in terms of increased training. Command interfaces are hard to learn. Managers must attend training workshops and read documentation. Most people never learn more than a fraction of the commands in any command language and make frequent mistakes in command entry. While command entry mistakes can usually be corrected, they create a cost for users and companies in terms of productive time lost, and frequent mistakes can make users feel frustrated and even incompetent.

Menu Interfaces

In a menu interaction, a user selects from a list of possible choices the task or function to be performed. The ordered list of functions or tasks is called a menu. The user makes a choice among items by manipulating an input device or entering a menu item number. Menus should appear in a logical, hierarchical order, starting with a main menu and going to subordinate or submenus. Menus can become tedious and time-consuming when complex situations are analyzed, since it may take several menus to use a system and the user must shift back and forth among the menus. A pull-down menu is a submenu that appears as a superimposed drop-down menu on a screen, usually after an entry has been made in a high-level menu. A tool bar with graphical icons can also serve as a menu.

Menus are often effective because they rely on recognition rather than recall. Working with menus reminds users of available options. The menu designer must consider the conflicting needs of both experienced and inexperienced users.

Graphical Interfaces

A graphical user interface (GUI) is an interface system in which users have direct control of visible objects. Users point and click to initiate actions rather than enter complex commands. Two well-known GUI are the Windows 95/98/2000/XP operating systems and the Macintosh OS. The major GUI elements are windows, icons, pull-down menus, and dialog boxes. A window is an area of the computer screen that behaves as if it was an independent computer terminal. Icons are small pictures that represent windows or actions. Some of the icons frequently used in Microsoft applications are shown in Figure 5.1. Clicking on an icon initiates opening a window or running a command. In the graphical or object manipulation interface style, the user directly manipulates objects represented as symbols called icons.

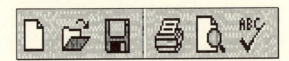

Figure 5.1 Examples of Icons

User interfaces can be enriched with the use of multimedia and hypermedia technologies. Multimedia refers to many media, including graphic materials, audio, and images, including motion pictures and animation. Hypermedia describes documents that contain several types of media linked in documents. The World Wide Web is an example of a hypermedia delivery system. Web documents can include explicit internal and external links, multimedia content, and interactivity with databases.

Question-and-Answer Interfaces

A question-and-answer interface dialogue begins with the computer asking the user a question. The user answers the question with a phrase or a sentence. A dialogue then occurs between the computer and user. The computer's questions are a function of prior responses of the user and the processing needs of the application. A related interface style is called form interaction; in form interaction style, the user enters data or commands into designated spaces (fields) in a form. The headings of the form serve as a prompt for the desired input. A human-computer interaction that is similar to a human-human dialog is referred to as natural language dialogue. The major limitation of using natural language responses is the inability of the computer to really understand unstructured or unanticipated natural language. The programmer must anticipate user answers and program responses.

The following example shows a simple question and answer dialogue:

>*dss*	What is your name?
>*user*	Daniel Power
>*dss*	What is your age?
>*user*	51 years old
>*dss*	Please enter a number
>*user*	51

A question and answer dialogue is one of the oldest types of interfaces; it is not used as frequently today in building DSS, but it may be revived by improvements in speech recognition technologies.

Another new type of interface is called a three-dimensional or virtual reality (VR) interface. It is being used in a number of research settings. With a VR interface, a user interacts with a computer-generated environment. A user wears a headset and hand-position sensor to interact with the decision support simulation. A user can walk around, grasp, and move objects, and, in general, alter the environment. A VR interface may become a viable DSS user interface in the future, but for the next few years managers and DSS analysts should focus on the interfaces discussed in preceding paragraphs. In most DSS more than one interface style is implemented.

ROMC DESIGN APPROACH

Sprague and Carlson (1982) presented an approach for designing DSS and especially the user interface called ROMC. Their approach has four user-oriented entities: 1) Representations for conveying information to the user, 2) Operations for manipulating data displayed as representations, 3) aids for a user's Memory, and 4) aids for helping users Control a DSS.

This section describes the four components of Sprague and Carlson's approach and provides contemporary examples of each component. ROMC was intended as a process-independent approach for identifying the necessary capabilities of a DSS. It can also serve as a framework for creating screen designs and for building the user interface of a DSS. DSS analysts can improve screen design and layout by focusing on these four components as user interface design elements.

Representations

In a DSS, decision-making activities take place in the context of a conceptualization of the information used in the activity. The conceptualization may be an icon, a chart, a map, a text document, a form, a spreadsheet, a picture, a table of numbers, or an equation. The conceptualization is a physical representation that helps a decision maker communicate about the decision situation with another person.

Representations provide a context in which users can interpret DSS outputs and select DSS operations. Representations also can be used to supply parameters for DSS operations. For example, a point selected on a graph or a map can be linked to a data value, a document, or a database query. Also, prioritizing a list of employees may be the primary input for a personnel-scheduling DSS. Managers and DSS analysts need to evaluate and choose appropriate representations.

Operations

Operations are specific tasks that a decision maker can perform with a DSS. For example, a DSS may have operators to gather data, generate a report, retrieve alternatives, rate alternatives, add alternatives, etc. Note that an operation may be used in more than one activity and that there is usually no prespecified ordering of operations. Analysts need to decide how operations will be controlled from the user interface. Will menus be used? Icons? What names will be used for operations?

Memory Aids

Several types of memory aids should be provided in a DSS user interface to support the use of representations and operations. A symbolic link to a data warehouse is a memory aid for decision makers. Triggers or rules remind a decision maker that certain operations may need to be performed. A user profile or data filters may make operation of the DSS easier. User-established links or command sequences can make a specific DSS easier for that user to manipulate.

A trigger may invoke an operation automatically or remind the DSS user to invoke the operation. A profile can store initial defaults for using the DSS. Users' logs of actions taken and operations invoked are also memory aids, especially if the user can back up and undo or replay actions. DSS analysts should identify needs for memory aids and decide how reminders will be displayed. The help system is an important memory aid that must be designed as part of the user interface.

Control Aids

DSS control aids are intended to help decision makers use representations, operations and memory aids. Control aids help decision makers direct the use of the DSS. One type of control aid focuses on the standard conventions for user-system interaction, which are enforced across representations and operations. This type of control aid uniformly displays menus or defines guidelines for the design and behavior of icons. Some operations are more system-oriented than decision-process-oriented and these operations are also control aids. Edit, delete, and save operations are generic control operations and hence they are also control aids for the DSS. The tools used to create the user interface constrain the control aids. User interface design guidelines should also standardize the "look and feel" of the user interface.

BUILDING THE DSS USER INTERFACE

The ROMC framework can be a useful tool for designing the DSS user interface. Also, the ROMC specification of elements, along with screen layouts, can aid in implementing the actual DSS user interface. Every DSS will have a specific set of representations, operations, memory aids, and control aids. The generality and usefulness of a DSS will depend on the skill of the designers in selecting design elements.

Flow-charting the existing or a desired decision process can help develop the ROMC framework. A decision-process flowchart should focus on the inputs, operations, and outputs of each decision task. The resulting DSS design will likely follow the flowchart and its sequencing of tasks. The resulting representations may be effective, but the operations and control aids developed from this approach may provide limited flexibility to the decision maker. Creating prototypes of the DSS screens early in the analysis process, and then eliciting input from potential users, can reduce the problem of limited flexibility in the operations of a DSS.

Screen designs and layouts should be aesthetically pleasing. The design does not need to be "artistic," but it should not create a negative impression. Managers and designers should evaluate a DSS user interface in terms of balance, symmetry, proportion, and arrangement. Balance means the design elements are equally weighted on the screen. Symmetry refers to correspondence in size and shape of the design elements. Proportion is a harmonious relation among the parts. Arrangement is the ordering of elements. A balanced, symmetric screen design is the easiest screen layout to create and it is generally pleasing. Working with unbalanced and asymmetric screen designs is much more difficult for most of us. Figure 5.2 provides an example of a simple screen design. Does the design appear balanced and symmetric?

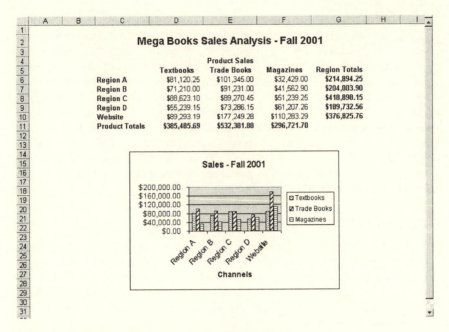

Figure 5.2 An Example of a Simple, Balanced Screen Design

Keen and Gambino (in Bennett, 1983, p. 168) provide the following suggestions for building a DSS user interface. They believe rapid prototyping and adaptive design is essential for building the user interface; they argue that a DSS analyst, programmer, or consultant who is building a DSS must do the following:

a. *Get started.* A DSS application does not usually come packaged with neat specifications. Start with an initial user interface design. It provides a means of learning from and responding to the user.

b. *Respond quickly.* A DSS user interface must evolve rapidly, and designers must learn quickly. The design structure and programming techniques must facilitate evolution and learning.

c. *Pay close attention to user-system interfaces and outputs.* A DSS is "a set of relatively simple components that must fit together to permit complex, varied, and idiosyncratic problem solving". A DSS analyst needs to get a very detailed understanding of the task to be supported and of the people who carry out the task.

According to Keen and Gambino, the "natural sequence and order of priority" in developing any type of DSS is the following four steps:

1. Design the user interface and dialog.
2. Design commands and operations in terms of the users' processes and concepts.
3. Define what the user does and sees when a command is invoked.
4. Work backward to create the program logic and data management.

Professor Mark Silver (1991) proposed an alternative design approach. He suggests the following steps as appropriate for developing a DSS user interface:

1. Determine who your user is.
2. Determine what the user will do with the system. What are the specific tasks?
3. Determine what sequence of steps the user must follow to accomplish a task.
4. Diagram the steps in item 3 and the decision tree involved. Review them with the user.
5. Determine which of these steps require interaction with the system.
6. Determine information and decision requirements for each interaction (both system and user).
7. Select the categories of dialogue (menus, prompts, forms, etc.).
8. Diagram the flow of dialogue, showing all decisions and their information requirements. Review these with the user.
9. Design screens.
10. Try it, analyze it, simplify it, change it, try it . . .
11. Update the decision diagrams.
12. Bulletproof the dialogue by asking what happens if the user does something unexpected?

While Silver's list focuses on a broad set of steps, steps 4 to 11 are an iterative design process. Even if a DSS analyst plans to develop a DSS user interface using rapid prototyping, it is important to understand who the DSS user is, what the system will be used for, and what sequence of steps a user will follow. A designer may be able to skip over some of the formal diagramming steps, such as steps 4, 8, and 11, in favor of creating a prototype, but some understanding of the task should be formalized and documented.

In general, a DSS analyst should complete the design of the user interface prior to building a database and implementing the design. During construction of a DSS changes will be made, but the interface design forces an analyst to deal with many practical issues. A DSS analyst can use a number of tools to assist in interface design including screen mock-ups, transition diagrams, and menu trees. When possible the software that implements the user interface should be decoupled from the DSS data, model and communication components.

COMMENTS ON DESIGN ELEMENTS

Graphics, including charts, enable the presentation of information in a way that can clearly show the meaning of data and permits users to visualize relationships. The importance of using charts and graphs in communicating numeric data has been recognized for many years. Since the mid-1970s, computer graphics have been used to aid in management decision making. Graphics help managers "visualize" data, relationships, and variances. Common types of computer graphs and charts include time-series charts, bar and pie charts, scatter diagrams, maps, hierarchy charts, and flow charts. Managers, business analysts, and corporate staff use computer-generated graphics in reports, presentations, performance tracking, scheduling, control, planning, modeling, and design. It is important to use graphics in the DSS user interface, especially in data displays. An end user tool like Excel has a wizard that helps create charts. Some of the charts available in Excel are shown in Figure 5.3.

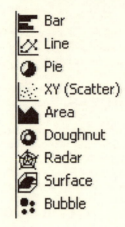

Figure 5.3 Some Excel Chart Types

Let's summarize some guidelines for graphical displays. Communicate only one major message on each chart or screen. Use an action heading in appropriate sized fonts for screen and chart headings. A line chart is appropriate for displaying time-related information, but analysts need to be careful to use appropriate labels and to avoid adding dissimilar quantities. Bar charts are more appropriate for comparing individual data values. Pie charts help show how the whole breaks down into component parts. You should limit the number of components or pieces in a pie chart to five or fewer.

Color is often recommended as a means of enhancing a user-interface design. Appropriate use of color can enhance the aesthetics of an interface for most people. Color can call attention to extreme or exceptional data values, help users differentiate among items on a chart, and convey information quickly. For example, research indicates blue creates a sense of trust, green means "go" or "all clear;" and red indicates danger. In general, the following guidelines related to the use of color are appropriate for DSS user interfaces:

1.   Do not allow color to be the only way your system conveys any information. Supplement the use of color with other cues that can be used by people who cannot perceive the color difference. Include numerical values in addition to color codes, provide cross-hatching on top of color, or make sure that the colors chosen are perceived as substantially lighter or darker than each other.

2.   Where computer hardware and software permit, allow the user to customize an application's use of color. Changing colors can compensate for some people's color vision deficiencies. In some systems, colors that cover an area, such as a region on a map, can be replaced by monochrome patterns such as dots, stripes, and cross-hatching.

3.   Use light pastel colors in screen designs. They create fewer annoying reflections than do dark colors. This is especially true in an office environment

with fluorescent lights. As a result, try to use light colors to cover large areas of the screen. Save darker colors for smaller "spot" usage.

The use of color in a DSS user interface can create accessibility issues for some people with vision impairments, but if multiple cues are used, the system remains accessible and added benefits can be gained from the appropriate use of color cues.

How people interact with a system (human-software interaction sequence) is also an important design issue. One issue, unique to DSS design and often inadequately considered, is the type and amount of guidance, called decisional guidance, that a DSS provides its users in the decision-making process (cf., Silver, 1991). Decisional guidance provided by a system can be unintended or inadvertent. For example, users tend to select the first or last items from menus. Putting a frequently used capability in the middle of a menu may not be planned, but it may cause problems. Decisional guidance can also be planned and deliberate. Designers can intentionally build guidance mechanisms into a system after determining that a particular decision approach or process is better than what many users would come upon by chance. This type of planned process guidance is distinct from the typical on-line help facility, which focuses on guidance in the mechanical aspects of operating the system. On-line help assumes that the user has already decided what to do, but does not know how to do it. Process guidance assumes the user needs direction in using the system for decision support.

Some DSS give the developer more of an opportunity to provide decisional guidance than do others. A DSS that does not provide for many discretionary user judgments during its use cannot benefit greatly from such a guidance facility. A DSS that lets users choose among several decision methods, alternative models, ways to cross-tabulate a set of data, forecasting techniques, or even alternative sequences of activities, does provide an opportunity to provide decisional guidance.

GUIDELINES FOR DIALOG AND USER INTERFACE DESIGN

This section is based on Ben Shneiderman's (1992) research and writings. He has developed some underlying principles of design that he argues are applicable in most interactive systems. The following underlying principles of interface design are derived heuristically from experience.

Strive for consistency. This principle is the most frequently violated one, and yet is the easiest one to apply. Consistent sequences of actions should be required in similar situations; identical terminology should be used in prompts, menus, and help screens; and consistent commands should be used in a DSS.

Provide shortcuts for frequent users. As the frequency of use increases, so does a user's desire to reduce the number of interactions and to increase the pace of interaction. Frequent knowledgeable users appreciate abbreviations, special keys, hidden commands, and macro facilities. Shorter response times and faster display rates are other attractions for frequent users. A system must respond to the differing needs of its users.

Provide informative feedback. For every user action, there should be some system feedback. For frequent and minor actions, the response can be modest, whereas for infrequent and major actions, the response should be more substantial.

Design dialogs to create closure. Sequences of actions should be organized into groups with a beginning, middle, and end. The informative feedback at the completion of a group of actions gives the user the satisfaction of accomplishment, a sense of relief, the signal to drop contingency plans and options from their minds, and an indication that the way is clear to prepare for the next group of actions. The "power" of a dialog and commands should be appropriate to the capabilities of the users. "Power" is a measure of the amount of work accomplished by a given instruction to a system (cf., Galitz, 1985).

Provide simple error recovery. Design the system so the user cannot make a serious error. If an error is made, the system should detect the error and offer simple, comprehensible mechanisms for handling it. A user should not have to repeat actions, but rather should need to repair only the faulty part. Errors should leave the DSS unchanged, or the system should give instructions about restoring the prior state.

Permit easy reversal of actions. A user's actions should be reversible. Following this guideline relieves anxiety, since the user knows that errors can be undone, and encourages exploration of unfamiliar options. The amount of reversibility may be limited to the most recent action or to only data entries, or it may be essentially unlimited.

Support internal locus of control. Experienced users want to feel that they are in charge of the system and that the system responds to their actions. Surprising system actions, tedious sequences of data entries, incapacity or difficulty in obtaining necessary information, and the inability to produce the action desired all build anxiety and dissatisfaction.

Reduce information load. Information load is a measure of the degree to which a person's memory is used to process information on a display screen. It is a function of the task being performed, a person's familiarity with the task, and the design of the user interface itself. The limitation of human-information processing in short-term memory requires that displays be kept simple and that sufficient training time be allotted for learning commands and sequences of actions. Where appropriate, on-line access to command-syntax forms, abbreviations, codes, and other information should be provided. Designers can reduce information load by providing graphic rather than alphanumeric displays, formatting displays to correspond to users' immediate information requirements, using words that are easy to understand, and providing simple dialogues (cf., Galitz, 1985, p. 21).

FACTORS INFLUENCING USER INTERFACE DESIGN SUCCESS

According to Larson (1982), user interface design success is influenced by 11 factors. Some of his factors overlap with Shneiderman's (1992) guidelines. System factors include uniformity of the commands and interface, adaptability, execution time, system versatility, and quality of help provided. Human factors include the learning time for the DSS, ease of recall, errors made by users, concentration required, fatigue from using the system, and the "fun" the user has while using the system. Larson and others have explained each of these factors that determine, or at least affect, DSS user interface design success.

Uniformity of commands and interface. Are the commands of the DSS identical to equivalent commands of other systems? If they want to, people can learn any idiosyncratic or esoteric interface; what is difficult is learning and remembering two, three, or more interfaces and switching frequently among them. A DSS developer must be aware of other systems used by the target managers and then strive for consistency in the user interface.

Adaptability. Does the system adjust to the end user's level of competence as he or she becomes more experienced? Does it tailor itself to the habits and styles of different users? Does the DSS provide shortcuts for frequent users? It may be difficult or impractical for a DSS to be "self-tailoring" in this sense. It is easier, and may be sufficient, to let an experienced user select an "expert user" mode in which prompts are minimized. In a graphical user-interface environment, it is helpful to provide keyboard equivalents for commonly used mouse-and-menu commands, as some users prefer using a mouse and others prefer using keystrokes.

Execution time. How long does it take the user to perform his or her decision support task? Decision task time is influenced by the choices made for software, hardware, and the user interface design. In general, faster execution times increase design success. User interface design can minimize time wasted by users.

Versatility. Can the DSS be used to perform a variety of tasks? A DSS must be versatile enough to accommodate the full range of tasks that need to be performed by a decision maker who wants to use it. Once a DSS becomes widely used, tasks related to its original purpose—but distinct from that purpose—may be performed by users. This is especially the case with data-driven and document-driven DSS. While it is possible these new tasks will require additional development work, it should be possible to incorporate them into the existing user interface.

Quality of Help provided. Does the system provide help when the user has trouble? On-line help facilities are becoming the norm for DSS. Many development tools make it easy to incorporate on-line help into a system. Wherever possible, help should be context-sensitive. The Help facility should recognize what the user is trying to do, or at least what screen the user is looking at, and provide help that is tailored as closely as possible to the current need.

Learning time for the DSS. How long does it take a novice to learn the system? A design that provides for rapid learning must take into account what the user knows and how the user's mind fits that knowledge together.

Ease of recall. How easy is it for an end user to recall how to use the system after he or she has not used it for some time? This is a more important factor for DSS than for transaction processing systems because managers often return to a DSS after a long interval of non-use. For example, some budgeting support systems are intended to help with decisions that recur predictably on an annual basis. Eleven months might elapse from a manager's last use of the system until his or her next use of it. A user interface that facilitates recall will reduce the time it takes to get back up to speed each year.

Errors. How many errors does a DSS user make, and how serious are those errors? Does the DSS provide simple error recovery? The most serious errors can lead to wrong decisions. Following closely behind in significance are errors that corrupt a corporate database. Then come errors that bring down or "crash" the computer, followed finally by errors that waste the user's time but have no other bad effects. Fortunately, most user errors will be in the last category. Understanding a user's usual decision-making process can help minimize errors.

Concentration required. How many things must a user keep in mind while using the DSS? Most people have difficulty keeping more than six or seven active facts in mind at any one time. One way to reduce the memory load is to label screens and output with informative labels like: "Profit Projections," "Sales Growth," and "Model 47 shipments start 4/94."

Fatigue. How quickly does the user tire while using the system? What is the information load created by the DSS? Physical fatigue is seldom a factor with DSS because usage frequency is not high enough to lead to such a problem. However, mental fatigue can occur. DSS analysts should minimize mental fatigue by examining the concentration required and keeping it within the capabilities of the intended users.

Fun. Does the manager enjoy using the DSS? This does not mean "funny" error messages or jokes on the screen. Such "humor" grows stale quickly. It means designers should keep users informed about what the system is doing, warn them of time-consuming operations, provide progress displays, and generally try to minimize frustrations that come from using an uncooperative system. Simulations and "what if" analyses can also help make a DSS "fun."

CONCLUSIONS AND COMMENTARY

Evaluating a DSS user interface is as important as designing it. Managers are the evaluators, and hence their evaluation during the development of a DSS interface design influences its success. Much guidance has been written about computer software user interfaces—because this topic is important—and much more can be written—because there remains so much to learn. The user interface is a critical component of all DSS. It facilitates communication between a DSS and its users. The intended user can, however, create unique design and development problems.

This chapter briefly examined and evaluated knowledge about user interface design. In general, it seems that managers are rarely comfortable with command-line or simple menu interfaces. It appears that a sophisticated graphical interface can increase a manager's use of computerized decision aids and Decision Support Software. DSS users seem to prefer easy to use, functional interfaces that use meaningful design conventions and standards. "Cute" user interfaces with funny graphics lose their appeal quickly and complex interfaces increase training costs and increase the burden to recall commands and conventions for the user. The use of graphics and other visual information displays seems to appeal to many managers. GUI seems here to stay.

A good DSS user interface can be built using a number of development environments. A Web-based "thin client" interface can be as powerful and as easy to use as a more traditional client/server interface with a "thick client" installed on each user's computer. But, in any development environment, extensive time and energy need to be spent on designing and evaluating the interface. A good interface needs to be planned and designed.

Finally, it is advantageous to use a checklist for evaluating a prototype or proposed DSS interface. The DSS User-Centered Design Guidelines in Appendix II provide a starting point for creating a more specific list. Determine that the DSS content is easy to understand, that the DSS is robust and resilient, that it has an appropriate orientation and useful navigation tools, and then check the impact on productivity, the impact on data integrity, and the control capabilities for users. Overall, if DSS analysts improve user interfaces, then the usefulness of a new DSS and its value to decision makers should increase.

Chapter 6

Understanding DSS Architecture, Networking, and Security Issues

INTRODUCTION

Information technology (IT) architectures and computing infrastructures are evolving rapidly in corporations. In some companies, the IT infrastructure is being built in an uncoordinated, opportunistic manner. This approach is understandable given the rapid pace of technological change, but companies need much more than a "Web server here and a router there" approach to IT architecture and networking. Managers need to take steps to design an infrastructure that meets the following evaluation criteria: 1) minimizes support costs and maximizes user productivity; 2) avoids system crashes and other performance problems; and 3) reduces infrastructure impediments that delay the deployment of new IS/IT applications, especially Decision Support Systems (DSS). A network is the critical element of the IT infrastructure that supports enterprise-wide and communications-driven DSS.

According to Evans and Wurster in a 1997 *Harvard Business Review* article, the "rapid emergence of universal technical standards for communication, allowing everybody to communicate with everybody else at essentially zero cost, is a sea change." They note, "It is easy to get lost in the technical jargon, but the important principle here is that the same technical standards underlie all the so-called Net technologies: the Internet, which connects everyone; extranets, which connect companies to one another; and intranets, which connect individuals within companies." Both managers and MIS staff need to understand the magnitude of this sea change in how people can communicate.

One could reasonably ask how the DSS architecture and IS/IT infrastructure is related to networking and security issues. First, part of a DSS architecture is the network design. Second, security issues for a DSS are directly affected by architecture and network choices. These three topics of architecture, networking, and security are closely intertwined and are very important issues for building DSS. Unless one builds a DSS on a stand-alone computer in a secured office environment and keeps the computer under the watchful eye of the manager who is using it, designers and managers need to address DSS architecture, networking, and security issues. If one wants to design, develop, and implement successful DSS, it is important to understand these three fundamental technical topics.

This chapter explores the basics of DSS architecture, enterprise-wide networks and extranets, and security issues. The linkages among these issues are also explored.

DSS ARCHITECTURE AND IS/IT INFRASTRUCTURE

Many academics discuss building DSS in terms of four major components - the user interface, a database, models and analytical tools, and the DSS architecture and network (see Figure 6.1). One can label these components collectively as the overall architecture of a DSS. This traditional view of DSS components remains useful because it identifies commonalities between different types of DSS, but it provides only an initial perspective for understanding the complexity of DSS architectures.

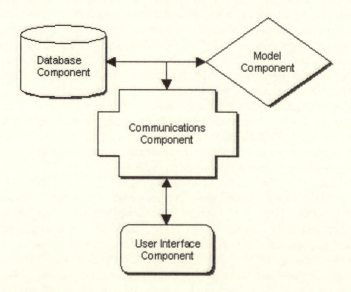

Figure 6.1 DSS Components

As noted previously, a major component in the design of a DSS is the user interface. The tools for building the user interface are sometimes termed DSS generators, query and reporting tools, and front-end development packages. DSS user interfaces can be distributed to clients in a "thick-client" architecture or delivered over a network using Web pages or Java applets in a "thin-client" architecture. A thin-client architecture, where a user interacts using a Web browser, has many advantages, but until recently, the sophistication of the user interface was limited, compared to a thick-client architecture, where a program resides on a DSS user's computer.

A DSS database is a collection of data organized for easy access and analysis. Large databases in enterprise-wide DSS are often called data warehouses or data marts. Document or unstructured data is stored differently than structured data. Web servers provide a powerful platform for unstructured data and documents. The architecture for a data-driven DSS often involves databases on multiple servers, specialized hardware and in some cases both multidimensional and relational database software. The extraction, transformation, loading, and indexing of structured DSS data is difficult, and there are as many data engineering strategies as there are data warehouses.

Mathematical and analytical models are an important part of many DSS, especially model-driven DSS. Model management software can be centralized on a server with a database, or specific models can be distributed to client computers. Java applets and JavaScript programs provide a powerful new means to deliver models to users in a thin-client architecture.

The DSS architecture and network component refers to how hardware is organized, how software and data are distributed in the system, and how components of the DSS are integrated and physically connected. A major issue today is whether a specific DSS should only be available using thin-client technology on a company intranet or available on the global Internet. This should depend on the needs analysis and feasibility study. Scalability is also an important DSS issue. Scalability refers to the ability to "scale" hardware and software to support larger or smaller volumes of data and more or fewer users. Scalability also refers to the possibility of increasing or decreasing size or capability of a DSS in cost-effective increments.

The DSS framework discussed in Chapter 1 showed the different emphases that are placed on DSS components when specific types of DSS are actually constructed. Architecture, networking and security issues vary for data-driven, document-driven, model-driven and knowledge-driven DSS. Multi-participant systems like group and interorganizational DSS rely heavily on network technologies. The architecture of a data-driven DSS emphasizes database performance and scalability. Most model-driven DSS architectures store the model software on a server and distribute the user interface software to clients. Networking issues create challenges for many types of DSS, but especially for a geographically distributed, multiparticipant DSS.

An architecture for any information system is a formal definition of its elements and subsystems, including decision support systems. A DSS architecture can often be diagrammed in terms of four layers: the business decision process flow chart, the systems architecture, the technical architecture, and a user interface design. The business decision process flow chart shows what tasks are completed. The systems architecture shows the major software components. The technical architecture focuses on hardware, protocols, and networking. The user interface design focuses on outputs and capabilities of the system (see Chapter 5). The architecture also defines the structures and controls that define how the platform can be used, and the categories of applications that can be created on the platform. It includes the hardware and software used to manage information and communication; the tools used to access, package, deliver, and communicate information; the standards, models, and control frameworks; and the overall configuration that integrates the various components (cf., Applegate et al., 1996). Table 6.1 identifies some of the architecture requirements for different categories of DSS.

Type	Network Needed	Components
Communications-driven and GDSS	Always	Message storage, process support for GDSS
Data-driven	Usually	Web-enabled data access
Document-driven	Usually	HTML, TXT and PDF file storage and searching
Knowledge-driven	Sometimes	AI, statistical models, Web delivery
Model-driven	Sometimes	Optimization, Simulation processing
Interorganizational	Always	Depends on purpose

Table 6.1   DSS Framework and Architecture Issues

Defining the DSS Architecture

A DSS architecture includes the IS/IT architecture components relevant to the DSS. A DSS may be a subsystem of a larger information system and a specific DSS may have multiple types of decision support subsystems. Having a well-defined and well-communicated DSS architecture provides an organization with significant benefits. An architecture document helps developers work together, improves planning, increases the development team's ability to communicate system concepts to management, increases the team's ability to communicate needs to potential vendors, and increases the ability of other groups to implement systems that must work with the DSS. Technical benefits of a DSS architecture document include the ability to plan systems in an effective and coordinated fashion and to evaluate technology options within the context of how they will work rather than from a more abstract perspective. A DSS vision and an architecture document help communicate the future, and provide a consistent goal for making individual design decisions. Achieving all these benefits requires that both information system professionals and prospective DSS users cooperate closely in developing the architecture.

An architecture drawing provides the grand scheme of a large-scale DSS project. The overall architecture of a DSS should be diagrammed and understood before specific decisions are made. The nature of the architecture depends on the DSS. Small-scale DSS developed by individuals for their own use do not justify a major architectural planning effort, although the overall information system architecture of the organization may constrain the capabilities of desktop DSS. Enterprise-wide DSS do require careful architecture planning if they are to succeed. Figure 6.2 shows a high-level enterprise-wide data delivery architecture. In general, more detail about the hardware, networks, and software is needed in specifying the architecture than is shown in Figure 6.2.

According to Mallach (1994), a DSS architecture should define and specify the following components:

1. Database or databases, including any existing databases internal or external to the organization, and any databases that are created specifically for DSS use. The architecture schematic should identify who is responsible for different types of databases, including their accuracy, currency, and security.
2. Model or models, including information about their sources of data, processing, the organizational unit responsibility for maintaining them, and limits on access to them.
3. Software tools for users to access the database and the models, and software tools that system administrators can use to manage the database and the models.
4. Hardware and operating system platforms on which the databases and models reside, on which the programs run, and through which users access the DSS. Any constraints, such as a policy to standardize on products of a particular vendor or products that use a particular operating system, should be stated.
5. Networking and communication capabilities needed to connect the hardware platforms. These capabilities must support needs to connect to one or more servers and databases, needs of work group members to communicate within the group, and enterprise needs to link work groups to each other or to shared data. In many DSS situations the corporate network is used. In this case the network must be examined to make sure it meets present and future decision support traffic needs.

Mallach also claims potential users should be specified when a DSS architecture is designed. The specifications should state any assumptions about users' locations, jobs, levels of education, and any other factors that may affect their use of a specific DSS.   This information can be part of the business decision process diagram or data flow diagram.

Bob Lambert, in a paper titled "Data Warehousing Fundamentals" (1996), has a similar list of architectural issues that need to be addressed. Lambert argues, "An architecture is a design completed early in a project that encompasses (but not necessarily in detail) all aspects of the finished product."

According to Lambert, a completely specified DSS architecture addresses a number of topics including:

•   Major system components and the interfaces, connections, or communication paths among the components;
•   Anticipated system enhancements, migration paths, and modifications.

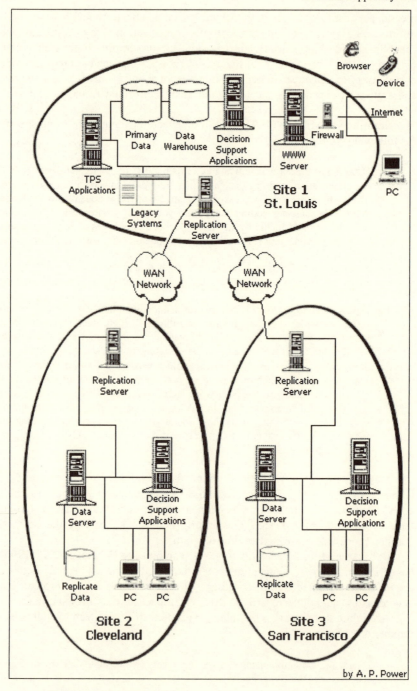

Figure 6.2 High-Level DSS Architecture

Lambert notes, "All project participants should understand and accept the architecture. The architectural design should set a common level of understanding among technical, non-technical and management participants."

A Client/Server Architecture

Most DSS are built within the context of a corporate-wide client/server architecture. Based on Taylor (1998), client/server refers to a computational architecture that involves client processes requesting service over a network from server processes. Ravi Kalakota in the Client/Server FAQ (Taylor, 1998) explains that client/server architectures are:

1) A combination of a client or front-end portion that interacts with the user and a server or back-end portion that interacts with the shared resource. The client process provides the interface between the user and the rest of the application system. The server process acts as a software engine that manages shared resources such as databases, analytical processors, or printers.

2) The client and server have fundamentally different requirements for computing resources such as processor speeds, memory, disk speeds and capacities, and input/output devices.

3) Scalable. An important characteristic of client-server systems is scalability. They can be scaled horizontally or vertically. Horizontal scaling means adding or removing client workstations with only a slight performance impact. Vertical scaling means migrating to a larger and faster server machine or to multiple servers.

A common error in client/server development is to prototype an application in a small, two-tier architecture environment and then scale up by simply adding more users to the server. This approach usually results in an ineffective system because the server becomes overwhelmed. A three-tier architecture with a second "agent" server between the client and the server can support hundreds or thousands of users.

The Gartner group proposed terminology for describing different client/server styles, or organizing schemes, based on the distribution of the three components of an application: user interface, business analysis or application logic, and data management. The descriptive styles are distributed presentation, distributed function, and distributed data management. Distributed presentation is when only the user interface is processed on the client either using a Web browser or thick client interface. In a distributed function design, one part of the application processing is on the client, additional application processing is on one or more servers. Distributed function applications are the most complex type of design. In distributed data management, the entire application resides on the client, and data management is located on one or more remote servers/hosts. Web-based DSS are implemented using a distributed presentation design, but a DSS may also have distributed functions and distributed data management.

As noted, networks are a major element in the technical specification of a DSS architecture. The next section discusses this key architecture component.

NETWORKING ISSUES

Enterprise-wide DSS have interconnected servers, databases, and workstations. In many DSS development situations, an existing corporate network is used as part of the DSS architecture. In this situation the corporate network must be examined to make sure it meets present and future DSS traffic needs. Also, many DSS proposals are recommending Web-based DSS that are accessed from a client computer connected using the global Internet to a Web server. This architecture uses a public network based on the TCP/IP communications protocol.

This section summarizes a number of major issues in networking and computing communications that managers and DSS analysts should be familiar with so they can participate in networking discussions with network technical specialists. The following discussion is based on Frisch (1995), Nemeth, Snyder, Seebass, and Hein (1995), Kirkner, Ladd, O'Donnell, et al. (1996), and Jones (1997). The three major aims of this section are to:

1. Explain the basic concepts of networking;
2. Provide an explanation of what TCP/IP is and how it works;
3. Define some major networking terms.

Overview

A client/server architecture is based on having a physical network where computers act as either a server managing files and network services or as a client where users run applications and access servers. Clients rely on servers for resources like Web pages, databases, files, printing, and on-line analytical processing.

A network is a collection of computers connected in a way that allows them to communicate with each other and share information. To communicate, the computers need an agreed-upon language for communication. Networked computers are often referred to as hosts. Each host on a network must have some unique identifier that allows other hosts to communicate with it. Typical physical connections for hosts include Ethernet, token ring, serial line, and modems. Communication languages on computer networks are referred to as network protocols. A network protocol is a set of rules and formats that governs how information is sent and in what format it is sent. Some of the different network protocols used today include TCP/IP (Internet and UNIX), IPX (Novell), and Appletalk (cf., Hunt, 1992).

A number of technologies provide sharing of information, capabilities to distribute a DSS, and communications connectivity. These technologies include the Internet, private Integrated Services Digital Networks (ISDN), and remote access dial-up servers. Broadband service is another form of data transmission that uses cable television coaxial and fiber optic cables. Currently, the favored technology for many new DSS is the Internet because it is inexpensive, it is low risk, and it is a mature technology. Managers, customers and suppliers can use a dial-up or high-speed modem to connect to an Internet service provider or to their main office intranet. A major concern with using the Internet for DSS is managing security problems.

Sharing Resources

The fundamental purpose of computer networks is to provide access to shared resources, including storage for decision support data and information. One type of network for providing shared resources is a local area network (LAN). A LAN has several primary components:

- A network interconnection and hubs (for example, copper wire, fiber optic cable, infrared, or radio).
- Network Interface Circuitry (NIC) in the individual personal computers connected to the network.
- The shared resources, like a database server, each with their own NIC connected to the network.
- Software on a personal computer that uses the NIC to access the shared resources. This software is typically arranged to present the appearance to the rest of the operating system that these resources are directly connected.
- Software on the shared resource that coordinates with the software on the individual machines to provide access to the shared resources for users. This type of software is called a multi-user operating system. UNIX is a common operating system for DSS, but Windows NT is used in some architectures and for implementing some DSS packages.

The most common network design is for the server in a LAN to be the same sort of personal computer hardware as the individual personal computers on the network. In this case, the operating system is called a Network Operating System (NOS) to emphasize the difference from the single-user operating system of the personal computer. Novell Netware is an example of this approach. A NOS is an operating system that manages network resources. The NOS is like a traffic cop, controlling the exchange and flow of files, electronic mail, and print jobs. It manages multiple requests concurrently and provides the security needed in a multi-user environment.

A LAN is a communications network that serves users within a specific geographic area. It is made up of servers, workstations, a network operating system and a communications link. A wide area network (WAN) is a much larger network than a LAN, and all machines are not directly connected. A group of LANs are often connected to form a WAN. LANs and WANs can be directly connected to the global Internet.

Connecting the Resources: TCP/IP

The Transmission Control Protocol/Internet Protocol (TCP/IP) is the most widely used set of standard networking protocols. A networking protocol enables computers to communicate with one another.

The general concept of connecting a network of dissimilar computers arose from research conducted by the U.S. Defense Advanced Research Projects

Agency (DARPA). During that research, DARPA developed the TCP/IP suite of protocols to communicate among networks, and implemented an network called ARPAnet, which later evolved into the Internet. The TCP/IP suite of protocols defines formats and rules for the transmission and receipt of information independently of any given network organization or computer hardware. Although the protocols were developed for the Internet, they are also applicable to other cases where networks must be connected, including internal organizational networks called intranets. The Internet is a collection of networks and gateways that use the TCP/IP protocol suite.

Also, the Internet is a packet-switched network. A packet-switched network transmits information in small segments, called packets. If one computer transmits a lengthy file to another computer, the file is divided into many packets at the origin and then reassembled at the destination. Protocols define the format of these packets, including the origin of the packet and its destination, length, and type, as well as the way computers on the networks will receive and retransmit packets. TCP/IP routing capabilities allow forwarding of traffic from one network to another.

TCP/IP Protocol

The objective TCP/IP is to get data from one host to another host, with the assumption that the connection may be difficult. IP provides three capabilities: 1) a delivery service; 2) a means to fragment and reassemble data packets; and 3) routing functions to move data packets on the network.

Data might start out in Seattle with a final destination in Australia. Along the way, many computers called routers with varying capabilities will be encountered. There might be heavy traffic that causes a particular route to be suboptimal, so the data might have to take another route. In addition, the router may not be able to transfer all the data, so the data has to be fragmented before continuing.

The TCP/IP protocol suite includes a number of protocols or rules. The Internet Protocol is a low level protocol that transports raw data over networks. The Transmission Control Protocol (TCP) sends data between programs using IP. As with all other communications protocol, TCP/IP is composed of layers.

TCP/IP assigns a unique address to every workstation in the world connected using TCP/IP. This "IP number" is a four-byte value that is created by converting each byte into a decimal number from 0 to 255 and separating the bytes with a period. For example, 131.123.2.25 is an IP number. Machines using TCP/IP also have natural language host names. A host name under TCP/IP follows the format hostname.site.domain.country. IP always uses the IP address and not the host name when it is sending information.

Why TCP/IP?

The growing acceptance of TCP/IP is due to several factors. First, TCP/IP has been used since the early 1970s. Second, in the early 1980s it was distributed as a core part of Berkeley's UNIX Version 4.2 and UNIX workstations became primary servers on the Internet. TCP/IP was initially successful in the mid-1980s because it delivered a few basic services that many users needed (file transfer, electronic mail, remote logon) across a very large number of client and server systems. Several computers in a small department can use TCP/IP (along with other protocols) on a single LAN. The IP component provides routing from the department to the enterprise network, then to regional networks, and finally to the global Internet.

Third, TCP/IP is dependable. On the battlefield a communications network can be damaged, so DARPA researchers designed TCP/IP to be robust and to automatically recover from any node or phone line failure. This modular design allows the construction of very large networks with less central management. Because of its proven capabilities over Internets, its wide availability and support for routing, it has become an accepted standard for interconnecting heterogeneous environments from multiple vendors. Fourth, when organizations use TCP/IP, they can choose to use it exclusively over their own private intranet or as part of the global Internet.

The Internet Protocol was developed to create a network of networks called the Internet. Individual machines are first connected to a LAN. TCP/IP shares the LAN with other uses, for example, a Novell file server or a Windows for Workgroups peer-to-peer system. One hardware device provides the TCP/IP connection between the LAN and the rest of the Internet world. To insure that all types of systems from all vendors can communicate, TCP/IP is standardized on the LAN. TCP/IP and the Internet are not as secure as some alternative systems, but the system is available worldwide, and it is inexpensive. So managers and MIS professionals need to be concerned with maintaining security on networks using TCP/IP.

IMPROVING SECURITY FOR DECISION SUPPORT SYSTEMS

Security is a very important issue associated with building, managing, and using DSS. Reports of computer crime are increasing at a rate of more than 150 percent a year. Viruses and worms attack computers from e-mail message attachments. Hackers disrupt Web sites. Customer and credit card data have been stolen from Web servers. Company and customer data is valuable to competitors and thefts by unhappy employees, and hackers of company data do occur. Security *is* important.

Improving security for DSS involves addressing a number of issues. First, managers and MIS staff must determine security needs. Managers should ask what are the current security problems. This task is often called security evaluation. Based on the diagnosis in the evaluation stage, they need to implement the required security measures and fix any problems. These two tasks occur in what has been called the implementation stage. Once appropriate security is in place, one must monitor the system, and any new security problems need to be fixed. This is the feedback stage. Finally, managers and MIS staff need to stay informed about new security problems and methods for breaking into information systems. Both managers and MIS staff need to assume shared and equal responsibility for the security of DSS.

There are four major stages involved with implementing security for information systems and especially DSS. The four major stages are: evaluating security needs (evaluation), remedying problems and implementing solutions (implementation), observing and monitoring the operation of the system (feedback), and finally, staying informed (research) on security issues (cf., Jones, 1997).

Evaluation: Evaluating Security Needs

Before implementing any form of security, MIS staff need to decide how important security is for the company and identify any current security problems that need attention. This section examines these two steps, looks at some of the possible threats, and introduces some ways to evaluate security problems.

Information systems and especially DSS can be made very secure if enough effort is expended. A very secure system, however, is usually too inconvenient for managers to use. According to Jones (1997), when implementing a security plan, both system administrators and managers must weigh the following costs and factors:

- the importance of the system, its availability, and the data stored on it,
- the amount of effort required to make and keep the system secure, and
- how the security features will affect the users of the system.

A computer containing the plans for Intel's next computer chip or sensitive financial data should be carefully secured. On the other hand, it does not make sense to spend hundreds of thousands of dollars securing a computer used for e-mail by business students. A system can be made as secure as is necessary, but, in doing so, you might lose the ability to make effective use of it. Managers and systems administrators must balance the need for convenience against the need for security.

To implement security on a system, one should first identify the possible threats to the system. There are three major types of threats to a computer system: physical threats, denial of service, and unauthorized access. Physical threats include fire, theft of equipment, and vandalism. Denial of service means that people are unable to use a system because of some type a security breach. One way to deny service for Web servers is repeated and ongoing attempts to access the server that overwhelm its ability to meet legitimate requests for service. Unauthorized access means a "hacker" or a former employee has broken into a company's computers or Web site.

Not all denial of service attacks rely on expert knowledge of computer hardware and software. The quickest way of denying service is to steal or destroy the physical hardware. Mechanisms should be in place to prevent access to the physical hardware of a system. Network cables also create a security risk. The simplest way to disable a computer network is to take a shovel and dig up or cut a few of the cables used for a computer network. This problem may occur by design or accident.

To break into a DSS and gain access a hacker will generally go through a number of stages. The first stage is information gathering. During this phase, a hacker is trying to gather as much information about a site as possible, for example, what are the users' names, their phone numbers, office locations, what machines are there. Second, using the information gathered about a DSS or transaction processing system, a hacker tries to get a login account. It usually doesn't matter whose account. At this stage, the hacker is just interested in getting onto a specific machine.

Third, a hacker tries to get administrator privileges for the system. Hackers exploit bugs in programs and operating systems. Finally, a hacker makes changes to gain access and control of the system. Social engineering is one of the most used methods for gaining access, and it generally requires very little computer knowledge. The most common form of social engineering is for a hacker to impersonate an employee, usually a computer support employee, and obtain passwords or other security related information over the phone. Hackers also sift through the trash of an organization looking for passwords or other information. Some hackers actually get a job at a targeted site. Most hackers consider people to be the weak link in security.

Security threats are also caused by problems with computer software. These problems are caused either by misuse, by hardware incompatibilities, by people, by mistakes in programs, or by program interactions with other programs. MIS professionals need to evaluate the possibilities of technical problems.

Passwords are the first line of defense in the security of a computer system. They are also usually the biggest security problem. The main reason is that users perform actions with passwords that compromise their security including:

- writing their password on a "post it" note and then leave it lying around,
- typing their passwords very slowly while someone is watching over their shoulders,
- choose "dumb" passwords like their first name, and
- log into their secure accounts across insecure connections.

These unfortunate actions by users make it easy for hackers to obtain passwords and bypass this important first line of defense. If a person has managed to crack someone's password and break into his or her account, the next step is to obtain an account with more access. The systems administrator is responsible for initially setting up file permissions correctly and then maintaining them.

The development of large-scale networks, especially global networks such as the Internet, has drastically increased the likelihood that a network-accessible DSS will be attacked. No longer is the worry only about people on site. All of the people on the Internet are now potential attackers. The security threat has increased.

Implementation: Remedying Problems and Executing Solutions

Having decided on an appropriate level of security and having identified security problems, MIS staff need to fix the problems and implement a security policy. A security policy can ensure the safe and organized use of resources. A computer security policy is a document that sets out rules and principles that affect the way an organization approaches security problems. Managers and MIS staff should specify the security rules for major Decision Support Systems. This section examines tools and methods that can be used to improve security with passwords, user education, file permissions, firewalls and secure servers.

Improving Password Security

There are a number of approaches managers and systems administrators can use to help make passwords more secure including: password user education, password generators, password aging, regular password cracking, and one-time passwords. Password generators create cryptic passwords for users, password aging forces periodic change of passwords, password cracking attempts to identify users with "bad" passwords, and one-time passwords are used only once. In some cases, a company wants to use one-time passwords. If a manager is traveling and needs access to sensitive data, we may want to change the password prior to each login.

User Education

Users do not want other people breaking into their accounts. If the users of a system are informed of the dangers of using "bad" passwords, most will choose "better" passwords. How an MIS staff performs user education depends on the users. Different users respond to different methods. System administrators must always remember that it is important not to alienate users, especially senior managers who need to use a DSS. User education is extremely important. DSS users need to learn about the importance of security and how to secure their passwords, equipment and data. One major problem is stolen portable computers. Managers can lose customer and decision support data and other important information.

File Permissions

Security is also related to the management of networked servers. The file system structure and file permissions are the fences of multiuser operating systems like UNIX and Windows NT. If used properly, permissions or rights to access files and directories and data can keep users in their own restricted areas on a server. The system administrator needs to monitor and maintain the rights and permissions granted DSS users. Inappropriate file permissions can lead to destruction of data and unauthorized use of data.

Firewalls

The Internet creates access for hackers who want to break into a DSS. By connecting to the Internet, a company opens a door for hackers. A firewall is designed to shut the doors. Basically, a firewall is a collection of hardware and software that forces all incoming and outgoing Internet data to go through one gate or door. It checks and logs requests made from outside the network to computing systems and requests made from internal users and systems to outside computing resources. The firewall software examines IP addresses and destinations of packets. Rules block access from certain IP addresses or block certain requests. For example, a rule may block file transfer protocol (FTP) requests from external IP addresses.

A firewall creates the following four advantages: protection of vulnerable or strategic services, concentration of security on the most important systems, enhanced privacy, and provision of logging and statistics on network use and users.

Secure Servers

Another security measure is to have a secure server and use encryption. A Web address for a secure server is displayed in a Web browser's location field beginning with "https" rather than "http" when one enters a secure area. Most browsers also show either a closed lock or a solid key symbol in the status bar at the bottom of the screen. Companies should have a secure server for DSS applications that can be accessed over the Internet.

Feedback: Observing Operations and Maintaining Security Solutions

Once a system has been secured, the job is *not* over. Managers and system administrators must observe what people are doing with a DSS and determine if someone may have compromised the security of a specific DSS. Also, ongoing maintenance of security solutions is important. Operating systems can have "security holes" that are discovered; problems then need to be "plugged" with patches, and eventually the operating system needs to be upgraded. If this is not done, all systems on the server can be compromised.

Stay Informed: Use Web Resources

Managers must also stay informed about security needs and issues and system administrators must research routinely security issues and threats. The Web is the best source of current, timely Internet security and computer security information. Some useful Web hyperlinks include:

CERIAS, the Center for Education and Research in Information Assurance and Security at Purdue University, has a security hotlist at URL http://www.cerias.purdue.edu/hotlist/.

CERT Coordination Center at http://www.cert.org. CERT is a security watchdog and reporting group. Staff members provide technical assistance and coordinate responses to security compromises, identify trends in intruder activity, work with other security experts, and disseminate information to the broad community. CERT also analyzes product vulnerabilities, publishes technical documents, and presents training courses.

Sun Security site at http://java.sun.com/security focuses on UNIX and Sun Solaris security issues.

U.S. Department of Justice Computer Crime and Intellectual Property Section (CCIPS) Web site is at http://www.usdoj.gov/criminal/cybercrime.

World Wide Web Security FAQ by Lincoln D. Stein is at http://www.w3.org/Security/Faq/. It attempts to answer questions relating to the security implications of running a Web server and using Web browsers.

Email lists also provide alerts for System Administrators. MIS professionals with security responsibilities need to try to keep middle-level and senior managers informed about possible security problems.

CONCLUSIONS AND COMMENTARY

It is absolutely essential that a DSS have an appropriate architecture, network design, and level of security. Managers need to realize that the more widely accessible a DSS is, the more security problems that can occur. Managers also need to recognize that the greater the importance of DSS data, the greater the level of security that is needed. By connecting to the Internet, it is no longer a case of "if" a system will be broken into but rather "when." Despite the risks, it is my opinion that we have no choice but to use the Internet for accessing interorganizational DSS and Web-based DSS.

A well-defined DSS architecture has many benefits. Developing a DSS should therefore include adequate attention to the many important architecture issues. Networks provide the high-speed data transmission that many people have come to depend upon. So, managers need to understand the basics of how networks function. Security is not some specialist's responsibility. Managers and MIS staff need to learn about security issues; security for DSS data and systems is a shared responsibility. Managers need to remember that passwords are the first line of defense against unauthorized use of a DSS. Also, DSS users themselves often weaken the defense provided by passwords. There are a number of strategies that can be used to increase the effectiveness of passwords, but the most important is user education. Educate DSS users and remind them regularly of the importance of passwords.

Companies have become very dependent on the Internet, and managers need to be vigilant in their use of it. Attacks on a company's network can be anticipated and should be prevented when possible. The Internet is more than a physical network connecting millions of computers that can exchange information.

The future of distributed DSS capabilities is only limited by a company's technology infrastructure. Technology for DSS is expanding and improving rapidly. Networking technologies will become better, faster, and cheaper. Future technology will provide much higher speeds for video teleconferencing. Communications links will be both wired and wireless. The Internet has proven it can connect managers globally. The security issues associated with the Internet are being addressed proactively, and the Internet is now an integral part of distributing DSS capabilities to users.

Architecture, network and security issues must be examined together during the planning for a new DSS. Once a DSS is implemented, network and security monitoring must then become an ongoing activity.

Chapter 7

Implementing Communications-Driven and Group Decision Support Systems

INTRODUCTION

Globalization and computing technologies have expanded product markets and changed business organizations. One change is that companies have become more geographically dispersed, and this has created new challenges for managers. Also, changes in organizations and changes in the nature of the work performed by teams have increased significantly the importance of effective teams. The concept of business relationships is also changing. Relationships between people inside an organization and people previously considered outside like customers, suppliers, and other stakeholders are increasingly important.

Because of these changes, many organizations have discovered the value of collaborative work. Also, there is an increased emphasis on computer-supported business decision processes. Many companies want to make the knowledge of managers and experts available to those who could benefit from that knowledge.

The interaction of these various forces has resulted in an increased use of participatory decision making, temporary teams, and technology to support geographically dispersed teams. Work groups, task forces, and teams have become important means to improve the performance of organizations. For some groups and teams, Group Decision Support Systems (GDSS), groupware, and other communication and collaboration tools can improve the performance of team members.

For all of the above reasons, managers are implementing communications-driven DSS. Because communications-driven DSS are usually purchased, rather than developed in-house by companies, the focus in this chapter is on how products are implemented and used, rather than on building a proprietary group support system. This chapter emphasizes the various categories of group decision support situations, specific examples of group decision support tools, a managerial perspective on group decision support, a contingency theory of group support, the benefits of GDSS, the evolution of so-called virtual organizations, and evaluating communications and group support tools. A good starting point is to review key terms.

KEY TERMS

Managers spend a significant amount of time working with other managers and staff in teams and work groups. Cross-functional business teams, project teams, new product teams, and even crisis management teams operate in businesses today. Many of these groups use e-mail, bulletin boards, and groupware systems. Group support systems, video conferencing, and GDSS are especially valuable in helping teams where members are geographically separated or where they cannot meet face-to-face. GDSS also have been shown to improve the effectiveness and productivity of some types of face-to-face meetings.

Meetings can now occur when participants are separated by distance and computer-supported meetings can occur at various times or asynchronously. Full-motion video, audio, and Web-based meeting tools support these electronic meetings or e-meetings. The business and social changes created by implementing these tools to support group communication, collaboration, and knowledge sharing are many. One set of significant changes that has resulted from implementing collaborative computing technologies is the creation of virtual organizations.

Communications-driven DSS is a category of DSS that uses network and communications technologies to facilitate collaboration, communication and shared decision-making support. Communications technologies are central to supporting decision making and provide the dominant decision support functionality. A simple bulletin board or threaded e-mail is the most elementary level of functionality. Communications-driven DSS are multiparticipant DSS that enable two or more people to communicate with each other, share information, and coordinate their activities.

A number of terms are used to describe software that supports groups in decision-making and knowledge-work tasks. Some examples include electronic meeting system, collaborative workgroup software, groupware, and GDSS. All of these terms refer to tools intended to help members of a group make better decisions and perform tasks better than they could working alone without computer support. All of these technologies can be incorporated in a communications-driven DSS.

Groupware is any software that can be used to support and assist groups in completing tasks. Groupware helps users coordinate and keep track of ongoing projects and tasks. Such applications are not meant to replace people in an interactive situation; rather, groupware refers to tools that extend or enhance collaboration. Groupware products are very different from single-user decision support applications.

GDSS are a hybrid type of DSS that allows multiple users to work collaboratively using various model-driven software tools. GDSS are specifically designed to support a group rather than an individual. DeSanctis and Gallupe (1987) defined a GDSS as "an interactive computer-based system to facilitate the solution of unstructured problems by a set of decision-makers working together as a group." GDSS provide software tools to assist communication, collaboration, and decision making in groups. GDSS are often used in a decision room which is a specially arranged room designed for computer supported meetings. In the room, computer workstations are available for use by meeting participants. A facilitator helps the participants use the GDSS and manages the use of the system. The objective for using a decision room is to enhance and improve a group's decision-making process and the quality of its decisions.

A term that overlaps communications-driven DSS is "multimedia decision support." Multimedia decision support refers to the integration of video, computer, and decision-support technologies to help decision makers. In multimedia decision support, a decision makers' actions, choices, and decisions affect the way in which the group interaction occurs, the information that is reviewed and discussed, the analyses that are performed, and the actions that are agreed upon. Company intranets provide a viable, affordable delivery mechanism for the deployment of multimedia decision support applications to a manager's desktop and to decision rooms.

The Web and intranet infrastructures are important factors enabling development of more powerful communications-driven DSS. The most powerful group support software is now based on these communications technologies. Communications-driven DSS software has at least one of the following characteristics: it enables communication between groups of people; it facilitates the sharing of information; it supports collaboration and coordination between people; and/or it supports group decision tasks.

GROUP DECISION SUPPORT SITUATIONS

Situations that might benefit from communications-driven decision support can be analyzed in terms of time and place. Traditionally a 2 by 2 matrix is used to represent the four possible situations with the time dimension running on the Y-axis and the place dimension running along the X-axis. Table 7.1 categorizes GDSS, groupware and other communications tools by time and place of use. The four situations include: same time/same place, same time/different place, different time/same place, and different time/different place.

In same time or real time meetings, communication occurs at the same time for all participants. In different time or asynchronous time meetings, communication occurs at different times. In same place meetings, people meet in the same room. In different place meetings, a meeting occurs and participants are in geographically distributed locations. In real time meetings, we try to establish a WYSIWIS (What You See Is What I See) interaction. This concept is analogous to having two people at their own homes watching the same television show at the same time. Computer technologies, especially video conferencing, chat, and tools like Microsoft NetMeeting extend this concept and allow people to interact and communicate in a WYSIWIS environment.

	Same Place	**Different Place**
Same Time	Decision rooms Computers with projector displays Voting tools	Two-way video Audio conferencing White boards Screen sharing Chat
Different Time	Workstation software for shift work Document sharing	Conferencing Bulletin boards Email Voice mail

Table 7.1 Four Combinations of Group Decision Support

Same Time and Same Place

In this situation, support at the low end of the technology spectrum includes tools like computer projection systems that display computer images on a traditional white screen. On the high end are meeting rooms where each person has her own computer with appropriate software to assist during a meeting.

Same Time and Different Place

Studying same time and different place situations is an important research area. We need to understand how technology can support the growing business need for remote meetings. Shared workspaces are one such technology that is based on the concept of WYSIWIS. The idea is to allow people in geographically distributed locations to work together at the same time and see what other participants are doing. Video teleconferences allow participants to see and hear each other across great distances and give users more of a feeling of being in the same meeting room as the other participants. In a video conference, participants can observe the facial expressions and body language that accompanies what participants hear. Video conferences are a richer communication channel than audio or text-based interactions. A multiparticipant video conference can provide support of a meeting where some participants are located at a distance from others. Time-zone differences can, however, become an issue in scheduling meetings of this type. Microsoft NetMeeting supports video conferencing and has groupware capabilities.

Flagstar Bank (FSB) won the 1997 *Computerworld* Smithsonian Award for its use of information technology in the Finance, Insurance, and Real Estate category. Flagstar Bank's Lenders' Interactive Video Exchange (LIVE) project used Intel ProShare conferencing systems with automated underwriting DSS technologies. With LIVE, a homebuyer at a branch bank and a loan underwriter at the central bank location can meet face-to-face using interactive video and get loans approved within an hour. Usually, the loan approval process takes weeks, and the prospective homeowner has no contact with the person who makes the decision.

Different Time and Same Place

Managers sometimes need to share information with a manager who worked on a prior shift. They need to investigate how computer software can support existing administrative, sequential, decision making, and information filtering needs. Some groupware systems attempt to help managers make smooth transitions in shift work situations at places like hospitals and factories by facilitating group memory and charting progress so that there is a quick and smooth transition from one shift to the next.

Different Time and Different Place

Some managers need to collaborate over large distances and across time zones. The need for research in this group situation is increasing because of an ongoing need for more coordination between geographically dispersed team members. Group voice mail, e-mail, fax, conferencing software, internets/intranets, and hypermedia allow users to communicate at different times even though they are in geographically distributed locations.

Buckman Laboratories, an industrial chemical company based in Memphis, Tennessee, has over 1200 employees around the world. The concept of sharing knowledge and best practices has been a concern at Buckman for many years. Buckman has a knowledge transfer system called K'Netix, the Buckman Knowledge Network. When employees need information or help, they just ask for it via forums, which are Buckman-only on-line forums. Conversations are the basis for transferring knowledge around the company. So, the important conversations are captured. Volunteer experts identify the conversations that contain valuable information and, more importantly, valuable streams of reasoning. These are then edited to remove extraneous material, given key words, and stored in the forum library. This system combines document and communications-driven DSS.

A business team or task force may need communications-driven decision support in all four of the above situations.

COMMUNICATION AND GROUP SUPPORT TOOLS

Communication technologies can be used to support many different purposes in companies. It has become important to manage and support communications among team members as well as communication between the organization and its stakeholders, like customers and suppliers. Creating an integrated communications-driven DSS strategy, which addresses all these needs, is important.

Multiparticipant systems like group and interorganizational DSS create complex implementation issues. Networking issues create challenges for many types of DSS, but especially for systems with many participants. An enterprise-wide DSS grows and inevitably becomes a major part of the overall information systems infrastructure. One can identify four communications-driven DSS architectures: decision rooms, local decision networks, teleconferencing, and remote decision making (cf., DeSanctis and Gallupe, 1985). Some architectures seem to work best for ongoing decision support and others are limited to groups where member are in close physical proximity to each other (see Figure 7.1).

When group members are in close proximity, and ad hoc or one-time decision support is needed, then a decision room with a GDSS is the best choice. When ongoing support is needed, decision support on a local area network with groupware or a GDSS often has advantages over repeated use of the decision room. When group members are widely dispersed, video conferencing decision support can provide participants needed face-to-face interaction. When the support needed is more ongoing, then it may be advantageous to use a Web-based communications-driven DSS. The following paragraphs explain in more detail group DSS, groupware, and video conferencing.

Group Decision Support Systems

GDSS aid groups, especially groups of managers, in analyzing problem situations and in performing group decision making tasks. Common GDSS components include: an agenda tool; a whiteboard, an opinion meter, an idea categorizer, electronic brainstorming, a group outliner, a topic commenter, voting tools, a survey tool, and alternative analysis tools.

In a GDSS you can create an agenda with a listing of the activities you want to accomplish, such as brainstorming, categorizing ideas, and voting. GroupSystems, a GDSS product, offers a variety of voting methods including Yes/No responses, rank ordering alternatives, True/False responses, and rating on a 10-point scale.

Electronic Brainstorming is the most popular GDSS tool. Meeting participants are given stimulus questions like "What are possible new products our customers might buy?" All participants concurrently respond to the question for a fixed period of time, usually about 10 minutes. A participant types in an idea, anonymously submits it, and then types in another.

People from outside of a company can participate using GDSS. They can come to a company's group decision room or participate remotely using a Web-based GDSS. People unfamiliar with GDSS should visit GroupSystems at http://www.groupsystems.com. According to their Web site, the ability to help a group develop consensus is one of the key features that distinguishes GroupSystems from data-sharing software such as Lotus Notes or conferencing programs.

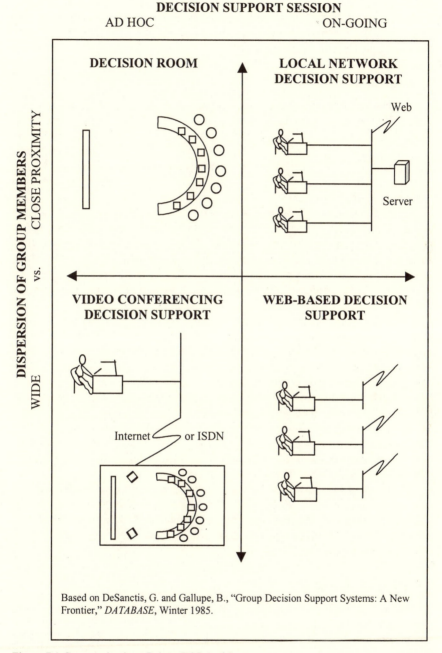

DECISION SUPPORT SESSION
AD HOC   ON-GOING

DISPERSION OF GROUP MEMBERS
CLOSE PROXIMITY   vs.   WIDE

DECISION ROOM

LOCAL NETWORK DECISION SUPPORT

Web

Server

VIDEO CONFERENCING DECISION SUPPORT

WEB-BASED DECISION SUPPORT

Internet   or ISDN

Based on DeSanctis, G. and Gallupe, B., "Group Decision Support Systems: A New Frontier," *DATABASE*, Winter 1985.

Figure 7.1 Communications-Driven DSS Architecture

GDSS have lost some of the excitement they generated in the early 1990s, but a number of organizations still actively use decision rooms, including: Air Force Innovation Center, IBM Global Services, SABRE Group, and Southern New England Telecommunications.

Groupware

Computer conferencing provides meeting participants with connectivity and with a database of comments and interactions. Electronic bulletin boards are a simple type of groupware. Email is also a groupware tool. Other capabilities of groupware software includes information sharing, joint document authoring, shared calendars, and project management. Groupware provides support for communication and collaboration among group members, and it provides coordination for group tasks.

A conferencing or messaging system or what is also known as a bulletin board is a widely used communication support tool. It allows posting of messages that can be read and responded to by team members and meeting participants at any time. A conferencing system can be searched for content, sender, and date. Also, posted articles or messages can have embedded hyperlinks. Most conferencing systems can have any number of topics or forums.

Most managers use some type of electronic mail. An electronic mail facility is needed to provide one-to-one message transfer among team members. Some systems are better than others, but e-mail remains an important communication and collaboration tool.

A chat tool is also sometimes useful. A chat tool provides real-time text-based communication among participants. People can type in a message, and they can "chat" with others in the chat session.

An interesting meeting support tool is a whiteboard. A whiteboard allows for real-time communication among meeting participants, using a graphical drawing or painting interface. A person draws on the whiteboard and all other participants "see" what is drawn on their computer screens.

Most groupware programs let users transmit e-mail, but they also tend to have such features as group calendars, databases and message boards. Groupware programs let users check other staff members' schedules in order to plan meetings. One of the biggest strengths of groupware programs is their messaging capability.

Video Conferencing

AT&T demonstrated the first Picture Phone at the 1964 World's Fair in New York and in 1970 AT&T offered its Picture Phone for lease at $160 per month. In the next 15 years, developments in interactive video seemed to stagnate. In September 1992, CU-SeeMe was introduced for the Macintosh and in December 1996 Microsoft NetMeeting with video was released. Today, interactive video is supported by a number of vendors. For example, Microsoft's NetMeeting software is available for use on LANs and the Internet. There are also dedicated video conferencing systems from a number of vendors like Polycom and Intel that can support same time/different place meetings with full-motion video.

Video conferencing decision support is designed to assist when business operations are widely dispersed. Current technology supports two distinct types of video conferencing. One type links one personal computer to another and allows two people to interact. The second type supports multiple individuals or individuals and groups in conference rooms or at PC's. A video conference room has a large video display, multiple microphones, and high-speed transmission of video images.

The most important factor to consider in choosing between video conferencing systems is the quality of the audio. Out-of-sync and poor quality audio is unacceptable. Audio must provide rich and fully synchronized sound for participants.

Video conferencing and Web-based tools can potentially speed up decision making while reducing time and other costs for meetings. Also, video conferencing with Web-based tools can provide managers access to computer-based resources and Web-based materials during meetings. Video conferencing for decision support makes it possible to involve more people in decision meetings and it may reduce the stress associated with travel. This type of decision support is, however, inappropriate when there is insufficient network bandwidth.

A MANAGERIAL PERSPECTIVE ON COMMUNICATIONS-DRIVEN DSS

Using alternative communications media raises very different sets of questions for managers. The important task for a manager who is implementing communications-driven DSS is to ask relevant questions related to how a proposed technology can support a decision group or work team. Let's examine some questions that should concern managers about group decision support technologies.

Bulletin boards and Web-conferencing. Is a threaded discussion forum needed for posting questions and comments? Will managers use the technology? If so, how can a team leader encourage an interesting and engaging conversation among people who don't access comments at the same time? How does a team leader know when it's time to make a decision and when there is consensus about a choice? How does a team leader deal with conflict when everyone is participating at different times? What is the virtual equivalent of eye contact? How can participants build a culture that will support a distributed decision-making process?

Document sharing. Do managers need to collaborate on documents and other files from distributed locations? Will document sharing help or harm relationships and trust among team members? Does document sharing help or hurt team building? Is document sharing different for internal and external users? What happens when a documents is incorrect? Who's responsible?

Electronic mail. Are managers currently using e-mail? What norms need to be established for things like response time and whether e-mail can be forwarded to others? What norms are important about who gets copied on e-mail messages and whether or not there are blind copies? How does the style of e-mail messages influence how people feel about the team? How can does a team leader discourage "flaming" or the sending of harsh and inflammatory messages?

GDSS and computer-supported face-to-face meetings. If one holds such a meeting supported by GDSS, how does the ability to contribute anonymous input affect the team? How can one test whether consensus in the group is meaningful or an artifact of the computer-supported session? How much training is needed? How much will the software be used?

Interactive video. In a decision conference with video conferencing, will participants feel comfortable with being on TV and being recorded? How can one manage a meeting with multiple remote participants at different locations to make sure that everyone has a chance to be heard? How much training is needed for a team leader and for team members?

The overriding question facing managers is "What group communication and collaboration support tools are appropriate or 'best' in a given situation?" In some ways, even this question is becoming less important because all of the above tools are converging in an integrated group support product. Having an integrated group support tool set will let participants choose different tools during a meeting without needing to change the software meeting environment.

A CONTINGENCY THEORY

Communications-driven DSS address a number of problems associated with group communication and group decision making. The most basic systems address the problems of communication barriers and emphasize improving communication, idea formation, discussion, and messaging. More sophisticated systems add decision-support modeling and group decision techniques to enhance the system. The most sophisticated systems provide for automated group communications, as well as include capabilities for selecting and arranging rules for a meeting.

Research suggests that a meeting supported by a GDSS can improve productivity of participants and result in more ideas (cf., McGoff, Hunt, Vogel, and Nunamaker, 1990; Gray and Nunnamaker, 1996). The effectiveness of a GDSS is a function of the design of the software, the composition and skills of group members, the task that is being supported, and the context of the meeting. Context refers to situational factors like the meeting room design, time pressures, and experience of and use of a facilitator.

Intuitively, we know that no one set of tools or processes is best in all group decision-making circumstances. DeSanctis and Gallupe (1987) presented a typology with three dimensions that they argued are crucial for designing or choosing group support software. The three dimensions are task type, group size, and group proximity.

Task Type

The particular group task is an important factor to consider in communications-driven DSS and GDSS evaluation and selection. The attributes of the task determine the need for information and the communication practices in the group. Group goals and tasks include:

- Generating ideas and actions, includes planning and creativity tasks.
- Choosing alternatives, includes intellective tasks like choosing the right answer, and preference tasks.
- Negotiating solutions, includes resolving differing viewpoints as well as dealing with conflicting motives.

Group Size

Very small groups of 2 to 3 members that can meet face to face generally do not need extensive support from computerized tools. Very large groups may need much more sophisticated decision support tools than medium sized groups. The experience of group members with computerized tools also appears to impact performance with them. Some tools can be learned much more quickly than others.

Group Proximity

Decision room groups that can meet at the same time and same place probably do not need as many communication and decision-aiding tools as distributed groups that are meeting at different times and in different places. When groups are in close proximity, they can use synchronous decision support, like a decision meeting room, or asynchronous decision support, like email or bulletin boards. When group members are widely dispersed, video conferencing or interactive Web-based conferencing can provide synchronous support and the same asynchronous tools can support widely dispersed groups.

Task Type and Media Type

As mentioned in an earlier section, a wide variety of tools can support group communication and collaboration. A number of studies have examined the relationship between task type and media type. Hollingshead, McGrath, and O'Connor (1993) explored the relationship between communication technology and group task performance. They found that the amount of experience with the computer technology and the group membership had a larger impact on performance than task type. The task/media fit model (Daft and Lengel, 1986) was generally supported. Table 7.2 summarizes current thinking about what media best fits which types of decision tasks. In general, computer-mediated communication is a good fit for generating ideas and plans. Negotiating conflicts of interest should be done face-to-face, and computer support is not necessarily helpful.

	Asynchronous Decision Support	Synchronous Decision Support	Face-to-Face Meetings
Generating ideas and actions	More ideas Experienced users satisfied	More ideas Experienced users satisfied	Acceptable
Choosing alternatives	Good for rating and ranking by experienced users	Good for rating and ranking	Can be more time consuming
Negotiating solutions	Hard to conduct negotiations	Possible with interactive video and white board	Preferred approach

Table 7.2 A Matrix of Task Types and Media Types

In general, communications-driven DSS are most successful when the people who do the work to support the system are hired for that purpose or are beneficiaries of the system. For example, the automatic meeting and scheduling feature of an electronic calendar is not always used in companies. The immediate beneficiary of the system is often the manager or secretary who initiates a meeting. Group members must do additional work to enter their schedule information so they may resist using the application. The primary beneficiary of most project management applications is the project leader or manager. Other team members must enter considerable information about their tasks and completion times. If team members are rewarded for entering information, the quantity and quality of information entered will increase over a period of time.

In order to have productive conversations among members of virtual teams, you need to create a common or shared understanding for the group. Group support systems succeed when managers, developers, and users adhere to social conventions. For example, in a Group DSS the explicit record of opposing positions may be politically unacceptable to some managers. If so, the information should not be recorded.

Communications-driven DSS succeed when their use is built around specific structured work procedures that allow or even encourage exception handling and task modification. For example, arrangements that are in the best interest of a group may not be compatible with the structure, procedures, and processes imposed by a group support system. Unless the system is strongly supported by senior management, the system will not be used because it is not compatible with the group's preferences and procedures.

GROUP DECISION SUPPORT SYSTEMS BENEFITS

One of the best-known GDSS is a product called GroupSystems. The product was initially developed at the University of Arizona; currently GroupSystems is marketed by a company called GroupSystems (check http://groupsystems.com). It is used at a number of corporations, government agencies, and universities. A computer-supported meeting room is typically set up with a workstation computer for each participant in the meeting. A large public screen provides viewing of shared information for participants in the meeting. The computer hardware is connected by a local area network (LAN). Meeting software provides support for creating an agenda, generating ideas, organizing ideas, evaluating and rating ideas, and other group-decision tasks. Each participant in a face-to-face computer-supported meeting can use the software concurrently and, if desired provide input anonymously. Also, voting and rating of ideas usually occurs anonymously in GDSS.

McGoff and his colleagues (1990) reported success with the use of the GroupSystems application at IBM. The most prominent benefit reported was saving an estimated 56 percent in work/meeting hours. Their research estimated that the savings were so great that the return on investment for a decision room was one year. Computer-supported meetings seem to be helpful in keeping a meeting on track and on reducing the amount of unrelated discussions about outside issues. IBM was also been able to resolve issues in a shorter time span, because meetings were longer in length but fewer in number, allowing problems to be resolved faster.

Anonymity of participants resulted in many positives in the IBM research studies. First, there was greater participation. The increased participation rate carried over into the work culture with members approaching their leaders more often to stay involved with related issues. Also, there was less group think (Janis and Mann, 1977). The system was designed with easy-to-use graphical interface; thus, low levels of computer literacy did not deter use of the system. According to McGoff et al., the most surprising benefit of the software was the uses of the session data after a meeting. This data was used to support managerial decisions, to document future sessions, in presentations and project management workshops, for technical reviews, and in bimonthly meetings to keep the group focused on the project until completion.

Jessup and Valacich's (1993) book *Group Support Systems* reports many experimental and field studies on group support technologies. The research paints a "rather cloudy picture," but in "most field research, GSS use appeared to improve meeting outcomes such as performance, efficiency, and satisfaction" (p. 73).

Many companies created decision rooms in the late 1980s and early 1990s. For example, managers at Mariott reported that in the first 2 months of use, 1,000 people used the new meeting room for generating ideas. Boeing used a version of Ventana GroupSystems and claimed that using a group support system reduced the total time spent in meetings by 71 percent. Team projects involving meetings at Boeing were also accomplished more quickly by using computer support. GTE used GroupSystems.com's products to generate ideas. Agilent Technologies recently migrated from GroupSystems to GroupSystems OnLine. According to a vendor case study, the result has been an increase in the sharing and capturing of knowledge as well as an increase in productivity. Agilent has customized planning and project management methodologies built on GroupSystems to meet various department needs.

Before communications-driven DSS are implemented, it is essential that management support its use. If top management does not believe GDSS, groupware and communications-driven DSS will benefit the organization, it will be difficult to persuade people to use the system. However, if management is behind the implementation and use of the new tools, several positive effects may be noticed. First, when group support is introduced in a company, it should increase the productivity of its users. This occurs because an increased amount of work can be accomplished in shorter amounts of time and because of enhanced communication between employees. Second, group support software facilitates teamwork through open communication. Third, some groupware products help document important work information in a convenient location. Finally, communications-driven DSS can enhance communication between upper management and the rest of a company's employees.

According to many proponents of computerized support, the main benefit of a GDSS is that it saves time and money. How does it accomplish this? Here are a few of the ways:

- Simultaneous input leverages a team's time and creates better quality ideas.
- The computer system records ideas for distribution and future work.
- Process support facilitates completing team tasks faster.
- In some cases, a GDSS provides access to information that lets a group use outside data while working in the system.
- Meetings can be held with the participants in the same room or spread around the world. Travel costs can be reduced.
- A video conference allows a team member to discuss alternatives with remote team members.

The anticipated benefits of communications-driven DSS and GDSS are many. Actually realizing them can be somewhat challenging, and it may be disruptive to the current operations of a company. One major change that has resulted from computerized group support is the creation or enabling of virtual organizations. The next section discusses the changes in organization structure facilitated by computing and communications technologies.

VIRTUAL ORGANIZATIONS

According to Hatim Tyabji, retired CEO of VeriFone, a virtual organization is a company that operates continuously through traditional barriers of time and distance. The entire company communicates around the clock via electronic mail and other information systems and tools. Managers converse via e-mail, by the transmittal of internal documents, or by the company-wide combined usage of a single informational database (cf., Galal, Stoddard, Nolan, and Kao, 1996). Tyabji said in an interview "E-mail is powerful in this company because there are no exceptions. There is no paper. There are no secretaries. Period" (Taylor, 1995, p. 115). Virtual organizations are dependent on communications-driven DSS for their existence and their effective functioning.

Alternative Definitions

One can also view a virtual organization as a network of independent organizations linked together by information systems and information technology to exploit market opportunities by sharing skills, costs, and market access. Some virtual organizations operate on a project-only, temporary basis. Many so-called virtual organizations operate as permanent companies. According to Vine (1995), "a virtual organization uses technology to create new arrangements among employees, suppliers, customers, and others to quickly gain new opportunities with greater efficiency and lower cost."

A Simple Example of a "Virtual Organization"

A small consulting firm might use the Internet to faciliate collaboration by its employees who are professionals working at home offices and at client sites. Even the owner of the consulting firm could work in a home office and communicate and collaborate with the other members of the firm.

Employees could perform their work and send e-mail memos and reports to the owner, who in turn would supervise the operation and meet with the other members face-to-face at a weekly breakfast meeting or as needed. Team members might subscribe to a listserv mailing list or another information resource to obtain advice or even locate specialists for project work. This strategic use of the Internet reduces overhead and commuting time while increasing flexibility, speed, and overall effectiveness.

Benefits of a Virtual Organization

According to Peter Drucker (1988), by the year 2008 the typical large business will have half the levels of management and one-third the managers of its counterpart of today. Specialists will be brought together in task forces that cut across traditional departments. Coordination and control will depend largely on employees' willingness to discipline themselves. According to Drucker, behind these changes lies information technology. Information-based organizations pose their own management challenges: motivating and rewarding specialists; creating a vision to unify an organization of specialists; devising a management structure that works with task forces; and ensuring the supply, preparation, and testing of top management people.

What are the anticipated benefits of virtual organizations? There are eight major benefits discussed in the literature including: increased effectiveness, reduced costs, improved client satisfaction, reduced capital investment needs in new businesses, expenses are greatly reduced, lead times are shortened, inventory is better managed, and a direct connection is established with the customer.

According to Charles Handy (1995) in a *Harvard Business Review* article, the technological possibilities of the virtual organization are appealing, but it is easy to ignore the potential problems. He argues the managerial and personal implications that result from the new technologies require rethinking old notions of control. He notes that as it becomes possible for more work to be done outside the traditional office, trust will become more important to organizations. Handy proposes seven rules of trust that when violated reduce the effectiveness of a virtual organization. First, he says, trust is not blind—it needs fairly small groupings in which people can know each other well. Second, trust needs boundaries—he suggests managers should define goals, then let workers try to achieve them. Third, trust demands learning and openness to change. Fourth, "trust is tough"—when trust turns out to be misplaced, people have to be fired. Fifth, trust needs bonding— the goals of small units must fit with those of the larger group. Sixth, trust needs touch—workers must sometimes meet in person. Finally, trust requires leaders. Technology can undermine trust, only people can create and maintain trust in work groups.

There will be many types of virtual organizations. Some will succeed and realize the anticipated benefits; other types will fail for lack of trust and a lack of technological expertise.

Aligning Information Systems and Organizational Structures

Identifying all possible alignments of information technologies and decision support implementations in organizations is beyond the scope of this chapter, but it is useful to discuss and examine four organization structures that may result from implementing communications-driven DSS. The metaphorical labels for these are a community structure, a federation structure, a mobile structure, and a skyscraper structure (cf. Power, 1988).

A Community Structure

A large "community" of organizations can potentially achieve economic efficiencies in providing goods and services. In a community organization, a large number of interdependent organizations can be grouped into a multilevel hierarchy where individual organizations retain extensive autonomy. A communications-driven DSS is the key to providing coordination and control for the management group of the community. A sophisticated infrastructure of communication and information systems is vital to creating a large grouping of supplier and buyer organizations. The corporate telecommunications network and information systems can facilitate coordinated purchasing, exchanges, and sales by community members. Also, various DSS can facilitate centralized strategic planning and monitoring. Maintaining discrete organizational entities in the community should facilitate management control and, if needed, reorganization of the community. Measurement and reward systems can be linked to the "profits" of each member organization. Stock options and other equity arrangements linked to unit performance should encourage the best managers to remain with the community.

A Federation Structure

Organizations without hierarchies may evolve in response to improved communication and information technologies. Private, centralized computing resources can also help small business owners and professionals coordinate their businesses. Information and communication technologies can help them share knowledge and more efficiently use and obtain resources. These new "federation" organizations can be managed using communications-driven DSS. Intelligent management support systems can aid owner/managers in implementing collective actions on pricing, inventory management, or investment of resources. Rewards can be tied to the sales volume and profitability of each task entity, for example, of each office in a multi-office firm. Also, in professional service federations, the quality of work and the competence of each provider can be assessed by a committee of owner/managers using tools like Balanced Scorecard systems and EIS.

A Mobile Structure

This information-oriented structure can be visualized as a "mobile" organization. It is mobile both in the sense of being transportable or movable (at an economic cost and in a short period) and in the sense of being responsive or changeable, like an abstract sculpture with parts that can move rapidly and easily in response to the slightest breeze. Portable and handheld computing technologies, the Internet and Web, and cell phones and public telecommunications networks increase the viability and practicality of implementing mobile organization structures.

A Skyscraper Structure

Concerns about status and prestige may motivate managers to increase the number of upper-middle and top management positions in a company. Communication and information technologies can facilitate this type of multi-level structure. The structure that results could be called a "skyscraper." Managers at the top would supervise very few people, and the number of management levels in the organization would be very large. Computerized systems would do much of the routine transaction processing and would create value for the organization. The number of operating personnel would be a much smaller percentage of all employees than is currently found in the most automated manufacturing and oil refining companies. Centralized and integrated communications and information systems help ensure that everyone knows about everyone else's actions and performance. Information technology makes this structure possible and potentially efficient for some organizations like financial institutions.

EVALUATING COMMUNICATIONS AND GROUP SUPPORT TOOLS

Implementing communications-driven DSS in a traditional organization or implementing these tools to create a virtual organization or innovative organization structure is a major technology decision. Because these tools are purchased and installed rather than built by information systems staff, the evaluation focuses on products from vendors. The following six criteria should be carefully considered when evaluating any of the group support tools mentioned in this section.

Reliability. Many companies want a solution that has proven it can meet their needs. Managers want to know what software is going to perform the necessary tasks without failing. Some innovative companies will be early adopters of unproven technologies. Reliability should, however, still be evaluated.

Cost. Given the significant costs of technology and the rapid advances of new technologies, companies want an affordable package. Managers should examine the cost per user for a system as well as the total cost of the system. Also, ongoing operation costs such as hardware and software maintenance and support staff of a proposed communications-driven DSS need to be considered when solutions are compared.

Scalability. Companies need a package that will easily integrate with existing software applications and hardware platforms. Also, the systems should support all of the anticipated users. Managers do not want to purchase separate components to connect legacy systems with new group support applications.

Security. Many organizations and individuals are beginning to increase the amounts of shared data and number of transactions being executed across firewalls and geographic regions through the Internet. With this increase in shared data, there is an increasing concern regarding the security of this information.

Development features. Many vendors produce standard packages to run on many different platforms. It is important to most organizations that the package allows for development of some customized capabilities.

Ease of installation and use. Companies and managers are under extreme pressure to do things rapidly. With this pressure, managers want a software package that is easy to install and requires minimal amounts of training for its users.

CONCLUSIONS AND COMMENTARY

Managers and academic researchers are in the early stages of a process of accumulating knowledge about communications-driven DSS. Much more needs to be learned about how communications-driven DSS affect group meeting processes and team and organizational outcomes. There is some evidence that communications-driven DSS are, however, changing organizations.

Communications-driven DSS help in communication, collaboration and coordination. A fit between task type, group size and group proximity when selecting communications-driven decision support technologies increases the effectiveness of the decisions and improves group performance. Group support systems succeed when people who do work to support a system are hired for that purpose or are beneficiaries of the system. Also, communications-driven DSS and group support systems succeed when managers, developers, and users adhere to social conventions. Finally, communications-driven DSS are most effective when their use is built around specific structured work procedures that allow or even encourage exception handling and task modification.

Structural changes that are possible from improved information technologies are still somewhat difficult to anticipate. Managers must act now to create changes; they cannot rely on circumstance and chance to create a new organization structure. Information technology facilitates structural changes, and structural changes affect how and when information technology can and will be used in an organization. Aligning organization structures with information technologies is a reasonable but difficult goal. The different types of structural responses to information technologies—the community, the federation, the mobile, and the skyscraper—can help planners and organization theorists design companies that are aligned with and exploit group support systems and information technologies. Often, the most difficult issue facing business strategists when they attempt to align an organization to information technologies is identifying new, interesting, or innovative structures worth investigating and implementing.

Chapter 8

Building Data and Document-Driven Decision Support Systems

INTRODUCTION

In recent years, most large companies and many other large organizations have implemented database systems called data warehouses and some have also implemented document management and On-line Analytical Processing (OLAP) systems. Some organizations have implemented Business Intelligence (BI) technologies and some have created Executive Information Systems (EIS). Many managers and information systems specialists are interested in learning more about these relatively new types of data-driven and document-driven Decision Support Systems (DSS). For many years, the prospects and problems of providing managers with real-time management information have been discussed and debated (cf., Dearden, 1966). The debate about costs, advantages, problems, and possibilities must continue. Managers need to retrieve and analyze large structured and unstructured data collections for decision support.

The expanded DSS framework categorizes business intelligence systems, data warehouses, EIS, spatial DSS, and OLAP systems as data-driven DSS. In general, a data-driven DSS is an interactive computer-based system that helps a decision maker use a very large database of business data and, in some systems, data about the external environment of a company. For example, a system may have data on both a company's sales and on its competitors' sales. Some of the data is very detailed transaction data and some is a summary of transactions. In most implementations of data-driven DSS, users of the system can perform unplanned or ad hoc analyses and requests for data. In a data-driven DSS, managers process data to identify facts and draw conclusions about relationships and trends. Data-driven DSS help managers retrieve, display, and analyze historical data.

Document-driven DSS are defined as systems that integrate "a variety of storage and processing technologies to provide complete document retrieval and analysis." The Web now provides access to large document databases, including databases of hypertext documents, images, sounds, and video. Examples of documents that could be accessed by a document-driven DSS are policies and procedures, product specifications, catalogs, news stories, and corporate historical documents, including minutes of meetings, corporate records, and important correspondence. A search engine is a powerful decision-aiding tool associated with a document-driven DSS (cf., Fedorowicz, 1993, pp. 125–136; Swanson and Culnan, 1978; Power, 2001). Knowledge management, Web, and DSS technologies are used to build document-driven DSS.

Data and document-driven DSS are often very expensive to develop and implement in organizations. Despite the large resource commitments that are required, many companies have implemented these types of DSS. Technologies are changing and managers and MIS staff will need to make continuing investments in these categories of DSS software. So, it is important that managers understand the various terms and systems that use large databases to support management decision making. This chapter emphasizes: comparing data and document-driven DSS; identifying subcategories of data-driven DSS, comparing structured DSS data and operating data, understanding an interconnected data-driven DSS architecture, implementing data and document-driven DSS, and finding success in building DSS with large structured and unstructured databases. Now, let's begin our exploration of these two general categories of DSS by discussing the differences and similarities between them.

COMPARING DATA AND DOCUMENT-DRIVEN DSS

Document-driven DSS is a relatively new category of decision support. There are certainly similarities to the more familiar data-driven DSS, but there are also major differences. Document-driven DSS help managers process "soft" or qualitative information, and data-driven DSS help managers process "hard" or numeric data. Both categories of DSS come in various shapes and sizes. Some systems support senior managers and others support functional decision makers on narrowly defined tasks. The Web has increased the need for, and the possibilities associated with, document-driven DSS.

A defining difference between the two categories of DSS is that data-driven DSS help managers analyze, display and manipulate large structured data sets that contain numeric and short character strings while document-driven DSS analyze, display, and manipulate text including logical units of text, called documents (cf., Sullivan, 2001).

Another defining difference is the analysis tools used for decision support. Data-driven DSS use quantitative and statistical tools for ordering, summarizing, and evaluating the specific contents of a subject-oriented data warehouse. Document-driven DSS use natural language and statistical tools for extracting, categorizing, indexing, and summarizing subject-oriented document warehouses.

What are the similarities? First, both systems use databases with very large collections of information to drive or create decision support capabilities. Second, both types of systems require the definition of metadata and the cleaning, extraction, and loading of data into an appropriate data management system using an organizing framework or model.

Third, building either type of system involves understanding the decision support and information needs of the targeted users. Also, because user needs are hard to anticipate the tendency is to store large amounts of data or documents that may not be immediately needed. Rapid application development or prototyping is sometimes possible for small scale systems, but a more structured SDLC approach is needed for enterprise-wide data or document-driven DSS. Neither type of system can meet all of the decision support needs of all managers in an organization. The best approach is to try to meet a specific, well-defined need initially and then incrementally expand the structured data or documents that are captured and organized in the foundation data/document management system.

DATA-DRIVEN DSS SUBCATEGORIES

The broad category of data-driven DSS generally includes tools to help users "drill down" for more detailed information, "drill up" to see a broader, more summarized view, and "slice and dice" to change the data dimensions they are viewing. The results of "drilling" and "slicing and dicing" are presented in tables and charts. There are four main subcategories of data-driven DSS; data warehouses, OLAP systems with multidimensional databases, Executive Information Systems (EIS), and spatial DSS.

Data Warehouses

A data warehouse is a specific database designed and populated to provide decision support in an organization (cf., Gray and Watson, 1998). It is batch-updated and structured for rapid on-line queries and managerial summaries. Data warehouses contain large amounts of data—500 megabytes and more. According to data warehousing pioneer Bill Inmon (1995), "A data warehouse is a subject-oriented, integrated, time-variant, nonvolatile collection of data in support of management's decision making process."

What does Inmon mean by his four characteristics of a data warehouse? *Subject-oriented* means it focuses on subjects related to business or organizational activity like customers, employees and suppliers. *Integrated* means the data from various databases is stored in a consistent format through use of naming conventions, domain constraints, physical attributes, and measurements. *Time-variant* refers to associating data with specific points in time. Finally, *nonvolatile* means the data does not change once it is in the warehouse and stored for decision support. Ralph Kimball (1996), another data warehousing pioneer, states that "a data warehouse is a copy of transaction data specifically structured for query and analysis."

A related term is a "data mart." A data mart is a more focused or a single-subject data warehouse. For example, some companies build a customer data mart rather than a multi-subject data warehouse. Such a focused data mart would have all of the business information about a company's customers. Many organizations and businesses are starting their enterprise-wide data warehouses by building a series of focused data marts. Data warehouses and data marts are often accessed using ad-hoc query or report and query tools. Some authors have combined data warehousing and OLAP. The two terms should be recognized as different subcategories of data-driven DSS.

On-Line Analytical Processing (OLAP)

OLAP and multidimensional analysis refers to software for manipulating multidimensional data. Even though one can have multidimensional data in a data warehouse, OLAP software can create various views and more dimensional representations of the data. According to Nigel Pendse at the OLAPReport.com, OLAP software provides fast, consistent, interactive access to shared, multidimensional information. Pendse calls these characteristics the FASMI test, an acronym for fast analysis of shared, multidimensional information test. What does the FASMI test mean?

FAST means that the system delivers most responses to users within about five seconds. ANALYSIS means that the system can cope with any business logic and statistical analysis that is relevant for the application and the user. SHARED means that the software has security capabilities needed for sharing data among users. MULTIDIMENSIONAL is an essential requirement. An OLAP system must provide a multidimensional, conceptual view of the data. INFORMATION means the software can support all of the data and derived information that managers need.

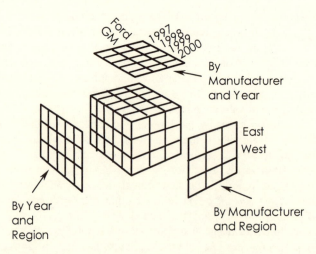

Figure 8.1 An Example of a Multidimensional Data Cube

OLAP software usually accesses a multidimensional database. A multidimensional database captures and presents data as a multidimensional array or data cube. Variables hold data in the database. The multidimensional database management system creates arrays of values, usually numeric, that are "dimensioned" by relevant attributes. For example, the attributes "year," "manufacturer," and "region" are dimensions of a "units sold" variable. This three-dimensional array can be visualized as a cube of data (see Figure 8.1). Arrays with more dimensions are often created, but such arrays are harder to visualize.

Multidimensional databases can have multiple variables with a common or a unique set of dimensions. A multidimensional view of data is especially powerful for OLAP applications. For example, one can sum units in dimensions. A relational database software package can also be used to structure data to support rapid, multi-dimensional queries. A Star schema is a typical structure implemented for multidimensional data using a relational database management system (cf., Gray and Watson, 1998). A Star schema has a central table of facts, often called a Fact Table, and dimension tables linked to it by foreign keys like StoreID or ProductID (see Figure 8.2). The star is a picture of the way the data is being stored. The basic factual information is in the middle of the star. This type of application, where multidimensional data is stored in a relational database management system has been called ROLAP, short for Relational OLAP.

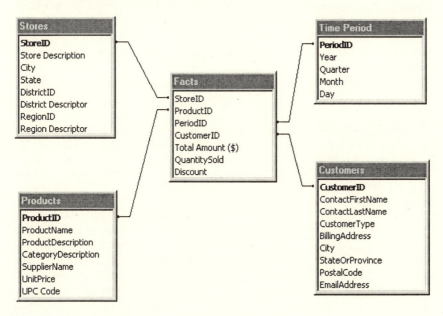

Figure 8.2 Star Schema Diagram

Like other data-driven DSS, OLAP usually provides drill-down and drill-up capabilities. Software reviewer Jay Tyo (1996) divided OLAP tools into five broad types that he labeled: stand-alone desktop OLAP tools; integrated desktop tools; relational OLAP tools; personal multidimensional databases; and other OLAP tools. The variety of products has only expanded in recent years with the introduction of Web-based OLAP. Categorizing data-driven DSS products is complex and difficult. New products are continually being introduced. So, managers and DSS analysts are confronted with a wide array of different types of OLAP and Business Intelligence products. The OLAP vendors have created a number of technical terms that can be somewhat confusing; for help with OLAP and data-driven DSS terms, check the *Guide to OLAP Terminology* created by the OLAP Council and the DSS Glossary at DSSResources.COM.

Business Intelligence (BI) is sometimes used interchangeably with OLAP and other synonyms for DSS. BI is a popularized umbrella term introduced by Howard Dresner of the Gartner Group in 1989 to describe a set of concepts and methods to improve business decision making by using fact-based support systems. A Business Intelligence system is a data-driven DSS. The most common "business intelligence" software is for querying a database and creating a report.

Executive Information Systems

Executive Information Systems (EIS) are computerized systems intended to provide current and appropriate information to support executive decision making for managers (cf., Watson, Rainer, and Houdeshel, 1992). The emphasis is on graphical displays and an easy-to-use interface that present information from the corporate database. EIS are designed to provide canned reports or briefing books to top-level executives. They offer strong reporting and drill-down capabilities.

EIS differ from traditional information systems in a number of ways (Kelly, 1997):

1. EIS are specifically tailored to an executive's information needs.
2. EIS are able to access data about specific issues and problems as well as aggregate reports.
3. EIS provide extensive on-line analysis tools including trend analysis, exception reporting, pivot tables, and "drill-down" capability.
4. EIS access a broad range of internal and external data.

Differentiating EIS from other sub-categories of data-driven DSS has historical value in that such systems were developed separately from model-driven DSS and report and query tools, but it also helps analysts understand that senior manager's have different decision support needs. EIS are intended to help senior executives find problems, identify opportunities, identify trends, and make fact-based decisions. EIS usually let managers pivot and change dimensions and "drill down" for more information in structured information displays. EIS are designed to avoid data overload for busy managers.

EIS and data-warehousing technologies are converging in the marketplace. EIS used proprietary databases that required many staff people to update, maintain, and create. This was very expensive. In addition, the data became obsolete quickly. New Business Intelligence and OLAP systems require much less staff support. Data warehouse and OLAP technologies have made EIS more powerful and more practical.

EIS report key business results to managers. The performance measures in the EIS must be easy to understand and collect. Whenever possible, data should be collected as part of routine work processes. An EIS should not add substantially to the workload of managers or staff. Balanced Scorecard measurement software can be used in some firms to expand the measures used in an EIS (check balancedscorecard.org).

In general, EIS are enterprise-wide, data-driven DSS that help senior managers analyze, compare, and highlight trends in important variables so that they can monitor performance and identify opportunities and problems. EIS increase the ability of senior executives to monitor many activities and may help in reducing the number of management levels in an organization.

Geographic Information Systems and Spatial DSS

The final subcategory of data-driven DSS that should be recognized is a spatial DSS (cf., Crossland, Wynne and Perkins, 1995) built using Geographic Information Systems (GIS) technologies. A GIS is a support system that represents data by using maps. Spatial DSS help a manager access, display, and analyze data that have geographic content and meaning. This type of system has been available for many years (cf., Sprague and Carlson, 1982). Some examples of spatial DSS include systems for crime analysis and mapping, customer demographic analyses, and political voting patterns analysis.

Spatial DSS applications are common in routing and location analysis, marketing, and traditional application areas of GIS in disciplines such as geology, forestry, and land planning (cf., Keenan, 1997).

GIS software provides a development environment for spatial DSS. Even limited functionality GIS software provides the ability to zoom in on a map and to display or highlight different data. A GIS provides database support that is designed to allow for the effective storage of spatial data. Also, GIS software provides a link between the user interface and database so a user can query and analyze the spatial data.

The developments and improvements in GIS software since 1990 make it practical to use off-the-shelf software to build a spatial DSS (cf., Keenan, 1997). An example of this type of software is the ArcInfo8 enterprise GIS software from ESRI (www.esri.com). ArcInfo is intended to help users view and query spatial data. Another widely used desktop mapping product is MapInfo (www.mapinfo.com). Also check Peter Keenan's excellent Web Resource on Spatial DSS at URL mis.ucd.ie/iswsdss/. Another major related Web site is Geographic Information Systems Resources and Links maintained by the U.S. Geological Survey at URL info.er.usgs.gov/research/gis/title.html.

Data-driven DSS have captured the imagination of managers because they can provide much easier access to a vast amount of business data. In a world of speeded-up competition, rapid changes in markets and products, and increased electronic communication, managers want to find their own answers to business questions. Managers are *not* willing or able to wait while financial or marketing analysts create special reports from databases. Managers are the customers and advocates for data-driven DSS. Because data is the driver of such systems it is important to identify and organize decision relevant data or what might be called DSS data. Matching decision situations and DSS data is the key to building data-driven DSS and making better fact-based managerial decisions. Now let's compare and contrast DSS data and operating data.

COMPARING DSS DATA AND OPERATING DATA

First, it is important to remember that operating data and DSS data serve different purposes. In general, DSS data is data about transactions and business occurrences; operating data is a detailed record of a company's daily business transactions. DSS data is created to provide tactical and strategic business meaning to operating data and relevant external data. The difference in purpose means that the data formats and structures will likely differ. Managers and DSS analysts must recognize that DSS data and operating data differ in terms of six major factors: the data structures, the time span, the summarization of data, data volatility, data dimensions, and metadata (cf., Rob and Coronell, 1997). Table 8.1 is a summary of the factors and the differences between operating and DSS data. The next six sections examine these differences in more detail.

Factors	Operating Data	DSS Data
Data Structures	normalized	integrated
Time Span	current	historical
Summarization	none	extensive in some systems
Data Volatility	volatile	non-volatile
Data Dimensions	one dimension	multiple dimensions
Metadata	desirable	required and important

Table 8.1   Comparing Operating and DSS Data

Data Structures

What are the differences between operating and DSS data structures? It is useful to examine the extent and nature of the differences in format and structure. Often, operating data are stored in a relational database management system. These relational transaction systems have data structures called tables that have been highly normalized. The tables are normalized to avoid anomalies in the data when transactions like updating, adding records, and deleting records occur. Normalization is the process of reducing a complex data structure into its simplest, most stable, structure. The process involves removing redundant attributes, keys, and relationships from a conceptual data model.

In general, in an operating data storage or transaction system, both the software and the hardware are optimized to support transactions for the daily operations of a company. For example, each time an item is sold, it must be recorded and accounted for in appropriate transaction tables. Also, related data like customer data and inventory data are updated in transaction processing systems. In order to provide effective and efficient update performance, transaction systems store data in many small tables, each with a minimum number of fields. Thus, a product purchase transaction might need to have data elements recorded in five or more different tables. For example, records may be added or updated in an invoice table, an invoice line table, a discount table, a store table, and a department table.

Although this structural approach of creating many small tables is effective in a transaction database, it is not appropriate for DSS data. Queries will tend to be slow, and, in many cases, tables will need to be joined to complete a query. For example, to create an invoice from an operating database to mail to a customer, all of the tables may need to be joined. In a large database of transactions, joining tables is time-consuming and uses extensive computing system resources. Operating data are usually stored in many tables and the stored data relates to a specific transaction. DSS data are generally stored in many fewer tables. DSS data does not always include the details of each operating transaction but does include transaction summaries. In general, DSS data are integrated from multiple operating databases, and are sometimes aggregated and summarized in the database to support predefined decision support needs. Also, DSS data may have data redundancies in the data structures if that will speed up queries.

The different data components of data warehouses often include: metadata, current detail data, older detail data, lightly summarized data, and highly summarized data. Extensive normalization is not appropriate for DSS data, and some normalization will actually reduce the processing efficiency of a data-driven DSS. Normalization is not needed because the data will not be changed once it is in the database, and hence, anomalies or errors from updating will not occur.

Time Span

Operating data shows the current status of business transactions. DSS data are a snapshot of the operating data at given points in time. Therefore, DSS data are an historic time series of operating data. In a DSS data store, operating data are stored in multiple "time slices." Inmon (1993) says the DSS data is "time-variant." This characteristic is analogous to putting a time stamp on DSS data when it is loaded in the database or data store.

Summarization

DSS data can be summarized in the DSS data store, and disaggregated data can be summarized by analytical processing software. Data can be brought from a DSS database into a multidimensional data cube to speed up analysis. Some DSS databases consist exclusively of summarized—or what is often called derived—data. For example, rather than storing each of 10,000 sales

transactions for a given retail store on a given day, a DSS database may contain
the total number of units sold and the total sales dollars generated during that
day. DSS data might be collected to monitor total dollar sales for each store or
unit sales for each type of product. The purpose of the summaries is to establish
and evaluate sales trends or product sales comparisons that will serve decision
needs. Managers may want to ask questions like: What are sales trends for
Product X? Should Product X be discontinued? Has advertising been effective
as measured by sales changes? All of these questions can be answered using
summarized data. Operating data is not summarized within in a transaction
database.

Data Volatility

Only two kinds of operations occur in a data warehouse or DSS database:
loading of data and accessing data. Data can be added in batches but there is no
on-line updating and changing of data. So the DSS data is non-volatile. Once it
is loaded it does not change. Operating data, on the other hand, is volatile.
Operating data changes when a new transaction occurs.   The database
management system for a transaction system records new transactions and
changes in transactions.

Data Dimensions

Having multiple dimensions is probably the most distinguishing
characteristic of DSS data. From a manager's and a DSS analyst's point of
view, DSS data are always related in many different ways. For example, when
managers analyze product sales to a specific customer during a given span of
time, they are likely to ask multidimensional questions. A manager may ask,
"How many products of type X were sold to customer Y during the most recent
six months?" DSS data can be examined from multiple dimensions, for example,
product, region, and year. The ability to analyze, extract, and present data in
meaningful ways is one of the major differences between a data-driven DSS and
a transaction processing system. In contrast to DSS data, operating data has only
one dimension.

Metadata

In a data-driven DSS it is important to develop and maintain metadata about
the DSS data. Metadata is defined as "data about the data" in a DSS database.
Data dictionaries are often created for transaction systems, but because DSS data
may come from many sources, creating a new dictionary and metadata is
especially important for a data-driven DSS. Also, the database designer must
integrate DSS data that comes from different sources. The data dictionary
provides a reference about how data has been combined from various data
sources.

Metadata provides a directory to help the Database Management System for
the data-driven DSS locate the contents of a data warehouse or data store.

Metadata is a guide to mapping data as it is transformed from the operating environment to the data warehouse environment, and it serves as a guide to the algorithms used for summarization of current detailed data. Metadata is semantic information associated with a given data element. Semantic information explains the meaning of what is recorded and stored in a DSS data store.

Metadata must include business definitions of the data and accurate, understandable descriptions of data types, potential values, the original source system, data formats, and other characteristics. Metadata also includes the names of variables, length of fields, valid values, and descriptions of data elements. Metadata protects a data warehouse or database from changes in the schema or design of source systems.

Data-driven DSS must have high quality data; inaccurate data can result in incorrect or poor decisions. High quality data is accurate, timely, meaningful, and complete. Assessing or measuring the quality of data sources is a preliminary task associated with evaluating the feasibility of a data-driven DSS project.

The above comparison of DSS data and operating data suggests some architectural issues related to building a data-driven DSS. The next section addresses some data-driven DSS software architecture issues more systematically.

AN INTERCONNECTED DATA-DRIVEN DSS ARCHITECTURE

DSS designers should begin building a new data-driven DSS by researching other data-driven DSS to identify a data model and an appropriate DSS architecture. The overall goal should be to understand a typical data-driven DSS's components and interfaces, how it fits into the typical organization, and what the typical reasons are for success or failure. In some cases vendors have developed data models and designs for specific industries and applications that can serve as a guide. After understanding data-driven DSS architectures in general, developers should map a template onto their company's specific situation. Developers need to determine the subjects that will be included and the questions that may be asked by decision makers.

A useful starting point is to examine the components in a data-driven DSS software architecture. At a minimum, DSS designers need to provide data structures for a data store, guidelines for a data extraction and filtering management tool, interfaces for a query tool, and some predefined charts and tables for use with a data analysis and presentation tool. The following paragraphs examine these four interconnected software architecture components.

The data store component consists of one or more databases, built using a relational database management system, a multidimensional database management system, or both types of systems. As noted, business data is extracted from operating databases and from external data sources. The external data sources provide data that cannot be found in company transaction systems but that are relevant to the business, such as stock prices and market indicators. The data store is a compilation of many "snapshots" of a company's financial, operating, and business situation. When developers create DSS data for the data store, they summarize and arrange the operating data in structures that are optimized for analysis and rapid retrieval of data. The "aging process" developed for a data store moves current detail data to older detail data based on when the data was loaded. This archiving occurs each time a batch update is performed. In most situations only summarized data is indexed in the data store.

The data extraction and filtering component is used to extract and validate the data taken from the operational databases and the external data sources. For example, to determine the relative market share by selected product line, the DSS requires data about competitors' products. Such data may be located in external databases provided by industry groups or by companies that market such data. As the name implies, this component extracts the data from various sources, filters the extracted data to select the relevant records, and formats the data so it can be added to the DSS data store component.

A decision support analyst or a manager can create the queries that access the DSS database using a report and query tool. Developers usually customize the query tool interface for managers so it is easier to use. The query tool actually accesses the data store and retrieves requested data.

Finally, an end user analysis and presentation tool helps a manager perform calculations and select the most appropriate presentation format. For example, managers may want to display data using a pivot table summary report, a map, or a bar chart. The query tool and the presentation tool are often the "front end" of a data-driven DSS. Client/server and Web technologies enable these end-user components to interact with the other components to form a complete data-driven DSS software architecture.

Once the software architecture is developed for a specific DSS, designed for a specific company and a specific purpose, a DSS development team still faces many challenges associated with implementing a new data-driven DSS.

IMPLEMENTING A DATA-DRIVEN DSS

Organization-wide Information System (IS) development projects like data-driven DSS are subject to numerous constraints. Some of these constraints are based on available funding. A large data warehouse can cost USD $2 to 3 million for software, hardware, staff development time, and training costs and can take two to three years to build. Other constraints are a function of management's view of the role played by an IS department and of management information and DSS requirements. Also, constraints may be imposed by corporate culture conflicts. It is important to identify issues that must be confronted when implementing a data warehouse, OLAP system or other data-driven DSS.

It is very important to remember that a DSS data store is not a static database. Instead, it will be supplemented regularly with new data. Because the data store is a foundation of a modern data-driven DSS, the design and implementation of a sophisticated data store provides an infrastructure for company-wide decision support. The decision support infrastructure also includes hardware, software, people, and procedures. A data store is a critical component, but it is not the only important component. The structure of the data store and its implementation must be examined in the context of the entire DSS infrastructure.

The technical aspects of creating a new database must be addressed. A new data-driven DSS must provide required analysis capabilities with acceptable query performance, and the DSS must support the data analysis needs of decision makers.

Traditional database design procedures must be adapted to fit the requirements of building a large DSS data store. Data is derived from transaction databases, so a DSS analyst must understand the transaction database designs. It is difficult to produce good DSS data when transaction databases are of poor quality or are inaccurate. So how should a data warehouse or data-driven DSS be developed?

A General Data-Driven DSS Development Process

Various consultants have customized their data-driven DSS development processes. Chapter 4 discussed the two general approaches called Systems Development Life Cycle and Rapid Prototyping. For small projects like a data mart, one can use Rapid Prototyping. For large projects, the following steps, based on a typical data warehouse development process (see Rob and Coronell, 1997), are appropriate. This decision-oriented design and development process includes five steps (see Figure 8.3).

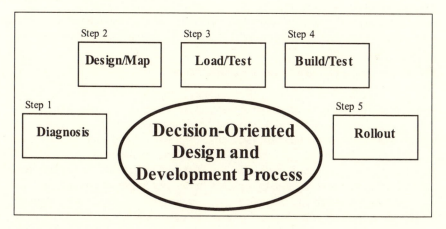

Figure 8.3 Decision-Oriented Process for a Data-Driven DSS

The first step is *Initial Data Gathering or Diagnosis*. This step involves identifying and interviewing key future DSS users, defining the main subjects of the DSS, identifying the transaction data model, defining ownership of data, assessing frequency of use and updates, defining end user interface requirements and defining any outputs and representations. The emphasis on decision makers and decisions should be maintained in subsequent steps.

The second step is *Designing and Mapping the Data Store*. In a relational DBMS environment, the first step is to design the Star Schema and identify facts, dimensions, and attributes. Then, one creates Star Schema diagrams, attribute hierarchies and aggregation levels. These conceptual models then need to be mapped to relational tables. In a multidimensional database environment, the key variables and dimensions need to be defined. The data store houses the relevant DSS data.

The third step is *Loading and Testing Data*. Creating the DSS database involves preparing to load data, defining initial data to load, and defining update processes. Then analysts define transformations of the transaction and any external data, map from the operational transaction data, integrate and transform the data. Next, analysts load, index and validate the data, and finally verify metadata and data cubes or Star Schemas.

The fourth step is *Building and Testing the Data-driven DSS*. Analysts need to create menus, develop output formats, build anticipated queries, test interfaces and results, optimize for speed and accuracy, engage in end user prototyping and testing, and provide end user training in a development environment. Decision makers need to be heavily involved in building and testing the new data-driven DSS.

The final step is *Rollout and Feedback*. This step involves actually deploying the DSS, providing additional training, getting user feedback, maintaining the system, and in many cases expanding and improving the DSS. One expects that the new DSS improves decision making and benefits the company and decision makers.

The above five-step development process needs to be altered in some important ways when one is building an Executive Information System.

Developing an Executive Information System

Information needs of executives change rapidly, so many Executive Information Systems are developed using rapid prototyping tools. Usually, a staff group creates screens and information displays for use in the EIS. The group needs to experiment with how data is presented and receive feedback from users. Determining executive information requirements can be an especially challenging task. Some of the systematic methods like structured interviews may need to be used to supplement reviews of prototype screens.

Although data-driven DSS using query and reporting tools are sometimes developed by end-users as desktop systems, EIS are traditionally more elaborate networked systems developed by IS professionals in cooperation with financial and staff professionals. Determining the critical success factors for an organization can help analysts determine what information should be presented in the EIS. Critical success factors are variables like earnings per share, market share, productivity, or units delivered that influence performance and success for a firm (cf., Rockart, 1979).

If a company wants to update its EIS or create a new capability, a small project team should be organized. According to Kelly (1997), a project leader should organize and direct the project. An executive sponsor or project champion is needed to promote the project in the organization and review project progress regularly. A technical leader participates in gathering requirements, reviewing plans, and ensuring technical feasibility of all proposals during EIS requirements definition. As the focus of the project becomes more technical, the EIS project team should be expanded to include additional technical staff who will be directly involved in extracting data from legacy systems and constructing the EIS data repository and user interface. An EIS project is similar to data warehouse projects with additional emphasis placed on the design of the user interface.

A well-known example of an EIS is the Lockheed-Georgia Management Information and Decision Support (MIDS) system (cf., Watson, Rainer and Houdeshel, 1992). MIDS was upgraded to a commercial system from Comshare in the early 1990s. A more recent example is an EIS was deployed at Pizzeria Uno (www.pizzeriauno.com). In an attempt to boost its competitiveness and profitability, Pizzeria Uno's management requested an EIS that would give executives and field management access to timely information on sales and labor costs. The company installed OLAP server software to support the EIS. Marketing, operations, and finance executives at Pizzeria Uno headquarters access the server's database from their PCs. Regional managers dial into the server each day to download up-to-date data onto their laptop computers. Executives can drill through data hierarchies, manipulate data, view data from different dimensions, such as deep-dish pizza take-home sales versus retail sales, and create reports tailored to their specific informational needs (based on a case at the Pilot Software Web site).

FINDING SUCCESS

Data or document-driven DSS development is usually a company-wide effort and requires many resources, including people and technologies. Building an effective enterprise-wide DSS is usually much harder than implementing a communications-driven DSS or developing a model-driven DSS using rapid prototyping. First, providing company-wide decision support requires a sophisticated information technology architecture. Creating such an architecture requires a mix of people skills, technologies, and managerial procedures that is often difficult to find and implement. For example, storing a large quantity of decision support data is likely to require purchasing the latest hardware and software. Most companies need to purchase high-end servers with multiple processors, advanced database systems, and very large capacity storage units. Some companies need to expand and improve their network infrastructures.

For a data-driven DSS, MIS staff need to develop detailed procedures to manage the flow of data from transaction databases to the data store. Data flow control includes data extraction, validation, and integration. A successful implementation of an enterprise-wide DSS architecture requires the support of people with advanced database design and data management skills.

How can managers increase the chances of completing a successful data- or document-driven DSS project? A number of authors have suggested some lessons they have learned from implementing their data warehouse, document warehouse and DSS projects. After evaluating the suggestions, the following recommendations seem especially useful for completing a successful data- or document-driven DSS project.

The first recommendation that makes sense is to *identify an influential project sponsor or champion*. The project champion must be a senior manager. For a high-cost, highly visible data or document-driven DSS project, the champion can deal with political issues and help insure that all involved realize they are part of a DSS team. All managers need to stay focused on a company's decision support development goals.

Second, managers should *be prepared for technology shortfalls*. Technology problems are inevitable with enterprise-wide DSS projects. Many times, the technology to accomplish some of the desired DSS tasks is not currently available or is not easily implemented. Unforeseen problems and frustrations will occur. Building any type of DSS requires patience and perseverance.

A third recommendation is to *tell everyone as much as possible about the costs* of creating and using the proposed data or document-driven DSS. Managers need to know how much it costs to develop, access, and analyze DSS data and documents. Remember: These systems can be very expensive.

Next, be sure to *invest in training*. Set aside adequate resources, both time and money, so users can learn to access and manipulate the data or documents in the new DSS. From the start, with a data-driven DSS, get users in the habit of "testing" complex questions or queries. With document-driven DSS, users need to learn how to conduct advanced searches.

Finally, *market and promote* the new data or document-driven DSS to the managers who are the intended users of the system. Both types of systems are somewhat novel and manager "buy-in" is important. A data or document-driven DSS is not usually tightly integrated with a single business process so market a new system widely to all who might benefit from access to its capabilities.

CONCLUSIONS AND COMMENTARY

Many different terms are used for the systems labeled in this chapter as data-driven and document-driven DSS, and that is OK. What is important is understanding the concepts associated with helping people access, analyze, and understand large amounts of complex data or documents. Some vendors advertise business intelligence (BI) software, data warehouse systems, multidimensional analysis software, OLAP or EIS. Some people would say that rather than document-driven DSS, the term should be "knowledge management" or "document management" or "knowledge management" systems.

What is fundamental is recognizing that different technologies are needed for systems built using structured data versus documents. Data-driven DSS have evolved from simple verification of facts to analysis of the data and now to sophisticated analysis of very large historical data sets. Data-driven DSS software products are also evolving to better support this wide range of activities. Managers can verify facts using intuitive, easy-to-use query and reporting tools. Decision makers can conduct analyses using OLAP and statistical tools. Also, managers and DSS analysts can discover new relationships in specific data sets, using knowledge discovery and data-mining tools.

Data and document-driven DSS are evolving in terms of technology and architecture. In recent years, systems have been delivering these decision support capabilities using Web technologies to managers located almost anywhere in the world. The Web is an exciting frontier that is broadening the use of data and documents in decision making. Web-based DSS will be discussed further in Chapter 11.

Data and document-driven DSS are important systems for providing managers with the information they want, when they want it, and in a format that is "decision impelling." Despite these benefits, many companies have difficulties developing, implementing, and maintaining enterprise-wide DSS at an acceptable cost. For large-scope decision support projects, cost control largely depends on the management and political skills of the project manager, the restraint of targeted user managers, and the technical skills of the MIS staff on the project team. Once the diagnosis and needs analysis tasks are completed for a project, future DSS users need to restrain their desire for more information and resist changing the requirements for the data- or document-driven DSS.

When building data-driven DSS, relevant data are organized and summarized in multiple dimensions for fast retrieval and ad hoc analysis. With a document-driven DSS, documents and unstructured data are organized and summarized for fast retrieval and ad hoc analysis. The primary goal of these systems is to help managers transform data and documents into information and knowledge. Both management control and strategic planning activities can be supported by such systems.

Chapter 9

Building Knowledge-Driven DSS and Mining Data

INTRODUCTION

Some people claim "controlling knowledge leads to power." Even if that claim is true, companies only "win" when relevant knowledge is shared among employees and other stakeholders. Today, sharing knowledge when making decisions is more important than most people recognize. One way to share knowledge is to build document-driven DSS. Another way is to build computerized systems that can store and retrieve knowledge codified as probabilities, rules, and relationships. Specialized software can process this knowledge and assist managers in making decisions. Specialized decision support and artificial intelligence (AI) tools can also help create knowledge. An umbrella term that describes these systems is knowledge-driven Decision Support Systems (DSS). These DSS provide suggestions to managers, and the dominant component is a "knowledge" capture and storage mechanism. Knowledge and suggestions are the two major themes that link these different knowledge tasks.

Knowledge-driven DSS, suggestion DSS, rule-based DSS and intelligent DSS are overlapping terms for DSS built using artificial intelligence technologies. Expert system development shells and data mining tools are often used to create these systems. Also, business and decision support analysts conduct special decision studies to identify relationships in very large databases using data mining or knowledge discovery tools. When a manager or knowledge worker uses a DSS with a data mining tool, the results from an analysis may suggest relationships and new knowledge.

This chapter is an introduction to and overview of knowledge-driven DSS technologies and applications. The first part of the chapter emphasizes expert system technologies and the second part emphasizes data mining techniques and tools. The overall thrust is to provide a foundation for building knowledge-driven DSS with specialized artificial intelligence tools. These technologies have been "hyped" by some vendors as solutions to a wide variety of problems, but artificial intelligence technologies are still "leading-edge" capabilities for most businesses. At some point in the future, all managers and knowledge workers may be using knowledge-driven DSS and mining data, but that future is still over the horizon, waiting to be implemented.

So, the focus in this chapter is on examining how software can be used to store, process, find, and derive knowledge to support business decision making. The following sections emphasize terms, characteristics of knowledge-driven DSS, project management and examples of knowledge-driven DSS, an introduction to data mining, examples of data mining, and development tools evaluation.

KEY TERMS AND CONCEPTS

Holsapple and Whinston (1996) discuss artificially intelligent DSS that "make use of computer-based mechanisms from the field of artificial intelligence." These DSS provide suggestions for business decision makers. When the dominant component of a DSS uses artificial intelligence (AI) technologies, including expert system technologies and some data mining tools, to assist business decision makers, one can call the system a knowledge-driven DSS. Artificial intelligence is a branch of computer science that studies how computer software can imitate the cognitive activities of people. Every application of AI technologies should not be called a decision support system. This section discusses key terms associated with knowledge-driven DSS.

Knowledge-Driven DSS and Management Expert Systems

Knowledge-driven DSS store and apply knowledge for a variety of specific business problems. These problems include classification and configuration tasks, such as loan credit scoring, fraud detection, and investment optimization.

Until recently, human experts had to perform classification and configuration tasks without computer support. Most of us identify a human expert as someone who is very knowledgeable in a particular area or subject. This human expert knows the appropriate questions to ask in order to draw a particular conclusion. In a similar way, one major type of expert system is a computer program that asks questions and reasons with the knowledge stored for the program about a narrow, specialized subject. This type of program attempts to solve a problem or give advice using heuristics.

In general, expert systems are programs with specialized problem-solving expertise. The expertise consists of three components: 1) knowledge of symptoms and indicators related to a particular topic or domain; 2) understanding of the relations among symptoms and of problems and solutions within that domain; and 3) "skill" or methods for solving some of the problems (cf., Power, 1985). An expert system is a knowledge-intensive program that captures the expertise of a human in a limited domain of knowledge and experience. It assists decision makers by asking relevant questions in a problem domain and by recommending actions and explaining reasons for adopting an action.

An expert system can explain the reasoning behind a conclusion it has reached. This explanation capability is extremely important in auditing and validating the results from a knowledge-driven DSS. It also helps ensure that the system is in compliance with applicable policies, regulations, or legal requirements.

Using knowledge-driven DSS and management expert systems results in a number of benefits. Such systems can improve consistency in decision making, enforce policies, and regulations, distribute expertise to nonexpert staff, and retain valuable expertise for a company when experts retire or resign.

Data Mining and Knowledge Discovery

Data mining and knowledge discovery are "hot" topics in the Information Systems and Marketing trade press. For many years companies have been storing large amounts of data, and more recently, companies have built large data warehouses. Now managers want to take advantage of the data they have collected by analyzing it, using statistical and artificial intelligence tools (cf., Berry & Linoff, 1997). Data mining techniques can help managers discover hidden relationships and patterns in data. Some analysts feel data mining can help a company gain a competitive advantage. Data mining tools can be used for both hypothesis testing and knowledge discovery. When vendors discuss data mining, they may be selling a set of end-user tools or a decision support capability or both. Managers and business analysts can perform data mining activities. Target users of these tools include financial analysts, statisticians, and marketing researchers. People who use these tools should have experience interpreting data.

Other Important Terms

Artificial Intelligence researchers have a specialized vocabulary that has accumulated in the past 30 years. The following are some major terms that are relevant to developing knowledge-driven DSS. A *development environment* is used by a knowledge-driven DSS designer and builder. A development environment typically includes software for creating and maintaining a knowledge base and software called an inference engine. An *inference engine* reasons with a set of rules created by a developer.

A *domain expert* is a key person in a knowledge-driven DSS development project. A domain expert is the person who has expertise in the domain in which a specific system is being developed. A domain expert works closely with a *knowledge engineer* to capture the expert's knowledge in a knowledge base. This process is used especially for capturing rule and relationship information in a computer readable format.

Knowledge refers to what one knows and understands. It is sometimes categorized as unstructured, structured, explicit, or implicit. Knowledge-driven DSS are built using explicit, structured knowledge. *Knowledge acquisition* is the extraction and formulation of knowledge derived from various sources, especially from experts. A *knowledge base* is a collection of organized facts, rules, and procedures. A knowledge base has a description of the elements in the process along with their characteristics, functions, and relationships. It also contains rules about the actions to implement as a result of certain events. A knowledge base can also obtain its information from external programs and databases. When dealing with a particular task or problem, a knowledge-driven DSS constructs a number of hypotheses based on the external information supplied, its own knowledge, and the rules in its knowledge base.

If managers and MIS professionals want to build knowledge-driven DSS, they must have some familiarity with major AI terms. The key to success is learning some of the basic jargon and staying focused on the broader objective of building DSS that use software with "artificial reasoning" capabilities.

CHARACTERISTICS OF KNOWLEDGE-DRIVEN DSS

There are a number of characteristics that are common to knowledge-driven DSS. First, this category of software assists—it doesn't replace—managers in specific problem-solving tasks. Second, the systems use knowledge stored as rules, relationships or probabilities. Third, people interact with a knowledge-driven DSS when they are performing a specific decision task. Fourth, knowledge-driven DSS base recommendations on human expertise and derived knowledge and assist in performing very limited tasks. Fifth, a knowledge-driven DSS processes stored task relevant information and does *not* "think".

A knowledge-driven DSS differs from a more conventional model-driven DSS in the way knowledge is presented and processed. This difference exists because expert systems attempt to simulate human reasoning processes. A model-driven DSS has a sequence of predefined instructions for responding to an event. In contrast, a knowledge-driven DSS, based on expert system technologies, attempts to reason about a response to an event using its knowledge base and logical rules for problem solving. Expert system technologies use representations of human knowledge. These representations are expressed in a special purpose language such as OPS5, PROLOG or LISP. Expert systems can also perform standard numerical calculations or data retrieval. An expert system development environment uses heuristic methods to obtain a recommendation. A heuristic is an approximate method that identifies varying amounts of uncertainty in conclusions. A conventional model-driven DSS uses mathematical and statistical methods to obtain a more precise solution.

Figure 9.1 shows the components of a knowledge-driven DSS. The model component is called an inference engine and it is the software that actually performs the reasoning function. The inference engine is the software that uses the knowledge represented in the data or knowledge base to draw its conclusions. The design of the inference engine may limit the ways in which knowledge can be represented in the knowledge base so that certain shells are only suitable for particular types of applications. In small systems, this is sometimes called the shell of the expert system, though the shell can be considered to be everything except the knowledge base itself.

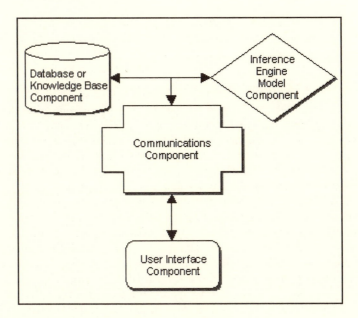

Figure 9.1 Components of a Knowledge-Driven DSS

In comparing and identifying knowledge-driven and model-driven DSS, one should remember that knowledge-driven DSS have a knowledge base and an inference engine, and model-driven DSS have a structured database and quantitative models. If one compares Figure 9.1 to Figure 6.1, it is clear that the components in knowledge-driven DSS are similar to the general DSS architecture.

MANAGING KNOWLEDGE-DRIVEN DSS PROJECTS

Knowledge-driven DSS should be initiated with a decision-oriented diagnosis and if the feasibility analysis is positive, then a small project team should complete a rapid prototyping development process. Many knowledge-driven DSS are built using rules and an expert system shell development environment. A knowledge engineer works with a domain expert to elicit rules and relationships. The testing and validation of the system may involve using prior examples and cases from the domain.

Several general rapid prototyping approaches for developing expert systems and knowledge-driven DSS have been proposed. Waterman (1986) proposed the following widely accepted approach:

1. Identification of a domain;
2. Conceptualization;
3. Formalization;
4. Implementation; and
5. Testing.

These five stages are highly interrelated and interdependent. An iterative process continues until the knowledge-driven DSS consistently performs at an acceptable level.

Choosing a Knowledge-Driven DSS Project

If a business decision problem cannot readily be solved and supported using traditional methods, it may be appropriate to try an expert system solution. How does one choose an appropriate knowledge-driven DSS project? In general, the "telephone test" can be used to help determine if a task can be supported with a knowledge-driven DSS built using expert systems technologies. What is the "telephone test?" To apply the test, one asks "Can a domain expert solve the problem and support decision making using a telephone exchange with a decision maker?" Sometimes, it is even helpful to ask the domain expert to interact with a potential user of a proposed DSS over the telephone and record the interaction that occurs. The domain expert should be told to ask structured rather than open-ended questions. If the answer is "Yes," the telephone exchange works; then a knowledge-driven DSS, based on expert systems technologies, can be developed to support the decision maker. On the other hand, if the decision maker is unable to describe the problem verbally, or if the expert is consistently unable to recommend a reasonable solution, then development of a knowledge-driven DSS will likely be unsatisfactory. The telephone test ensures that the expert is not gaining additional information about a problem from other senses and that the user is able to adequately describe the problem in words.

Using Rules for Knowledge-Driven DSS

Managers and developers should be familiar with the concept of a rule. A rule-based expert system has a large number of interconnected and nested IF-THEN statements or "rules" that are the basis for storing the knowledge in the system. Many expert system development environments store knowledge as rules.

The following is an example of a rule:

IF INCOME > $45,000 (condition)
AND IF SEX = "M" (condition)
THEN ADD to Target list (action)

A rule is a formal way of specifying a recommendation, directive, or strategy, expressed in an " 'if premise, 'then' conclusion" structure. Rules are one way of expressing declarative knowledge. For example, *if* a car won't start, *and* the lights are dim, *then* the car may have a dead battery. Thus, rules are relationships rather than instructions. Note this structure is different than the "if-then" structure used by procedural programming languages.

There are two ways an inference engine can manipulate rules. The first is forward chaining, where an inference engine starts from known facts and looks at the left-hand "if" side of the rules to find any matches and proceeds to find further rules that apply to the user's responses. The second method is known as backward chaining. This technique involves starting the inference engine with a hypothesized solution by looking at the right-hand "then" statements, then working backwards to find the starting conditions that are necessary to arrive at that solution and see how they match with the user's responses.

Let's examine the two approaches from a different perspective. Suppose someone wants to fly from Waterloo, Iowa, to Beijing, China. To find a "chain" of connecting flights one can search in one of two ways:

1.   Start with flights that arrive in Beijing and work backwards to eventually find a chain to Waterloo. This is a goal-driven, backward-chaining search.
2.   Or, start by listing all flights leaving Waterloo and mark intermediary cities. Look for flights out of intermediaries until all paths to Beijing are found. This approach is working with forward-chaining toward a goal. This is a data-driven, forward-chaining search.

Advantages and Limitations of Rules

Using an inference engine with rules is the most common development environment for knowledge-driven DSS. This preference for a rule technology is because rules are easy for managers and domain experts to understand. Also, using rules, it is easy to provide explanations to users of the DSS. From a developer's perspective, modification and maintenance of a knowledge base of rules is relatively easy. Also, a developer can combine information about uncertainty in conclusions with rules. Finally, a number of rule-based development environments are available for implementing systems. There are, however, a number of major limitations of using a rule-based development approach. First, and most important, complex knowledge is difficult to represent using rules. Also, when rules are used, the knowledge represented tends to be superficial. Knowledge-driven DSS builders usually like developing systems based on rules, but using rules will not work for all applications.

KNOWLEDGE-DRIVEN DSS EXAMPLES

More than 100 commercial expert systems were developed in the mid-80s in the first wave of enthusiasm about business applications of AI technologies. Many of these systems had fallen into disuse by the early 1990s. The systems generally failed because or managerial problems like lack of system acceptance or turnover of development staff. However, some systems were major successes (cf., Gill, 1995). Two classic examples of successful business expert systems are *TAXADVISOR* and XCON. More recent examples include a scheduling system for the Tomakomai paper mill, a customer support system at Compaq Computer, and an insurance plan selection system for Meiji Mutual Life Insurance Company.

TAXADVISOR was an expert system designed to assist an attorney with tax and estate planning for clients with large estates. The system collected client data and inferred actions the client needed to take to improve their financial profile, including insurance purchases, retirement actions, transfer of wealth, and modifications to gift and will provisions. TAXADVISOR used knowledge about estate planning based on attorneys' experiences and strategies as well as more generally accepted knowledge from textbooks. The system used a rule-based knowledge representation scheme controlled by backward chaining. TAXADVISOR was implemented in EMYCIN (cf., Michaelsen and Michie, 1983, Waterman, 1986). Accounting firm Coopers and Lybrand developed an early commercial expert system in this domain called ExpertTax.

XCON (eXpert CONfigurer of VAX 11/780 computer systems) was developed to configure computer systems. Based upon a customer's order, it recommended what components needed to be included to produce a complete operational system, and it determined the spatial relationships among all of the components. XCON was implemented in an expert system shell called OPS5 and developed through a collaboration between researchers at Carnegie-Mellon University and Digital Equipment Corporation (now Compaq). This commercial expert system configured VAX computers on a daily basis and was for many years the largest and most mature rule-based expert system in operation (cf., McDermmot, 1984).

Scheduling and control systems are needed in the paper production industry to ensure that all machines in the mill operate correctly. At Ohji Paper Company's Tomakomai Mill, an expert system developed by Toshiba is used to schedule the paper production machines. The Tomakomai Mill consists of ten paper-making machines, energy supply plants, and pulp supply plants. Two hundred paper products are produced per month. Each product has a specified production volume and due date, and requires a specified machine to produce it. In the Tomakomai Mill, a millwide production management system exists. The system has a planning level and a control/operation level. The scheduling system receives product orders from the headquarters office, makes a schedule, and delivers it to the other planning systems. Each system schedules and optimizes its operations based on the paper-making schedule. The paper production scheduling system consists of an expert system for automated scheduling and a data management system. The scheduling systems are implemented with an expert shell utility, ASIREX. This scheduling system has been in practical use since January 1989. The greatest advantage reported for this system is that it speeds up scheduling. The scheduling time for a monthly schedule was reduced from three days to two hours (cf., Nakayama and Mizutani, 1990; http://itri.loyola.edu/kb/toc.htm).

Toshiba also sells a small knowledge system with 110 rules called MARKETS-I. It is a decision support system to determine the suitability of opening a convenience store at a particular site.

Compaq Computer Corporation created and implemented a very successful Customer Support Intelligent System to provide computer users expert diagnosis and recommendations about problems. In 1989, the service department started by installing a call logging system. Then, an expert system was added. Most types of problems could be categorized as hardware, network, software, or general information (cf., Dhar and Stein, 1997).

The Meiji Mutual Life Insurance Company is one of the oldest life insurance companies in Japan with assets of around $74 billion. Meiji offers a wide range of insurance and pension products. In addition, the company is aggressively involved in developing and introducing new products. However, with the increasing number of products, the company was finding it difficult to ensure that all the insurance sales staff had the expertise and the latest knowledge required to provide the best advice and service to its customers. To overcome this problem, Meiji used XpertRule to develop the *Life Insurance Plan Selection Expert System*. The system can select the most suitable product, along with a reason for the choice, from Meiji's range of 37 individual-oriented products. Meiji began research into expert systems in 1986. Before using XpertRule, the company had completed a Lisp-based insurance plan selection system. This system, however, had a high delivery and maintenance cost and was not suited for distribution to all branches. Meiji adopted XpertRule because it allows for easy knowledge base construction. The knowledge base contained 47 decision tasks. The rules for selecting each plan were developed as a separate task. The system was structured so that when the details of a customer are entered, the system assesses the suitability of all the plans and reports on the best five. The system takes less than four seconds to make.

The above examples suggest the wide variety of knowledge-driven decision support applications that are possible to construct using expert systems technologies. A number of Web sites have examples of knowledge-driven DSS that provide a more concrete idea of what is possible. For example, the Department of Labor has developed an interactive compliance assistance tool called Elaws designed to help users understand their rights as employees or employers at URL http://www.dol.gov/elaws.

DATA MINING AND CREATING KNOWLEDGE

In the 1970s, companies employed business analysts who used statistical packages like SAS and SPSS to perform trend analyses and cluster analyses on data. As it became possible and affordable to store large amounts of data, managers wanted to access and analyze transaction data like that generated at a retail store cash register. Bar coding and the World Wide Web have also made it possible for companies to collect large amounts of new data.

Database marketing has also benefited from mining data. The information incorporated in the database marketing process is the historical database of previous mailings and the features associated with the (potential) customers, such as age, zip code, and their past responses. Data mining software uses this information to build a model of customer behavior that can be used to predict which customers are most likely to respond to a new catalog. By using this information, a marketing manager can target the customers likely to respond (cf., Thearling, 1998).

For many years, companies had statisticians study company data. When a statistician looks at the data, he or she makes a hypothesis about a relationship, then performs a query on a database and uses statistical techniques to prove or disprove the hypothesis. This has been called the "verification mode" (IBM, 1998). Data mining software works in a "discovery mode" and looks for patterns. A hypothesis is not stated before the data is analyzed.

There are two main kinds of models in data mining: predictive and descriptive. Predictive models can be used to forecast explicit values, based on patterns determined from known results. For example, from a database of customers who have already responded to a particular offer, a model can be built that predicts which prospects are likeliest to respond to the same offer. The predictive model is then used in a DSS. Descriptive models describe patterns in existing data, and are generally used to create meaningful subgroups such as demographic clusters. Once a descriptive model is identified it may be used for target marketing or other decision support tasks.

Data Mining Techniques and Tools

There are a wide variety of tools for data mining. The decision about which technique to use depends on the type of data and the type of questions that managers want answered by that data. Many commercial data mining software packages include more than one data mining tool. A summer 2000 Kdnuggets.com poll indicated SPSS's (spss.com) Clementine is the most-used data mining software package. It is targeted to business users and is a visual rapid modeling environment. Advanced sources of information on data mining tools include Berry and Linoff (1997) and Dhar and Stein (1997). This section examines five common categories for data mining tools: Case-Based Reasoning, Data Visualization, Fuzzy Query and Analysis, Genetic Algorithms, and Neural Networks (cf., Greenfield, 2000).

Case-Based Reasoning

Case-based tools find records in a database that are similar to specified records. A user specifies how strong a relationship should be before a new case is brought to her attention. This category of tools is also called memory-based reasoning. Software tries to measure the "distance" based on a measure of one record to other records and cluster records by similarity. This technique has been successful in analyzing relationships in free-form text. The Web site www.ai-cbr.org is a resource for the artificial intelligence and case-based reasoning technology fields.

A five-step problem-solving process is used with case-based tools:

Presentation: a description of the current problem is input to the system.
Retrieval: the system retrieves the closest-matching cases stored in a database of cases.
Adaptation: the system uses the current problem and closest-matching cases to generate a solution to the current problem.
Validation: the solution is validated through feedback from the user of the environment.
Update: if appropriate, the validated solution is added to the case base for use in future problem solving (cf., Allen, 1994).

Data Visualization

These tools graphically display complex relationships in multidimensional data from different perspectives. Visualization is the graphical presentation of information, with the goal of providing the viewer with a qualitative understanding of the information contents. Data visualization tools are data mining tools that translate complex formulas, mathematical relationships, or data warehouse information into graphs or other easily understood models. Statistical tools, like cluster analysis or classification and regression trees (CART), are often part of data visualization tools. Decision support analysts can visualize the clusters or examine a binary tree created by classifying records. In marketing, an analyst may create "co-occurrence" tables or charts of products that are purchased together. A good visualization is easy to understand and interpret, and it is a reasonably accurate representation of the underlying data.

Fuzzy Query and Analysis

Fuzzy data mining tools allow users to look at results that are "close" to specified criteria. The user can vary what the definition of "close" is to help determine the significance and number of results that will be returned. This category of data mining tools is based on a branch of mathematics called fuzzy logic. The logic of uncertainty and "fuzziness" provides a framework for finding, scoring, and ranking the results of queries. Fuzzy Tech, a company that develops Fuzzy query software, has a Web site with excellent information on this tool at http://www.fuzzytech.com/index.htm.

Genetic Algorithms

Genetic algorithms are optimization programs similar to the linear programming models discussed in Chapter 10. Genetic algorithm software conducts random experiments with new solutions while keeping the "good" interim results. A sample problem is to find the best subset of 20 variables to predict stock market behavior. To create a genetic model, the 20 variables would be identified as "genes" that have at least two possible values. The software would then select genes and their values randomly in an attempt to maximize or minimize a performance or fitness function. The performance function would provide a value for the fitness of the specific genetic model. Genetic optimization software also includes operators to combine and mutate genes. This quantitative model is used to find patterns, like other data mining techniques.

Neural Networks

Neural network tools are used to predict future information by learning patterns from past data. According to Berry and Linoff (1997), neural networks are the most common type of data mining technique. Some people even think that using a neural network is the only type of data mining. For example, with appropriate input data a neural network could be trained to predict the price or net asset value of a mutual fund in the next quarter. A neural network could also be trained to categorize applicants for admission to a college into various "success" categories.

Vendors make many claims for neural networks. One claim that is especially questionable is that neural networks can compensate for low quality data. Neural networks attempt to learn patterns from data directly by repeatedly examining the data to identify relationships and build a model. Neural networks build models by trial and error. The network guesses a value that it compares to the actual number. If the guess is wrong, the model is adjusted. This learning process involves three iterative steps: predict, compare, and adjust. Neural networks are commonly used in a knowledge-driven DSS to classify data and, as noted, to make predictions. Figure 9.2 shows that various inputs (from I_1 to I_j) are transformed by a network of simple processors. The processors combine and weight the inputs and produce one or more output values (O_1 to O_k).

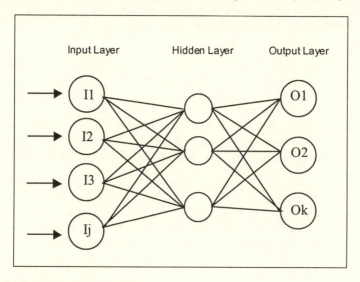

Figure 9.2 Neural Network Example

Data Mining Process

Data mining and knowledge discovery attempt to identify predictive relationships and provide managers with descriptive information about the subject of a database. There are a number of prescribed data mining processes. To make the best use of data mining, one must first make a clear statement of objectives. Researchers at IBM have described data mining as a three-phase process of data preparation, mining operations, and presentation. Analysts at the Gartner Group describes it similarly as a five-stage process:

1. Select and prepare the data to be mined.
2. Qualify the data via cluster and feature analysis.
3. Select one or more data mining tools.
4. Apply the data mining tool.
5. Apply the knowledge discovered to the company's specific line of business to achieve a business goal (Gerber, 1996).

These alternative processes can guide a special decision support study that uses data mining. In general, the first step is to select and prepare the data to be mined. Some data mining software packages include data preparation tools that can handle at least some of the preparation that needs to be done to the data. The second step is qualifying or testing the data using cluster and feature analysis software. This step takes some business knowledge about the question that one is trying to answer. This is the step where bias in the data should be detected and removed (IBM, 1998). In the third step an appropriate data mining tool is selected and used. Finally, the results are presented to decision makers, and if the results seem useful, a decision is influenced and one hopes business goals are achieved.

DATA MINING EXAMPLES

What are some examples of data mining decision support applications? Some applications include: predicting which customers are likely to buy which products and when; improving credit/loan/mortgage risk analysis; identifying new untapped market segments that might be profitable; predicting what securities to buy/sell and when; improving customer service, support, satisfaction, and loyalty; understanding what factors affect profit and productivity; and detecting fraud earlier to avoid losses.

One specific example is conducting a special decision support study to identify characteristics of users of ATM cards at points of sale. Some people never use their ATM cards at points of sale; others use their cards only a couple of times per month; and some use their cards quite frequently. Frequent users generate the most revenue for the financial institution that issues the card. At one company, genetic data mining was used to evolve prediction models for several levels of card usage, based on parameters such as customer age, average checking account balance, and average number of checks written per month. Using these models of frequent users, the financial institution was able to target people matching the frequent-user profile for promotional campaigns (cf., http://www.ultragem.com/sample.htm).

Firstar Bank used data mining to determine which customers were likely to be interested in a new service. Data mining allowed Firstar to do target mailings, saving the company time and money compared to broad mailings to all customers. As a result of the targeted mailing, the response rate to the mailings increased by a factor of four (Freeman, 1997).

Siemens uses a DSS, built with case-based reasoning, to aid technical customer support services staff. The program uses the results of previous customer inquires to help answer quickly questions from current inquires.

As the result of a data mining project done at ShopKo, managers discovered that the sale of film does not cause the sale of a camera; however, the sale of a camera generally causes the sale of film. Data mining may find relationships that managers already knew existed. One hopes new knowledge and relationships are also discovered. American Century Investments used data mining to find information to help them cross-sell financial products to existing customers (cf., http://www.spss.com).

Keys to Success

Developers at American Century shared a number of lessons they learned from this project. One lesson is that senior executive support, as well as IT support is necessary for success. Another lesson is that business issues must drive project development. If the project will not benefit the company, resources should not be allocated to it. They found that data mining often yields specific results rather than general rules. The quality of the data had a direct effect on the usefulness of the results. Finally, MIS staff at American Century found that data mining requires that analysts have statistical skills, business skills, and analytical skills in order for the company to get the most benefit from the tools.

EVALUATING DEVELOPMENT PACKAGES

The following five criteria should be carefully considered when evaluating vendor software for either mining data or building knowledge-driven DSS.

Cost. With the significant costs of technology and the rapid advancement of new technologies, companies want affordable packages. A development environment with multiple tools is often better than purchasing a more specialized development package. In general, MIS staff want to learn software that can be applied to a wide variety of problems

Scalability. Companies need development software that will easily integrate with existing software applications and hardware platforms. Many knowledge-driven DSS need to be distributed to users, so Web technologies are often appropriate. Some observers want more managers and analysts to have data mining tools, so a distributed, scalable solution is also an issue in statistical analysis and knowledge discovery.

Security. With the increase in shared data, there is increasing concern regarding the security of DSS knowledge and large databases. Both rule bases and behavioral data that will be mined need to be protected. Security is easily overlooked in developing knowledge applications.

Development features. Knowledge-driven DSS are not usually standard "off-the-shelf" packages. It is important that packages allow for easy development of customized capabilities, rule input, and maintenance. If uncertainties, frames, or other capabilities are part of the development environment, then the package needs to help ensure that features and capabilities are used appropriately.

Ease of installation and use. Managers and MIS staff want software packages that are easy to install and require minimal training. This criterion is especially important with end-user data mining tools.

CONCLUSIONS AND COMMENTARY

Knowledge-driven DSS and mining data are at the decision support frontier in organizations. During the 1980s, unrealistic expectations were created for expert systems and the recent "hype" about data mining has also created some skepticism. Managers and IS staff need to investigate how these technologies might solve real business problems, but caution should be used in selling knowledge-driven DSS and data mining projects.

Data mining techniques and tools are not fundamentally different from the older quantitative model-building techniques. The methods used in data mining are extensions and generalizations of analytical methods known for decades. Neural networks are a special case of what is called projection pursuit regression, a method developed in the 1940s. Classification and regression tree (CART) methods were used by social scientists in the 1960s (cf., http://www.twocrows.com/iwk9701.htm). The computing technology used to implement these underlying methods has, however, greatly improved.

For the foreseeable future, modest knowledge-driven DSS projects can provide some benefits and can help MIS staff develop experience using expert system and data mining tools. It is important for large companies to have projects in this category of DSS, but only modest resources should be committed in most companies. The list of possible applications in this chapter should guide the selection of new projects.

Some observers would include document-driven DSS as knowledge management tools. This may be the case, but more importantly, both types of systems can support decision makers.

Chapter 10

Building Model-Driven Decision Support Systems

INTRODUCTION

Many companies use models to assist in decision making. For example, Dresdner Bank uses a model-driven DSS when making credit and lending decisions. USA Truck uses OptiStop to generate optimal routes and fueling stop recommendations. Also, at USA Truck, managers use a DSS called Strategic Profitability Analysis to allocate equipment and establish pricing for customers. Jones Lang LaSalle uses a Web-based system for planning, budgeting, reporting, and analysis. Several Deere and Co. factories are using an optimization add-in to Microsoft Excel for balancing manufacturing constraints while achieving more production output. A number of railroad companies use DSS for train dispatching. This list of model-driven DSS could go on for many pages.

Many DSS use models. For example, a sales-forecasting DSS uses a moving average or econometric model; accounting and financial DSS generate estimates of income statements, balance sheets, or other outcome measures; representational DSS use simulation models; and optimization DSS generate optimal solutions, consistent with constraints and assist in scheduling and resource allocation. Model-driven DSS may assist in forecasting product demand, aid in employee scheduling, develop pro forma financial statements, or assist in choosing plant or warehouse locations. All of these systems are model-driven DSS.

Model-driven DSS provide managers with models and analysis capabilities that can be used during the process of making a decision. The range and scope of this category of DSS is very large. New commercial products are regularly announced, new Web-based applications are being developed for established tools, and companies are developing their own proprietary systems. To exploit these opportunities, DSS analysts and managers need to understand analytical tools and modeling. Building some types of models requires considerable expertise. Many specialized books discuss and explain how to implement specific types of models like simulation or linear programming. Companies use both custom and off-the-shelf model-driven DSS applications.

This chapter is only a starting point for those who want to build or buy model-driven DSS. It provides a brief overview of issues specifically relevant to building model-driven DSS. It summarizes commonly used models with a primary focus on terminology. The major objective is to help managers and DSS analysts evaluate model-driven DSS opportunities and work with model builders.

MODELING DECISION SITUATIONS

Mathematical and analytical models are the dominant component in a model-driven Decision Support System. If a model is needed to understand a situation, then a model-driven DSS can potentially deliver the needed representation to managers. DSS Analysts can create a wide variety of alternative model-driven DSS. So actually building a model-driven DSS involves resolving a number of important design and development questions.

Models can help managers understand financial, marketing, and many other business decisions. One major issue that must be resolved is the purpose of a proposed model-driven DSS. Is the purpose to assist in credit and lending decisions, budgeting, or product demand forecasting? Will the system be used routinely in a decision process or as part of a special study? Each model-driven DSS should have a clearly stated and specific purpose. To accomplish the specific purpose of a system, more than one type of model is sometimes used in building the model-driven DSS. So, a second issue is what models should be included in a specific system.

The tasks involved in building model-driven DSS are complex enough that a modeling specialist is usually needed on a development team for a large-scale system. End users should only develop model-driven DSS for one-time and special purpose decision support needs. Therefore, managers must confront the issue of who should build a planned or contemplated model-driven DSS.

In many specific DSS, a model produces outputs displayed for users. Also, the decision variables of model-driven DSS are frequently manipulated directly by managers. As mentioned in Chapter 4, DSS builders must determine the future users of the model.

Model-driven DSS have been built using statistical software packages, forecasting software, modeling packages, and end-user tools like spreadsheets. In all of these development environments, the goal is the same: to build a model that can be manipulated and tested. The values of key variables or parameters are changed to reflect uncertainty in supply, production, the economy, sales, costs, or other environmental and internal business factors. This capability of changing a parameter in a model-driven DSS is called "What if?" analysis and expanded testing of model parameters is called sensitivity analysis. The results from using a model-driven DSS in a situation are analyzed and evaluated by decision makers.

Modeling

A typical modeling process begins with identification of a problem and analysis of the requirements of the situation. It is advisable to analyze the scope of the problem domain and the forces and dynamics of the environment. The next step is to identify the variables for the model. The identification of decision variables and their relationships is very important. One should always ask if using a model is appropriate. If a model is appropriate, then one asks what variables and relationships need to be specified, using an appropriate modeling tool. An influence diagram can be used to examine the variables and relationships. Then a solution method or methods need to be chosen. Also, an analyst need to specify assumptions and make any needed forecasts. Forecasting variables or parameters is sometimes part of the construction of a model. Building a computerized system also involves integrating models and other DSS components like data files and data analysis procedures. Model-driven DSS need to be validated, evaluated, and managed. Model validation is the process of comparing a model's output with the actual behavior of the phenomenon that has been modeled. Validation attempts to answer the question, "Have we built the right model of the situation?"

Model Assumptions

Assumptions are untested beliefs or predictions. Assumptions are important in building many models because one is projecting or anticipating results. A decision maker can test assumptions using "what if" or sensitivity analysis before accepting the results of the model. DSS analysts and managers need to make assumptions about the time and risk dimensions for a situation. Model-driven DSS can be designed assuming either a static or dynamic analysis. Making either assumption about changes in a decision situation has advantages and disadvantages.

Static analysis is based on a "single snapshot" of a situation. Everything occurs in a single interval, which can be a short or long duration. A decision about whether a company should make or buy a product can be considered static in nature. A quarterly or annual income statement is static. During a static analysis, it is assumed that there is stability in the decision situation.

Dynamic analysis is used for situations that change over time. A simple example would be a five-year profit projection, where the input data, such as costs, prices, and quantities change from year to year. Dynamic models are also time dependent. For example, in determining how many cash registers should be open in a supermarket, it is necessary to consider the time of day. This time dependence occurs because in most supermarkets there are changes in the number of people that arrive at the market at different hours of the day.

Dynamic models are important because they show trends and patterns over time. Also, they can be used to calculate averages per period or moving averages, and to prepare comparative analyses. A comparative analysis might examine profit this quarter versus profit in the same quarter of last year. Dynamic analysis can provide an understanding of the changes occurring within a business enterprise. The analyses may identify possible solutions to specific business challenges and may facilitate the development of business plans, strategies, and tactics. DSS analysts and managers also must examine whether it is appropriate to assume certainty about model parameters in the decision situation. Many financial models are constructed under assumed certainty. "What if" analysis is the primary means of considering risk and uncertainty. As previously noted, "what if" analysis is the capability of "asking" or manipulating a model-driven DSS to determine what the effect will be on result variables of changing some of the decision variables.

The assumptions of DSS analysts and managers limit or constrain the types of models that can be used to build a DSS for the situation. Most of the rest of this chapter discusses various types of models.

General Types of Models

Models transform user inputs and data into useful information. A model represents a real situation as an abstract framework. A model may be specified in mathematical expressions, in natural language statements or as a computer program. Managers can manipulate the input to a model to change outputs. Models update files, provide responses to user actions, and perform recurring analytical tasks. Tool labels like optimization and simulation are often used to describe categories or types of models and those terms will be used in this chapter, but let's begin with some more general concepts.

An explanatory model describes what has occurred to create current results or outcomes, and it provides an explanation or analysis of a situation. For example, the model *Sales* = f (*Advertising, Number of Salespersons*) may be based on a correlation of advertising and the number of salespersons with sales in prior quarters

An algebraic model indicates which values must be introduced into a system of simultaneous equations to create a specific outcome. A manager specifies an outcome and a starting point, and then runs the model. This type of model helps managers gain insight about what variables must be manipulated and to what extent.

Explanatory models are descriptive models that describe situations. Algebraic models are predictive models (cf., Starfield, Smith, and Blelock, 1990; Codd, Codd, and Salley, 1993).

A DSS with Multiple Model Types

As noted, a model-driven DSS may include more than one of the above types of models. For example, a specific model-driven DSS may include:

1. An explanatory regression model that identifies relationships among variables,
2. A financial model of a pro forma income statement, and
3. An algebraic optimization model like linear programming.

Some models are standard components in DSS development packages, and some must be custom-programmed. A DSS analyst chooses appropriate models.

Once models have been chosen, a decision must be made to build the models, to use "ready-made" models, or to modify existing models. The software used for creating the model component also needs to be linked to any data and the DSS user interface. The user interface provides the functionality so that a decision support analyst or a decision maker can interact with the model.

General Problem Types

Management Scientists have been analyzing and trying to solve business problems for more than 50 years. During that time a variety of problem types that can potentially be analyzed with quantitative models have been identified. For example, Professor H. Arsham identifies a small set of Management Science problem types at his Web site (http://ubmail.ubalt.edu/~harsham/), including:

Cost-benefit analysis: Given the decision maker's assessment of costs and benefits, which choice should be recommended?

Forecasting: Using time series analysis to answer questions such as: What will demand be for a product? What are the sales patterns? How will sales affect profits?

Finance and investment: How much capital is needed? How much will the capital cost?

Inventory control and stockout: How much stock should be held? When to order more? How much should be ordered?

Location, allocation, distribution and transportation: Where is the best location for an operation? How big should facilities be? What resources are needed? Are there shortages?

Manpower planning and assignment: How many employees are needed? When?

Project planning and control: How long will a project take? What activities are most important? How should resources be used?

Queuing and congestion: How long are waiting lines? How many servers are needed? What service level is provided?

Reliability and replacement policy: How well is equipment working? How reliable is it? When should it be replaced?

Sequencing and scheduling: What job is most important? In what order should jobs be completed?

Each of these general problem types can occur in situations where a model-driven DSS could support one or more decision makers. These 10 common Management Science problem types can be analyzed using five general categories of quantitative models: accounting and financial models, decision analysis models, forecasting models, network and optimization models, and simulation models. The next five sections discuss each of these general model categories.

ACCOUNTING AND FINANCIAL MODELS

Many accounting and financial models are incorporated in specific model-driven DSS. For example, target return pricing is a popular method of choosing a selling price for a new product. This marketing analysis tool uses two models. An analyst determines a break-even point for a new product and then a target Return on Investment (ROI). After "what if" analysis, a selling price is established. Model-driven DSS can assist in analyzing the relationship between prices, advertising spending, and profits in brand and product planning. Models can assist in break-even analysis, cost-benefit analysis, and capital budgeting. A number of Decision Tools that use accounting and financial models are available on-line at DSSResources.COM.

Break-Even Analysis

A break-even calculation shows the level of operations in units produced at which revenues just cover costs (profit equals zero). The break-even volume can be computed in a number of ways. One approach divides fixed costs by the contribution margin to find the break-even quantity. The contribution margin is the selling price per unit minus the variable costs per unit. Also, the break-even quantity can be calculated by solving the expression: (Price * Quantity Sold) - (Fixed Cost + [Variable Cost per unit * Quantity Sold]) = 0.

A typical break-even model assumes a specific fixed cost and a constant average variable cost. The break-even quantity can be calculated in a spreadsheet by using a goal-seeking capability to set profit equal to zero, where profit equals revenue minus total costs. Figure 10.1 shows a model-driven DSS for break-even analysis developed in Excel.

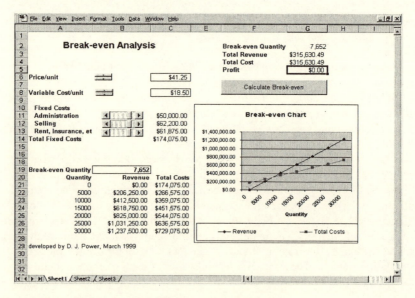

Figure 10.1 Break-Even DSS Developed in Microsoft Excel

A break-even model provides a quick glance at price, volume, and profit relationships. Actually determining fixed and variable costs can be difficult, but in most cases, managers can make reasonable assumptions. Also, break-even analysis ignores demand for a product, so it is often desirable for a manager to use various forecasting models in conjunction with a break-even analysis.

Budget Financial Models

Budgeting DSS are an especially popular enterprise-wide application. Lockheed Martin wanted to improve the quality of their budget information while they cut the number of staff hours needed to develop it. They implemented Comshare (http://www.comshare.com) BudgetPLUS. Sunoco Retail, a division of Suncor Energy, was burdened with an inflexible, labor-intensive in-house budgeting system. Comshare BudgetPLUS "has resolved Sunoco's budgeting needs and given the Company a centralized financial data repository, while empowering users who now have control over their own budgets." Budget models can also be built and tracked for divisions, products, or projects.

Companies are making major changes in their budget planning and forecasting processes. The process is becoming a company-wide effort, with many managers contributing inputs using Web-based support tools. Both large and medium-size companies are trying to combine the traditional bottom-up approach to budget preparation, in which department heads submit budget requests that are rolled up into a corporate budget, with a top-down approach in which budgets are prepared in line with strategic objectives outlined by top management. Companies are also revising budgets throughout the year. Using Web technologies, changes can be made quickly to the budget model estimates, and the cost of deployment is much less than with mainframe-based, enterprise-wide systems.

Products from a number of vendors support participative budget processes. Comshare, Adaytum Software, and Hyperion Solutions have products that assist in strategic planning, budgeting, management reporting, analysis, and financial consolidation, and are innovating with new Budgeting DSS. BudgetHub.org is an on-line resource for enterprise budgeting information.

Pro Forma Financial Statements

Financial analyses and projections can be very important in strategic planning. A projected or pro forma income statement summarizes the projected financial results for a specific future time period. Gross sales are forecasted, and costs are estimated based on historical data and projections. Profit or loss is calculated based on accounting relationships.

In many ways, developing financial projections using a model-driven DSS forces a manager to become concrete about revenues and costs and to deal with "business reality." Managers must quantify financial outflows and inflows to arrive at projected financial statements for a proposed plan. One can develop projections that are either revenue or profit driven. Also, the various pro forma statements can be linked together to speed up "what if" analyses in which assumptions and numbers are changed. Pro forma financial statements are useful for developing detailed financial plans, evaluating the progress of the strategic plan, pinpointing problem areas, and taking corrective action. The pro forma financial statements are also valuable when used as aids in the implementation of a strategic plan.

What are key questions to keep in mind when developing pro forma financial statements? What assumptions were made when the pro forma financial statements were prepared? How sensitive are these financial statements to changes in assumptions? Was a "what if" analysis conducted? Can we justify the numbers of the pro forma financial statements? For outside stakeholders, pro forma financial statements will be a critical part of their evaluation of a strategic plan, new venture plan, corporate acquisition, or new product introduction. For this reason, the statements must present a convincing case, be consistent with other elements of the strategic business plan, and present a realistic picture of the financial consequences of strategic actions.

Ratio Analysis

Financial ratio analysis is a process where an analyst or manager evaluates a firm's financial statements. Even though accounting differences can distort financial results, ratio analysis can be useful in a number of ways, and a model-driven DSS can assist in ratio analysis.

First, ratio analysis can aid in interpreting and evaluating company and competitor income statements and balance sheets by reducing the amount of data contained in them. After computing key ratios, a DSS can support a comprehensive analysis of a firm's financial position. For example, a DSS can show a time series of sales growth or a table of key ratios.

Second, financial ratio analysis can make financial data more meaningful. Any ratio shows a relationship between the numbers in its numerator and denominator. By selecting sets of numbers that are logically related, only a few ratios may be necessary to comprehensively analyze a set of financial statements. Lenders and some investment analysts use ratio analysis.

Third, ratios help to determine relative magnitudes of financial quantities. For example, the amount of a firm's debt has little meaning unless it is compared with the owner's investment in the business. Therefore, the debt/equity ratio shows a relationship that lets managers compare relative magnitudes rather than absolute amounts.

Because of these advantages, financial ratio analysis can help managers or business analysts make effective decisions about a firm's credit worthiness, potential earnings, and financial strengths and weaknesses.

There are many other specific accounting and financial models that can be incorporated in model-driven DSS. For example, cost-benefit models, portfolio models, and capital budgeting models have been used in DSS. The next section explores a more general category of models used in analyzing some decision situations.

DECISION ANALYSIS MODELS

Decision situations that involve a finite and usually small number of alternatives can be evaluated with decision analysis models. Decision analysts often help managers in novel decision situations identify alternatives and attributes. Decision alternatives are listed with their potential forecasted contributions to a goal or goals, and the probability of realizing such a contribution in a table or a graph. Then, one evaluates the results on some attributes to select the best alternative.

Single goal situations are approached by the use of a decision table or decision trees. Multiple goal situations can be analyzed by several techniques including multi-attribute utility analysis and the analytical hierarchy process.

The focus of decision analysis techniques is to help decision makers clarify their understanding of a problem, and separate facts from priorities and preferences. This result is achieved by structuring problems into a hierarchy of objectives and by studying the performance of decision alternatives on specific criteria. The interactive structuring and prioritization process encourages a user to keep a problem presentation simple and helps one extract the essentials decision elements.

A decision analysis is oriented towards finding the best alternative. The aim is to avoid eliciting any priorities that do not help to reach this goal. The modeling philosophy is to include only those goals that are relevant in each decision-making situation and that help to distinguish the alternatives from each other.

In general, computerized decision analysis tools help decision makers decompose and structure problems. The aim of these tools is to help a user apply models like decision trees, multi-attribute utility models, bayesian models, and Analytical Hierarchy Process (AHP). Examples of decision analysis software packages include AliahThink, BestChoice3, Criterium Decision Plus, DPL, Expert Choice, Strad, Supertree, TeamEC, and Which and Why. These tools may be used as part of a special decision study or more routinely as a DSS in reoccurring decision situations.

This section examines three decision analysis models: the analytical hierarchy process, decision trees and multi-attribute utility models.

Analytical Hierarchy Process (AHP)

The AHP technique (cf., Saaty, 1980; Saaty, 1990) can be characterized as a multicriteria decision technique that can combine qualitative and quantitative factors in the overall evaluation of alternatives. This section provides a brief introduction to AHP with an emphasis on a general decision process method.

The first step is to develop a hierarchical representation of a problem (see Figure 10.2). At the top of the hierarchy is the overall objective, and the decision alternatives are at the bottom. Between the top and bottom levels are the relevant attributes of the decision problem, such as selection criteria. The number of levels in the hierarchy depends on the complexity of the problem and the decision maker's model of the problem hierarchy. This step creates the model for a model-driven DSS.

Next, in Step 2, the DSS user generates relational data for comparing the alternatives. In step 3, the software determines the relative priority of each attribute using the comparisons of Step 2. A user of a model-driven DSS developed using software like Expert Choice (http://www.expertchoice.com) would have the option of redoing the comparison matrix. In Step 4, the priorities or weights of the lowest level alternatives relative to the top-most objective are then determined and displayed.

New Product Evaluation

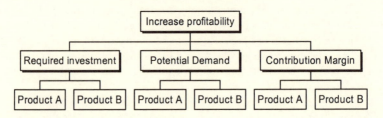

Figure 10.2 A Hierarchical Representation

A number of software packages implement AHP. The best known and most widely used is Expert Choice (visit URL http://www.expertchoice.com). Known for its user friendliness, it is the first fully graphical, mouse-driven implementation of AHP. A group support version Team Expert Choice, or TeamEC, is a software solution that is equipped with keypads for multiple voters. TeamEC can be used to create a communications-driven or group DSS.

Decision Trees and Multi-attribute Utility Models

A decision tree uses two types of nodes: choice nodes, represented by a square, and chance nodes, represented by a circle. An analyst constructs a decision tree. For the chance nodes, the probabilities along each outgoing branch must sum to one. One then calculates the expected payoffs for each branch in the tree. A decision tree has two major advantages. First, a decision tree shows graphically the relationships among the problem elements. Second, it can deal with more complex situations in a compact form.

Managers or decision analysts can use a generalized Decision Analysis Support System to develop a model of a complex, contingent situation. The off-the-shelf tool supports decision making for a special study or a non-routine problem analysis. For example, a company has two possible choices: Either introduce a product (A1), or not (A2). If the product is introduced, the firm incurs $100,000 in additional R&D costs. If the product is introduced, a competitor may introduce a competing product. So Alternative 1 can have two outcomes: Competitor introduces a competing product (O1), or not (O2). Based on knowledge of the marketplace, the competitor, and some marketing intelligence, the probability of O1 is 70 percent, and that of O2 is 30 percent. O1 and O2 are outcome or chance nodes. The final outcomes of the Promotional Campaigns (N1, N2, and N3) can depend on, among other things, the firm's actions, a competitor's actions, the size of the promotional campaign, and the size of a competitor's campaign. Thus, with a computerized model a decision maker can analyze the final outcomes in terms of possible promotional campaigns (based on Lee, Moore, and Taylor, 1985). The "best" strategy depends on the criterion the decision maker uses. In a marketing analysis, the criterion is typically maximizing Expected Monetary Value (EMV).

Multi-attribute utility analysis (MAUA) is a popular decision analysis tool. When this tool is used, the attributes are sometimes called decision factors or criteria. The attributes are then given importance weights. The decision maker provides information about each alternative on each attribute. This step involves measuring the decision maker's utility or perception of usefulness of an alternative in terms of the desired attributes. There is an extensive specialized literature on multi-attribute utility analysis (cf., Watson and Buede, 1987; Golub, 1997).

MAUA has traditionally been used in selection problems like choosing a site location in which there is certainty regarding the attribute levels of the alternatives. Another Management Science technique, subjective probability assessment, can be used to develop a distribution of attribute levels when there is uncertainty in these values. These probability distributions can be used in conjunction with MAUA to provide a consistent framework for making selection decisions.

FORECASTING MODELS

Forecasting models are an integral part of many model-driven DSS. One can build a forecasting model or one may use a forecasting software package. Forecasts may be made for a special decision study or a model-driven DSS for making forecasts may be used routinely in a business decision process. A forecasting model component may also be included in a broader purpose model-driven DSS. The quality of many decisions depends on the quality of a forecast.

The major use of forecasting is to predict the value of variables at some time in the future. The future time period of interest depends on when results will be evaluated. For example, in an inventory decision one may be interested in prices a year in the future, while in a capital investment decision one may be interested in prices and income five years in the future. Generally speaking, a decision analyst distinguishes between short-run and long-run forecasts.

Many types of forecasting models exist, but forecasting remains an extremely difficult task (cf., Makridakis and Wheelwright, 1982). What is going to happen in the future depends on many factors that are uncontrollable. Furthermore, data availability, accuracy, cost, and the time required to make a forecast play an important role in choosing a forecasting method. Forecasting methods can also be chosen based on convenience, popularity, expert advice, and guidelines from prior research. In general, the last two approaches should be used in building Forecasting DSS.

The best Web resource on forecasting models and methods is the Forecasting Principles site (hops.wharton.upenn.edu/forecast) maintained by J. Scott Armstrong. It provides a comprehensive review of forecasting. The site also provides: evidence showing the relevance of forecasting principles to a given problem, expert judgment about the applicability of forecasting principles, sources of data and forecasts, details about how to use forecasting methods, and guidance to locating the most recent research findings.

Forecasting methods can be grouped in several ways. One classification scheme distinguishes between formal forecasting techniques and informal approaches such as intuition, expert opinions, spur-of-the-moment guesses, and seat-of-the-pants predictions.

The following paragraphs review the more formal and analytical methods that have been used in building forecasting DSS, model-driven DSS for making forecasts. The methods reviewed include naïve extrapolation, judgment methods, moving averages, exponential smoothing, time series extrapolation, and regression and econometric models. Each method is discussed briefly, and major issues associated with using the methods are summarized. According to Scott Armstrong, given enough data, quantitative methods are more accurate than judgmental methods. He notes that when large changes are expected, causal methods are more accurate than naïve methods. Also, simple methods are preferable to complex methods since simple methods are easier to understand, less expensive, and rarely less accurate.

Judgment Methods. Judgment forecasting methods are based on subjective estimates and expert opinion, rather than on historical data. These methods are often used for long-range forecasts, especially where external factors may play a significant role. They also are used where historical data are very limited or nonexistent. A Group DSS could be used with a judgment method like the Delphi technique to obtain judgments. A communications-driven DSS can also collect estimates of sales staff. The results are not necessarily accurate, but the experts may be the best source of forecast information.

Naïve Extrapolation. This technique involves collecting data and developing a chart or graph of the data. The user extrapolates or estimates the data for future time periods. This technique is easy to update, and minimal quantitative knowledge is needed. It is easy and inexpensive to implement using a spreadsheet. It provides however, limited accuracy.

Moving Average. This type of forecast uses an average of historical values that "moves," or includes the new period in each succeeding forecast. It is for short-run forecasts and the results are easy to manipulate and test. Overall, a Forecasting DSS built using a moving average model will be easy to understand and inexpensive.

Exponential Smoothing. The historical data is mathematically altered to better reflect the forecaster's assumptions about the future of the variable being forecast. This model is similar to the moving average model, but it is harder to explain. A short-term forecast based on exponential smoothing is often acceptable.

Other Time-Series Extrapolations. Naïve extrapolation, moving average, and exponential smoothing are simple means to use a time series of data for forecasting. A time series is a set of values for a business or economic variable measured at successive intervals of time. For example, quarterly sales of a firm make up a time series. More complex methods are also used that are beyond the scope of this book. Managers use time-series analysis in decision making because they believe that knowledge of past behavior of the time series will help understand the behavior of the series in the future. In managerial planning, managers often assume that history will repeat itself and that past tendencies will continue.

Regression and Econometric Models. Data analysis tools like linear and multiple regression can be used in special studies to find data associations and, if possible, cause and effect relationships. Causal methods are more powerful than time-series methods, but they are also more complex. Their complexity comes from two sources: First, they include more variables, some of which are external to a decision situation. Second, they use sophisticated statistical techniques for evaluating variables. Causal approaches are most appropriate for intermediate term (3 to 5-year) forecasting.

In general, subjective forecasting methods are used in those cases where quantitative methods are inappropriate or cannot be used. Time pressure, lack of data, or lack of money may prevent the use of quantitative models. Complexity of historical data may also inhibit its use. Model-driven DSS primarily incorporate quantitative forecasting methods and often use multiple forecasting models.

NETWORK AND OPTIMIZATION MODELS

Project planning and control, location, allocation, distribution, and transportation problems can often be formulated using network and optimization models. These models can be used to determine: Where is the best location for an operation? How big should facilities be? What resources are needed? Are there shortages? Networks can define many relationships, and network problems are most often solved using optimization models.

For example, one can define and analyze a network of project activities using project management software. Project management is a popular category of off-the-shelf decision support software. The best selling package is Microsoft Project. It is a powerful application that can be used to efficiently plan, manage, and communicate project information. Project managers can enter actual costs for tasks and assignments. More information can be found at microsoft.com. While many computer users are familiar with project management software, not everyone realizes it is based on network flow models. These models are specially structured linear programming problems.

DSS analysts can define other networks. For example, one can develop a network of possible airline routes and schedules and compare costs. A set of routes or paths can be analyzed using a number of heuristic or quantitative tools. It has been estimated that 70 percent of all linear programming applications are network flow problems or have a substantial network structure. In addition to project management and aircraft routing, applications include: production planning and aggregate scheduling, personnel planning and scheduling, land use allocation, classroom scheduling, plant location, and multinational cash flow management.

Linear programming is the most widely known technique in a family of tools called mathematical programming. There are many possible uses of mathematical programming, especially of linear programming, in creating DSS. Many books have been written for courses in Management Science, Quantitative Analysis, and Operations Research. Managers and many DSS specialists are usually not experts in using optimization or simulation tools. Small-scale optimization DSS can be built using a spreadsheet program like Microsoft Excel.

Linear programming attempts to either maximize or minimize the values of an objective function. A solver program can be used for both equation-solving or goal-seeking and constrained optimization, using linear programming, nonlinear programming, and integer programming methods. An on-line Web-based tutorial on Using MS Excel Solver for Spreadsheet Optimization is at the Frontline Systems Web site (http://frontsys.com/).

Users of a model-driven DSS, based on a linear programming model, can find input values that satisfy a set of simultaneous equations and inequalities. When a user does this, there is usually more than one satisfactory set of input values. So, a solver can find the "best" set of input values that maximizes or minimizes some other calculated formula that a user specifies. This process is called constrained optimization; the equations or inequalities are called constraints. Every linear programming problem is composed of six elements (cf., Lee et al., 1985; Turban, 1995):

Decision Variables. These variables are values that a decision maker can change.

Objective Function. This is a mathematical expression that shows the linear relationship between the decision variables and the goal that is the focus of the model. The objective function is a measure of goal attainment. Examples of such goals are total profit, total cost, and market share.

Coefficients of the Objective Function. The coefficients of the variables in the objective function express the change in the value of the objective function by including in the solution one unit of each decision variable.

Constraints. Maximization or minimization is performed subject to a set of constraints. Constraints are most often expressed in the form of linear equation. Each constraint reflects the fact that resources are limited or that some requirement must be met.

Constraint Coefficients. Coefficients of a constraint's variables are called the input-output coefficients. They indicate the rate at which a given resource is depleted or used.

Capacities. The capacities or availability of the various resources are usually expressed as some upper or lower limit. When a problem is formulated, the capacities also express minimum requirements.

In Figure 10.3 the decision variables are the quantities of TVs, stereos, and speakers to build. The objective function is to maximize total profits. The constraints are from the parts inventory. Managers should be able to build a simple model-driven DSS like Figure 10.3 in Excel. A support person may need to help in conceptualizing the problem or in testing the end-user application. Most often optimization models are included in a DSS to assist in resource allocation. Managers are often required to allocate productive resources like raw materials, people, money, or time that can be used in a variety of different ways. The problem is to determine the best way to use the resources. Managers need to determine what "best" means, but usually it implies maximizing profits or minimizing costs. Optimization may be incorporated in a DSS used routinely in a firm or a management scientist may build an optimization model for a special decision support study.

	A	B	C	D	E	F	G	H
1								
2		**Product Mix DSS**						
3								
4								
5					TV Set	Stereo	Speaker	
6			Number to Build -->		100	100	100	
7		Part Name	Inventory	No. Used				
8		Chassis	450	200	1	1	0	
9		Picture Tube	250	100	1	0	0	
10		Speaker Cone	800	500	2	2	1	
11		Power Supply	450	200	1	1	0	
12		Electronics	600	400	2	1	1	
13								
14			Profits by Product:		$75	$50	$35	
15			Adjust per Unit Profits	◄ ►	◄ ►	◄ ►		
16								
17								
18			Total Profits:	$ 16,000			Solve	
19								
20								
21	developed by D. J. Power, 2001							
22								
23	This is a simplified version of a Microsoft Excel sample workbook.							

Figure 10.3 An Example Optimization Spreadsheet DSS

SIMULATION MODELS

Often, companies are faced with planning the production of a new product or building a new factory. Although these may seem like straightforward analyses, managers need to make many interrelated decisions. For example, production of a new product involves decisions regarding equipment, scheduling and control, and manufacturing philosophy. Many factors influence these decisions, including the need to meet production volume goals and costs associated with achieving these goals. Simulations can help evaluate complex, interrelated decision issues.

Simulation has many meanings, depending on the professional discipline where the term is being used. To simulate, according to many dictionaries, means to assume the appearance or characteristics of reality. It also means a model that generates test conditions approximating actual or operational conditions. In a DSS context, simulation generally refers to a technique for conducting experiments with a computer-based model. One method of simulating a system involves identifying the various states of a system and then modifying those states by executing specific events. A wide variety of problems can be evaluated using simulation, including inventory control and stock-out, manpower planning and assignment, queuing and congestion, reliability and replacement policy, and sequencing and scheduling.

Major Characteristics of Simulation

Simulation is a specialized type of modeling tool. Most quantitative models are an abstraction or simplification of reality, while simulation models usually try to imitate reality. In practical terms, this means that there are fewer simplifications in simulation models than in other quantitative models. Simulation models are generally complex.

Second, simulation is a technique for performing "what-if" analysis over multiple time periods or events. Therefore, simulation involves the testing of specific values of the decision or uncontrollable variables in the model and observing the impact on the output variables.

Simulation is a descriptive tool that can be used for prediction. A simulation describes and sometimes predicts the characteristics of a given system under different circumstances. Once these characteristics are known, alternative actions can be selected. The simulation process often consists of the repetition of a test or experiment many times to obtain an estimate of the overall effect of certain actions on the system.

Finally, simulation is usually needed when the problem under investigation is too complex to be evaluated using optimization models. Complexity means that the problem cannot be formulated for optimization because assumptions do not hold or because the optimization formulation is too large and complex.

Advantages and Disadvantages of Simulation

Recently, more model-driven DSS have been built using simulation models. The increased use of this approach can be attributed to a number of factors (cf., Render and Stair, 1988; Turban, 1995). First, simulation theory is relatively easy for managers to understand. A simulation model is a collection of many elementary relationships. Second, simulation allows the manager to ask "what-if" type questions. Third, DSS analysts work directly with managers because an accurate simulation model requires an intimate knowledge of the problem. The model is built from the manager's perspective, using his or her conceptual model of the system.

Fourth, a simulation model is built for one particular problem and, typically, will not solve any other problem. Thus, no generalized understanding of a problem is required of the manager; every component in the model corresponds one-to-one with a part of the real-life model. Fifth, simulation can handle an extremely wide variation in problem types, such as inventory and staffing, as well as long-range planning decisions. Sixth, managers can use simulation to experiment with different variables to determine which are important, and with different alternatives to determine which is best. Seventh, new software packages and tools like Java and C++ make it much easier to build simulations.

Finally, simulation allows for the inclusion of the real-life complexities of problems; simplifications are not necessary. Due to the nature of simulation, a great amount of time compression can be attained, giving the manager some information about the long-term effects of various policies. Also, with a simulation, it is easy to include a wide variety of performance measures.

There are three primary disadvantages of simulation. First, an optimal or "best" solution cannot be guaranteed. Second, constructing a simulation model is frequently a slow and costly process. Third, solutions and inferences from a specific simulation study are usually not transferable to other problems.

Types of Simulation

There are several types of simulation. The major types are probabilistic, time-dependent, and visual simulation. In a probabilistic simulation one or more of the independent variables is conceptualized as a probability distribution of values. Time-dependent or discrete simulation refers to a situation where it is important to know exactly when an event occurs. For example, in waiting line or queuing problems, it is important to know the precise time of arrival to determine if a customer will have to wait or not.

Visual simulation is the graphic display of computerized results. Software for visual simulation is one of the more successful new developments in computer-human interaction and problem solving. Animation and visual simulation helps explain results to managers. Eliot (1997) notes, "If you are analyzing a call center, you might show graphic icons of phones on the computer display and indicate the phones being answered as calls come into the call center. You could use colors, such as green for call completed and red for call abandoned, and otherwise make the simulation visually attractive to help other personnel understand just what the simulation is trying to do." (p. 14)

MODELING LANGUAGES AND SPREADSHEETS

Models can be developed in a variety of programming languages like Java and C++ and with a wide variety of software packages including spreadsheets and modeling packages. Spreadsheets are commonly used for desktop model-driven DSS. Modeling packages attempt to help users create and manipulate models. A model management system tries to provide support for various phases of the decision modeling life cycle.

Modeling and Data Summarization

DSS development packages for On-Line Analytical Processing (OLAP) and modeling have a variety of quantitative models in areas like statistics, financial analysis, accounting, and management science. These small models can be executed using a single command, such as AVERAGE or NPV. AVERAGE calculates the average of a number and may be used in a larger model; and NPV calculates the net present value of a collection of future cash flows for a given interest rate. It also may be a part of a make-versus-buy model.

Functions are often building blocks for other quantitative models. For example, a regression model can be a part of a forecasting model that supports a financial planning model. Several statistical functions are built into DSS generators. All major spreadsheet packages have extensive statistical tools. For example, Excel has analysis of variance, correlation, covariance, descriptive statistics, exponential smoothing, f-test, histograms, and moving average.

In addition, many DSS generators can interface with quantitative stand-alone packages. Such packages are usually much more powerful than the built-in routines. "Canned" or preprogrammed models can reduce the programming time of the DSS builder.

Electronic Spreadsheets

Spreadsheets are a very popular end-user decision support modeling tool. A spreadsheet is based on the structure of an accounting spreadsheet that is basically a column-and-row pad. In spreadsheets, reports can be consolidated, and data can be organized or sorted in alphabetical or numerical order. Other capabilities include setting up windows for viewing several parts of a spreadsheet simultaneously and executing mathematical manipulations. These capabilities enable the spreadsheet to become an important tool for analysis, planning, and modeling.

The current trend is to integrate spreadsheets with development and utility software, such as database management and graphics. Integrated packages like Microsoft Office with Excel are more popular in businesses than purchasing stand-alone spreadsheets. For more details on spreadsheets, see "A Brief History of Spreadsheets" at DSSResources.COM.

A major capability of spreadsheet programs is that numbers can be changed and the implications of these changes can immediately be observed and analyzed. Spreadsheets are used in almost every kind of organization in all functional areas. Managers can build small decision support applications on their own or with help from a DSS Analyst very quickly and inexpensively.

End-user developed model-driven DSS will have errors. All of the problems with this type of development that were discussed in Chapter 4 need to be addressed. One way to reduce errors and improve the usefulness of a model-driven DSS developed in a spreadsheet is to have an MIS staff member evaluate the application based on the following criteria:

- Accuracy. Are the results and calculations correct?
- Flexibility. Is it easy to change assumptions, parameters, and values? Is the application well documented?
- Understandability. Is it easy to understand the purpose of the model-driven DSS and how it is implemented in the spreadsheet?

- Auditability. Is it easy to audit the application? Is the organization of the workbook easy to understand? Can dependencies be traced in the application?
- Aesthetics. Are the spreadsheet screens attractive and well designed? Are any printouts easy to read?
- Documentation. Are formulas and related cells clearly defined and identified?

Development Packages

Many DSS applications deal with financial analysis, and some tools help develop such applications. While spreadsheet software can be used, specialized tools are often more efficient or effective. Since the 1960s, planning models have advanced from an obscure concept for large corporations to an appropriate tool for planning in almost any size company.

Some modeling packages require developers to enter equations. Spreadsheets, on the other hand, create their models with a computation or calculation orientation. The definition of a planning model varies somewhat with the scope of its application. For instance, financial planning models may have a very short planning horizon and a collection of accounting formulas for producing pro forma statements.

On the other hand, corporate planning models often include complex quantitative and logical interrelationships among a corporation's financial, marketing, and production activities. Most financial models are dynamic, multiyear models. Accounting formulas are true by definition, such as profit = revenue - expenses. Empirical relationships have been derived from past data, e.g. sales support expenses = \$48.50 * no. of salespeople. Managers hope empirical relationships remain valid long enough to use them for prediction or planning.

In addition to generic DSS-based planning models, there are several industry-specific ones for hospitals, banks, and universities. For example, many universities use EDUCAUSE's Financial Planning Model (EFPM). Comshare is a major vendor of planning and budgeting software.

There are few planning and modeling languages currently on the market. One of the best known such products was IFPS, interactive financial planning system, marketed by EXECUCOM. Gerald R. Wagner and his students originally developed IFPS in the late 1970s. Until a few years ago, an extended product, Visual IFPS/PLUS, was distributed by Comshare, which purchased EXECUCOM. A few of the current planning and modeling language products include Comshare Planning, Visual DSS from TrueBlue Systems, and CUFFS-88 from Cuffs Planning and Models, Ltd.

Typical decision support applications built using planning models include: financial forecasting; manpower planning; pro forma financial statements; profit planning; capital budgeting; sales forecasting; marketing decision making; investment analysis; merger and acquisition analysis; tax planning; lease versus purchase decisions; and new venture evaluation.

MODEL-DRIVEN DSS AIRLINE INDUSTRY EXAMPLES

Airlines are using decision support tools to project travel trends and to cut costs. Model-driven DSS benefit customers by reducing or controlling expenses, evaluating ticket prices, shortening lines in the terminal, and reducing delays. Also, airlines are using DSS to reduce their seat inventories and schedule flights.

Jessica Davis (1999) reported in *InfoWorld* that using the "Broadbase data mart, United's staff of 60 analyst/schedulers, typically MBA/economists, can load 'what if' scenarios—testing whether a new flight to Chicago would be more profitable using a larger or a smaller aircraft." She noted schedulers take into consideration passenger demand, constraints of airports, the maintenance needs of the aircraft, the cost of flying individual aircraft, crew resources, and other factors.

Another example of a model-driven DSS in the airline industry is a yield management system. This type of DSS uses a nonlinear, stochastic model that requires data, such as passenger demand, cancellations, and other estimates of passenger behavior. It had been estimated it would require approximately 250 million decision variables to solve the system-wide yield management problem. American Airlines developed a model that reduced the large problem to three much smaller subproblems that could be solved efficiently.

American Airlines' yield management system is called DINAMO (Dynamic Inventory and Maintenance Optimizer). It was fully implemented in 1988. Since then the system has improved productivity by automating the identification of critical flights and increasing pricing flexibility with a discount allocation process. Between 1988 and 1990 productivity for each analyst using DINAMO increased by over 30 percent. Overall, yield management provided quantifiable benefits of over $1.4 billion for 1988-1990 (Smith, Leimkuhler, and Darrow, 1992).

United Airlines deployed the System Operations Advisor (SOA), a real-time decision support system, at its operations control center (OCC) to increase the effectiveness of its operational decisions. United Airlines developed the SOA and implemented it in August 1992. From October 1993 to March 1994, this model-driven DSS application saved more than 27,000 minutes of potential delays, which translated into $540,000 savings in delay costs (Rakshit, Krishnamurthy, and Yu, 1996).

United Airlines also uses a crew scheduling DSS, a gate assignment and planning system and a customer service manager DSS. The crew scheduling system at United Airlines is estimated to save about $12 million annually in credit time for crewmembers and about $4 million annually in hotel costs.

Airline industry DSS vendors include: Airline Automation, Inc., Caleb Technologies, Carmen System, Sabre Technology Solutions, SH&E, Talus Solutions, and Trydon Airline Services.

CONCLUSIONS AND COMMENTARY

Learning to build models and model-driven DSS is a complex task that requires extensive preparatory work. In most situations, MIS professionals who want to build quantitative models need a strong background in management science and operations research. If managers and MIS professionals want to design and build successful model-driven DSS, they may need to expand their skills. If management scientists want to contribute more in building these model-driven DSS, they should develop a very broad understanding of DSS and focus less on using only specific quantitative tools and technologies.

Models are very important components in many DSS, but "bad" models result in "bad" decisions. Many models can be implemented quickly using prototyping. Using prototyping, a new DSS can be constructed, tested, and improved in just a few iterations. This development approach helps test the effectiveness of the overall design. The downside of prototyping is that a new DSS may be hard to deploy to a wide group of users. Managers and DSS analysts need to make sure the scaled-down DSS will work when it is deployed more widely in a company.

OLAP is one example of a hybrid system that uses simple analytical techniques to analyze large data sets. Many other model-driven DSS can be built that use a variety of organizational and external data sets. Managers should be consumers and developers of model-driven DSS. Widely used model-driven DSS need to be built systematically by a team of model specialists, MIS and network specialists and managers. Small-scale systems can be purchased or built using tools like Microsoft Excel. New model-driven DSS must capture the complexity of a decision and be easily implemented and integrated into existing systems.

Model-driven DSS remain important support tools for managers. The interest in data-driven DSS and GDSS should not distract managers from the need to update existing model-based systems and to develop new capabilities that can be implemented using Web technologies. The development environment for building model-driven DSS is powerful and increasingly "Web-friendly".

Historically, a small number of experts in management science and operations research have performed sophisticated special decision studies for companies. As the emphasis upon rapid response to competition increases, more and more individuals within companies will need to build and certainly use model-driven DSS. Managers and DSS analysts need to be actively involved in identifying the need for and the purpose of innovative model-driven DSS and Analytical Information Systems.

Chapter 11

Building Web-Based and Interorganizational Decision Support Systems

INTRODUCTION

In his 1995 book *The Road Ahead*, Microsoft Chairman Bill Gates argued the "information highway will extend the electronic marketplace and make it the ultimate go-between, the universal middleman. ... This will carry us into a new world of low-friction, low-overhead capitalism, in which market information will be plentiful and transaction costs low. It will be a shopper's heaven. (p. 158)" To exploit the plentiful market information and generate profits, companies will need to create and use sophisticated Decision Support Systems (DSS). These DSS will need to be available to both internal and external stakeholders. For many reasons, the logical technology to use for building these new DSS is the Internet or a corporate intranet built using Web technologies.

The dominant information technology platform in companies is changing from mainframes and LAN-based, client-server systems to Web and Internet technologies. This technology change is expanding what Peter Keen (1991) called "information reach" and "information range." The reach of information and decision support systems has expanded significantly to serve a very large group of internal and external stakeholders. The range and variety of decision support information that can be developed, delivered, and shared is also becoming much larger. Today, innovative Web-based examples of all five categories of DSS, including communications-driven, data-driven, document-driven, knowledge-driven, and model-driven DSS, can be found, and more innovative DSS of each type will surely be developed.

Data from various sources, including DSS vendors, The Conference Board, and PricewaterhouseCoopers, indicate that a technological shift to Web technologies is occurring in many corporations. In 1999, 58 percent of large corporations had intranets and 10 percent had extranets for business partners. A large majority had Web sites (72 percent) and used e-mail (92 percent). The growth of Web-based DSS was just beginning in 1999; only 8 percent of firms had We-enabled company data warehouses. Surveys indicate most large firms are planning to create intranets, establish extranets, and make company-wide data warehouses accessible on their intranets and extranets.

With Web technologies rapidly being implemented, it is important to monitor and explore the possibilities of Web-based DSS. Some evidence indicates that Web technologies can reduce the cost of building and delivering decision support. Managers need to know more about how to build Web-based and interorganizational DSS. And managers need to know how to create DSS that support customers and suppliers. In most companies it is important to explore the advantages of changing the technology of DSS to Web technologies. From a practical standpoint there are limits to the amount of knowledge of Web technologies most managers need. Managers should probably not be maintaining Web sites, but they often will be content providers. Finally, managers and MIS personnel need to "surf" the Web and try a variety of examples of Web-based and interorganizational DSS.

This chapter focuses on Web technologies and interorganizational DSS, especially topics like designing and managing Web-based systems; examples of Web-based DSS software; examples of Web-based and interorganizational DSS implementations; and advantages and disadvantages of Web-based and interorganizational DSS.

KEY TERMS

The World Wide Web is where the action is in developing enterprise-wide and interorganizational DSS. When vendors propose a Web-based DSS, they are referring to a computerized system that delivers decision support information or decision support tools to a manager, business analyst, or customer using a "thin-client" Web browser like Netscape Navigator or Internet Explorer. The computer server that is hosting the DSS application is linked to the user's computer by a network using the Transmission Control Protocol/Internet Protocol (TCP/IP). In many companies, a Web-based DSS is synonymous with an intranet and an enterprise-wide DSS that is supporting large groups of managers in a networked environment with a specialized data warehouse as part of the DSS architecture. This view is too narrow; Web technologies can be used to implement any category of DSS. Web-based means the entire application is implemented using Web technologies including a Web server; Web-enabled means key parts of an application like a database remain on a legacy system, but the application can be accessed from a Web-based component and displayed in a browser.

Some companies have created extranets for decision support as well as intranets. Interorganizational DSS serve a company's stockholders, bankers, customers, or suppliers. An interorganizational DSS may provide stakeholders with access to a company's extranet and authority or privileges to use specific decision support Intranet capabilities. For example, Artesyn Technologies (www.artesyn.com) has virtual design decision support tools to provide customers of its power supply products with pre-sales technical support. Wal-Mart Retail Link provides some suppliers with Web access to sales forecasts and decision support capabilities. Companies are creating Web-based, interorganizational DSS that customers can use to evaluate products or that suppliers can use to control costs or reduce inventories. These DSS may be data-driven or document-driven DSS, communications-driven or Group DSS (GDSS), model-driven DSS, or knowledge-driven DSS. The target users are managers and knowledge workers in a customer, supplier, or partner organization and, in some cases, retail customers. Some people would say these DSS are part of a company's external intranet or extranet.

As noted, only about 8 percent of firms had Web-enabled company data warehouses in 1999. A company intranet based on Web technologies can provide even more extensive management information and decision support than a data warehouse. Also, an intranet can provide decision support to a wide variety of internal users. An intranet is a secure, internal organizational network that uses TCP/IP with at least one Web server. It is important that an intranet is secure and accessible by only an organization's members or others who have specific authorization. A firewall and password protection should limit access to the network. An intranet is an internal information system based on Internet technology, Web services, and Hypertext Markup Language (HTML) or portable document format (PDF) publishing.

An intranet is used to share corporate information, including DSS capabilities. Most intranets have a main page called a portal. A portal is a simple, personalized Web front end that provides access to information from the global Internet as well as a wide variety of corporate systems, including document servers, business intelligence systems, groupware databases, and enterprise resource planning systems. A Web portal provides a means to implement the different generic DSS into a more complete management support system than any built in mainframe or client/server environments.

The above terms are evolving as quickly as the Web itself, and authors do not use them consistently. There will be some conceptual ambiguity in Internet and Web technologies for the foreseeable future.

DESIGNING AND DEVELOPING WEB-BASED DSS

A decision-oriented diagnosis approach is important for Web-based and interorganizational DSS. Simply making an existing DSS accessible by using a Web browser to managers, customers or other stakeholders will often lead to unsatisfactory results. Creating a Web-enabled DSS should be considered a "quick fix" rather than as a permanent means of deploying a decision support capability. Once diagnosis is complete, a feasibility analysis is definitely needed for an enterprise-wide DSS. A systematic development approach must be explicitly chosen, and managers must be involved in the development process.

Developing the user interface, models, and data store for Web-based DSS remain major tasks. A user interface remains important in a Web development environment, and it probably becomes more important because so many users of various levels of sophistication can potentially access some or all DSS capabilities. The representations available to user interface designers of Web-based DSS are comparable to those for stand-alone DSS, but the available operations expand enormously with the additions of hyperlinks and the availability of external data and document sources. Control and memory aids also change somewhat in a Web development environment.

The actual architecture implemented is usually simple. Most Web-based DSS are built using a three- or four-tier architecture. A person using a Web browser sends a request using the hypertext transfer protocol (HTTP) to a Web server. The Web server processes the request, using a program or script. The script may implement or link to a model, process a database request, or format a document. The results are returned to the user's Web browser for display (see Figure 11.1). Web applications are designed to allow any authorized user, with a Web browser and an Internet connection, to interact with them. The application code usually resides on a remote server and the user interface is presented at the client's Web browser.

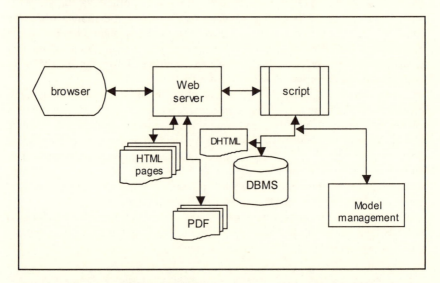

Figure 11.1 Web-Based DSS Architecture

The tools for building Web-based DSS are new and increasingly complex. Many people have heard of HTML, but it is only a small part of the development tool set. MIS staff and managers are bombarded with acronyms and terms like Extensible Markup Language (XML), Common Gateway Interface Scripts (CGI), Java applets, JavaScript code in HTML pages, and ActiveX components. The remainder of this section briefly explores some of these tools.

HyperText Markup Language (HTML) is designed to specify the logical organization of a Web document with hypertext extensions for hypertext links and user interaction. Web documents can be used for receiving input and showing output from a decision aid programmed in a programming language, such as Java or JavaScript. The most useful tags for entering input and displaying output are the Form tags.

Extensible Markup Language (XML) is a general syntax for describing data elements of a Web page. It is applicable to a wide range of DSS, including applications with databases and Web documents. It is similar to HTML; however, in XML one can create custom tags to show a document's structure. XML tags transform each Web page into a more structured document. For example, in a document consisting of employee information, there could be tags like <name> </name>, <position> </position>, and <streetaddress> </streetaddress>. In HTML, the information could only be separated with <br> or <p></p> tags. XML allows DSS to process documents, data, and information faster and more efficiently.

Common Gateway Interface (CGI) applications are server-executed programs used to dynamically create HTML documents. Many World Wide Web sites use CGI applications for dynamic Web page creation, for taking values from Web forms, and for providing a Web-based interface to other applications, such as databases. CGI programs provide the back-end processing for many Web-based decision aids and DSS.

Java is a general-purpose programming language. In "The Java Language: A White Paper" (Sun Microsystems, 1996), Sun developers describe Java as "a simple, object-oriented, distributed, interpreted, robust, secure, architecture neutral, portable, high-performance, multithreaded, and dynamic language." It is related to C and C++, but some capabilities are omitted and a few ideas from other languages are included. Java is categorized as a high-level programming language. Compiled Java code is computer architecture neutral, so Java applications can be used in a diverse operating system environment like the Internet. The Java language provides a powerful addition to the DSS development tools available for programmers. The official Java Web site is http://java.sun.com/. The largest directory of Java applets and Java-related Web sites is http://www.gamelan.com/.

JavaScript is a programming language that is highly integrated with Web browser objects. JavaScript is downloaded as part of an HTML page, and the Web browser processes it after it is received. JavaScript programs consist of functions that are called as a result of Web browser events like a mouse click. Some examples of JavaScript decision aids are at DSSResources.COM.

ActiveX controls are reusable software components developed by Microsoft. These controls can be used to add specialized functionality quickly to Web sites, desktop applications, and development tools. According to Webopedia, ActiveX is an "outgrowth of two other Microsoft technologies called OLE (Object Linking and Embedding) and COM (Component Object Model)." Most developers focus on ActiveX controls. An ActiveX control is similar to a Java applet. Related to ActiveX is VBScript. It enables one to embed interactive elements in HTML documents. Microsoft's Internet Explorer supports Java, JavaScript, and ActiveX, and Netscape's Navigator supports only Java and JavaScript, although plug-ins can provide support of VBScript and ActiveX.

Many desktop productivity tools like Microsoft Access, Excel, and PowerPoint have the capability to create Web documents. These HTML generator tools can let managers and analysts share decision support materials prepared on their personal PCs with others in their company. Web documents created with Microsoft applications often work best when viewed using Microsoft's Internet Explorer browser. In general, managers need to become more involved in working with desktop tools that can provide content for decision support intranets and extranets.

A number of specialized developer tools càn help implement Web-based DSS including Microsoft Front Page, Cold Fusion from Allaire (www.allaire.com) and Web DSS development software like dbProbe (internetivity.com). These tools can assist some experienced developers, but they can actually result in poorly developed DSS when used by people inexperienced in building DSS. End-users are building Web-based DSS using Front Page or even Cold Fusion, but these DSS often have more detractors than advocates.

When a company embarks on building Web-based DSS, some problems can be anticipated and minimized. First, Web-based DSS applications will probably encounter some peak load problems. During the business day, many managers will want to access the corporate intranet and so a "high performance" hardware architecture that can expand to serve a large number of concurrent users is needed. This load problem is associated with the "scalability" of the hardware and software and the planning of the developers.

Second, the Web is a "stateless" environment that does not automatically keep track of configuration settings, transaction information, or any other data for the next page request. To avoid requiring users to reenter information such as user name and password, Web-based DSS applications must keep state information from one Web page to another. This creates new security issues for companies wishing to make sensitive, internal data accessible to users. User authorization and authentication are challenging in the Web environment because of the large number of potential users.

Third, it is difficult to keep up with changing Web technologies. To cope, one must be selective in scanning and reading technical materials, and it is a plus to learn rapidly in such an environment. Both managers and technical staff need to learn about Web technologies and then be prepared to keep up with new developments as they occur. Despite these problems and challenges, the Web is and should be the platform of choice for new DSS.

MANAGING WEB-BASED AND INTERORGANIZATIONAL DSS

Companies are using both traditional Electronic Data Interchange (EDI) and newer Web-based extranet technologies to build "trading communities." These interorganizational systems can support both transaction processing and cooperative or shared decision making. Despite the possibilities, a number of real-world issues like reengineering or redesigning business processes and encouraging trading partners to participate in e-business relationships remain major challenges. Managers in interdependent organizations need to cooperate to build shared DSS, and suppliers need to consider what types of DSS can assist their customers. Also, managers must confront a variety of business, technical, and legal issues and impediments if they want to build effective interorganizational DSS.

The first major business issue that must be confronted is who will use the system: customers, suppliers or both? Then, managers need to ask a number of more specific questions: What is the cost of the proposed Web-based, interorganizational DSS, and who will pay the cost? Then managers need to ask: "Do we need to reengineer or redesign our processes? Does the Internet increase the speed of decisions and transactions and create efficiencies for our business? Will the use of networks, Web-based DSS and the Internet create new value for customers?" Too many "No" answers to the above questions, and proposed DSS projects will certainly fail.

In terms of technical issues, managers need to ask if the initiating company has the staff and technology in place to build the proposed interorganizational systems. Someone needs to determine what hardware and software the partners and participants will need to acquire. Technical issues can be overcome if potential problems and needs are identified early in the development process.

Finally, from a legal perspective, managers need to determine what material can be made available to external users, especially customers and suppliers, to support their decision making. And managers should ask: Do we have privacy or liability issues or copyright issues associated with the proposed DSS project?

Implementation can be especially difficult because a DSS project team needs the support of at least two sets of senior executives. Also, the team needs to address all of the above issues in terms of two or more different business and information technology cultures.

Advanced Interorganizational Systems

The most advanced interorganizational systems (IOS) use the public Internet to create communication links. The systems may involve any stakeholder with access to the Internet and authority or privileges to use specific capabilities. These advanced systems are associated with electronic commerce, DSS, and extranets. The increasing importance of easy and efficient access to information has lead many companies, especially large ones, to move toward more advanced Interorganizational systems. The increasing use of the Internet is significantly decreasing the costs of complex networks between suppliers, customers and manufacturers/retailers. The networked economy is creating electronic business communities—networks of suppliers, distributors, commerce providers, customers, and even competitors, according to the Alliance for Converging Technologies. The mission of the Alliance is to help companies collectively produce products and services by exchanging information online (see Tapscott, 1998).

Web technologies offer firms the opportunity to gather market intelligence and monitor consumer choices through customers' revealed preferences in navigational and purchasing behavior on the Web. Interorganizational DSS reduce costs to suppliers by letting them electronically access on-line databases of bid opportunities, online abilities to submit bids, and online review of awards. The Web facilitates cooperative processes and can include buyers, suppliers, and partners in redesigned business processes.

With Web-based DSS supporting value chains, the supply-chain management system and the customer support system can be integrated. Integration can provide sharing of manufacturing, inventory, and sales data. With such a system, suppliers build to order and do not stock inventory based on projections. A collaborative extranet supports relationships with key accounts. With an extranet, departmental peers in customer and supplier organizations are connected for real-time collaboration. A well-designed extranet with Web-based DSS should reduce cycle time and promote greater creativity in solving shared business problems.

Some Examples

According to John Webster (2000), PCS Health Systems, a prescription management company, issues plastic information cards to health-plan members. He notes, "When a patient fills a prescription, the pharmacist inputs patient information from the card, and PCS provides information such as eligibility, drug interactions and whether other drugs are preferred. Then the prescription can be dispensed, and PCS records the transaction and bills the health plan." Also, PCS provides analytical tools to its clients, the health plan managers, to help them understand how well their plan is performing. Clients use Web browsers to connect to the PCS network. Ron Merlino, senior vice president of technology infrastructure at PCS, said in Fall 2000 that PCS is giving more managers in client organizations access to data mining and analytical tools. A competing company, NDC Health Information Services, has a Web-enabled prescription data warehouse that it markets to pharmaceutical manufacturers.

Retailer Dayton Hudson has spent several years working to move its suppliers to EDI-based supply chains. It has standardized transactions on the delivery of Advanced Ship/Manifest documents based on Universal Product Codes (UPCs) to enable the retailer to keep track of its shipments and inventory. The retailer's EDI purchase order rollout began in January 1998, and the system currently supports 3,800 vendors with over one million UPCs cross-referenced. (Check http://www.internetwk.com) This large database provides extensive DSS possibilities similar to those in place at Wal-Mart and other retailers.

EXAMPLES OF WEB-BASED DSS DEVELOPMENT SOFTWARE

The DSS Vendor pages at DSSResources.COM include more than 75 companies that market decision support products. Many of these vendors have Web-based DSS products. The following paragraphs discuss a few vendors that have on-line examples or demonstrations of Web-based DSS development software. This information is quickly outdated so it will probably be necessary to explore the referenced sites to obtain current product information.

Arcplan, Inc. (http://www.arcplan.com) products include insight and dynaSight. The company Website claims dynaSight is the basis of a "New

Generation Corporate Information System that combines internal data sources and the Internet." It has a Java-based user interface and is able to analyze and structure the Internet dynamically, determine changes in information contents, and compress and store data in a database.

Business Objects (http://www.businessobjects.com/) has a number of Web-based decision support and business intelligence solutions. Its integrated query, reporting, and analysis tools are called WebIntelligence and BusinessObjects. WebIntelligence, Extranet edition, has "added security and audit features specific to extranets allowing organizations to share their data with their customers, partners, and suppliers."

Cognos (http://www.cognos.com/) DecisionStream is an application designed to build dimensional data marts. It integrates with Cognos Business Intelligence Web tools like Impromptu Web Query. There are two main parts to the DecisionStream architecture: a design client running on Windows or NT, and a Server Engine running on UNIX or NT.

Comshare MPC (http://www.comshare.com) is a Web-based application that provides management planning and control decision support. It has four modules for planning, budgeting, financial consolidation, and management reporting and analysis. All four modules share a common database.

Databeacon (http://www.databeacon.com) has a product called Databeacon 5.1. Written in Java, it is a cross-platform, corporate-wide tool for developing sales analysis, statistical analysis, financial analysis, inventory analysis, or data warehouse applications that needs multidimensional data analysis. This product is an excellent example of what is possible with Java applets.

Dimensional Insight has a dynamic Web-based, On-Line Analytical Processing (OLAP) tool based on Java applets. Web-enabled products include DI-WebDiver, DI-Discovery and DI-ReportDiver. With DI-ReportDiver, a user's password opens a Web page with a pop-down menu. The user selects a report that has been customized to answer his or her specific questions. The request is made to the server and the report is generated and sent back in compressed streams. Reports are generated in real-time.

Gentia (http://www.gentia.com/) markets a Web-based Enterprise Performance Management Suite based on the balanced scorecard concept and activity-based costing.

Hyperion (http://www.hyperion.com/) Web Gateway is a development platform for building Web-based analytic applications. It enables high-speed, interactive read-write access to Hyperion Essbase OLAP server across the World Wide Web. According to materials at the website, "The more than 800 licensees of Hyperion Web Gateway have built applications ranging from performance measurement to risk analysis to preparing the Federal Budget."

Hummingbird, Inc. (http://www.hummingbird.com) specializes in the development of decision-enabling Web-based work environments. Hummingbird's enterprise software solutions provide access to structured and unstructured data.

MicroStrategy (http://www.microstrategy.com) provides business intelligence technology. It's e-business decision support platform is called

MicroStrategy 7™. The primary application development capability is Web-based query and reporting.

Speedware (http://www.speedware.com) creates and markets client/server and Web solutions for application development and business intelligence systems. Speedware software products include Esperant, Speedware Autobahn.

The market for Web-based DSS development software is very competitive, highly fragmented, and rapidly changing. Vendors of packaged analytic applications include Informatica, Broadbase, e.Piphany, and Hyperion. Vendors of business intelligence software include Cognos, Business Objects, Brio, MicroStrategy, and Hummingbird. Vendors of tools for building Model-Driven Web-based applications include SAS and SPSS. Vendors of Web-based Groupware include Microsoft, Ventana and Netscape.

EXAMPLES OF WEB-BASED DSS

Many Web sites have decision support for customers or suppliers. Microsoft Carpoint at URL http://carpoint.msn.com demonstrates both data and model-driven DSS. Users can use a "Compare" feature to make pair-wise comparisons of car models across prespecified attributes.

A prototype Web-based, communications-driven DSS called TCB Works was developed by Dennis and Pootheri at the University of Georgia (cf., Dennis, Quek and Pootheri, 1996). TCBWorks is different from the typical discussion-oriented tools available on the Web. It is designed to enable people to interact, discuss issues, and make decisions. It can support both structured discussions and multicriteria decision making. When a user connects to TCBWorks a login screen requests the user's name and password. Once logged on, the user starts with a project screen. GroupSystems and other companies are developing similar Web-based GDSS.

Retirement and Investment planning is facilitated at a number of Web sites. Also, many 401K plans are supported by Web sites. Plan participants and sponsors do the work of entering data, transferring investments and researching investments. Model-driven DSS can show how an investment may grow over time; and knowledge-driven DSS provide advice. Some sites with DSS include Fidelity Investment's 401k.com, Principal Financial group at principal.com, and American Express at americanexpress.com. The Fidelity "Retirement Planning Calculator" is a model-driven DSS that helps a person decide how much to invest for retirement each month. Principal Financial has an "Investor Profile Quiz" that is a knowledge-driven DSS.

Netscape decision guides are good examples of model-driven and knowledge-driven DSS. One can find more than 25 decision guides at URL http://home.netscape.com/decisionguides. Topics of guides include choosing pets, bikes, and business schools.

Stockfinder at http://stockpoint.com has a data-driven DSS that helps investors identify stocks based on criteria like price, earnings, and type of industry. Stockpoint also has an Investment Profile knowledge-driven DSS. A user answers a short questionnaire about income constraints, personal financial goals and risk tolerance. The DSS processes the responses and provides a list of possible investments that match the person's personal goals and budget constraints. A number of investment web sites provide their users with DSS capabilities. Document-driven DSS provide company information from many sources, charting software lets users manipulate financial comparisons of large time series databases, and search and agent software that alert users to news, stock prices and changes in stock prices.

WATERSHEDSS (Water, Soil, and Hydro- Environmental Decision Support System) at URL http://h2osparc.wq.ncsu.edu/ is a model-driven DSS used to help watershed managers and land treatment personnel identify their water quality problems and select appropriate best management practices.

Finally, a cost/benefit analysis decision aid is at DSSResources.COM. It is a simple calculator built using JavaScript that structures information input and calculates some decision relevant information using a model. Figure 11.2 shows a screen shot. To try the application, JavaScript must be enabled and commas cannot be used in input fields. JavaScript decision aids at DSSResources.COM are provided for informational and instructional purposes only.

COMPANIES WITH WEB-BASED DSS

Many companies have implemented Web-based DSS. Universities are also making DSS available to stakeholders at Web sites. A number of DSS software companies provide case studies of successful Web-based DSS implementations at their Web sites. As one would expect, the vendors are reporting favorable results from Web-based DSS.

According to Arborsoft and Hyperion materials, Bell Canada implemented a Web-based DSS. In a press release, a Bell Canada spokesperson said that the cost of deploying traditional client/server OLAP software made it prohibitively expensive to enable the entire enterprise for OLAP. . . . "The Web dramatically alters the cost dynamics of delivering applications to users." He notes, "All users need are a Web browser and a laptop computer. There's almost no training required, very low client costs and zero infrastructure costs. The internet acts as a free wide area network." According to the release, "Hundreds of business, operation and sales managers will be able to compose their own interactive queries right from their Web browser rather than accessing static data reports prepared by financial analysts. They can navigate, analyze, and even update their sales forecasts without the need for proprietary client software."

In 1998, the Pharmaceutical Division of Bayer Corporation deployed a Web-based tool that allows managers at the company's 600+ cost centers to create yearly budget plans. Users access their planning information via Bayer's corporate intranet from any of the company's North American locations or its German headquarters. The planning tool was developed using arcplan's inSight interface development software with a back-end system based on an IBM RS 6000 server running Oracle® 7.4. The system also incorporates a firewall-protected intranet server, which subsequently feeds information to the Oracle server/data warehouse and then on to a Hyperion system for further reporting. The Web-based implementation was chosen due to the ease of distribution of applications over the Internet.

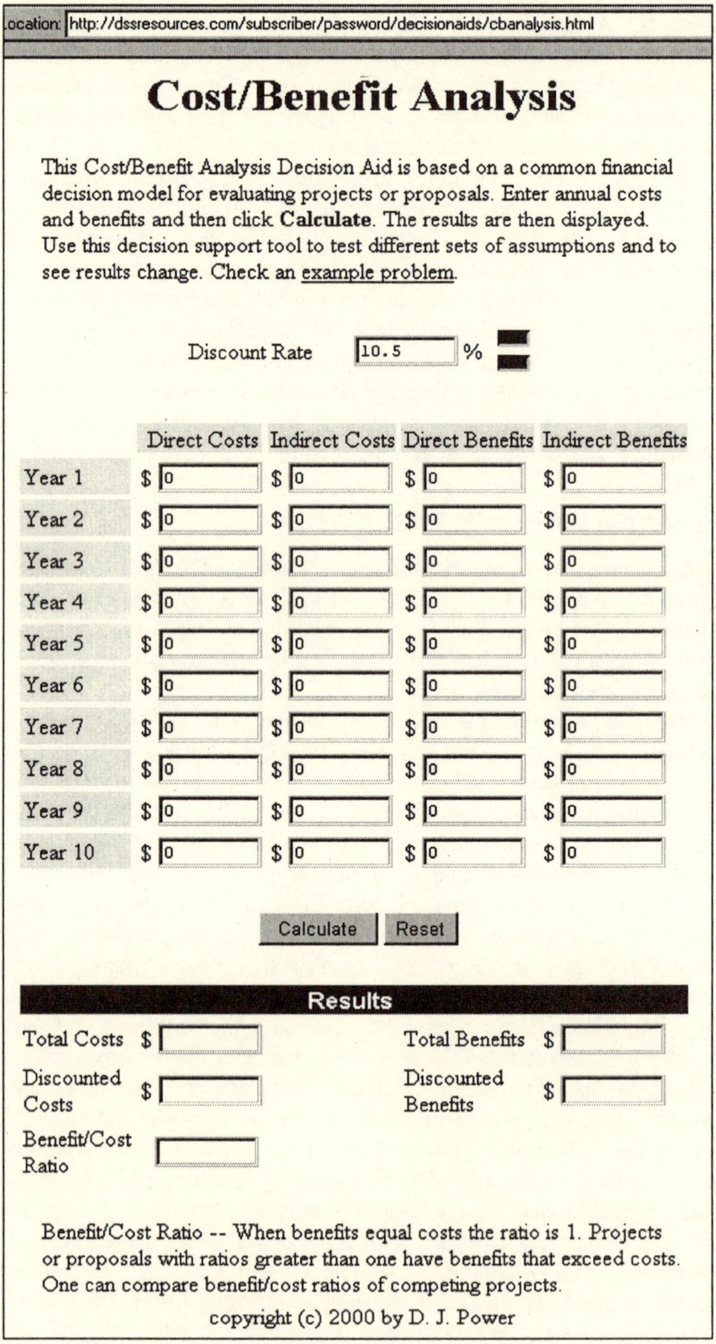
Location: http://dssresources.com/subscriber/password/decisionaids/cbanalysis.html

Cost/Benefit Analysis

This Cost/Benefit Analysis Decision Aid is based on a common financial decision model for evaluating projects or proposals. Enter annual costs and benefits and then click **Calculate**. The results are then displayed. Use this decision support tool to test different sets of assumptions and to see results change. Check an example problem.

Discount Rate 10.5 %

	Direct Costs	Indirect Costs	Direct Benefits	Indirect Benefits
Year 1	$ 0	$ 0	$ 0	$ 0
Year 2	$ 0	$ 0	$ 0	$ 0
Year 3	$ 0	$ 0	$ 0	$ 0
Year 4	$ 0	$ 0	$ 0	$ 0
Year 5	$ 0	$ 0	$ 0	$ 0
Year 6	$ 0	$ 0	$ 0	$ 0
Year 7	$ 0	$ 0	$ 0	$ 0
Year 8	$ 0	$ 0	$ 0	$ 0
Year 9	$ 0	$ 0	$ 0	$ 0
Year 10	$ 0	$ 0	$ 0	$ 0

Calculate Reset

Results

Total Costs $ Total Benefits $

Discounted Costs $ Discounted Benefits $

Benefit/Cost Ratio

Benefit/Cost Ratio -- When benefits equal costs the ratio is 1. Projects or proposals with ratios greater than one have benefits that exceed costs. One can compare benefit/cost ratios of competing projects.

copyright (c) 2000 by D. J. Power

Figure 11.2 JavaScript Decision Aid at DSSResources.COM

Deere & Co., Inc., Waterloo Works, is using Information Discovery's (http://www.datamining.com) pattern-based approach to data analysis to forecast tractor sales. Their system is Web-browser-based, and it allows users to access historical data. Business users can access information on the corporate intranet. A case study at the Information Discovery Website, Datamining.com, claims the application has lowered Deere's inventory and marketing costs and allowed Deere to better plan sales.

In January 1998, Information Advantage announced that EDS had chosen DecisionSuite and WebOLAP(tm) to support implementation of the EDS knowledge management strategy. "EDS is rolling out DecisionSuite to several hundred users performing on-line analyses on a 50 GB database. 1998 deployment could scale up to 9000 knowledge worker desktops." Larry Ford, president and CEO of Information Advantage said in the press release, "The Web enables multinational organizations, like EDS, to provide applications that deliver content to the end-user without the traditional, costly barriers of installation, training and maintenance."

Hannaford Brothers grocery chain developed a DSS using Microstrategy's DSS Web. At Hannaford, DSS Web provides store managers with access to the same data warehouse application relied upon by corporate decision makers. Utilizing DSS Web, managers receive detailed sales, cost, inventory, and budget reports and use this information to make decisions at the store level.

According to a MicroStrategy case study, Société Générale USA chose a multi-tier architecture that enabled the support of both client server and Web computing. MicroStrategy software enabled Société Générale USA to provide support for executive and power users, running on either PCs or UNIX workstations and using a Web browser interface.

Many other cases are available at Vendor Websites and at DSSResources.COM. For example, at DSSResources.COM, decision support applications at the following companies are summarized: ShopKo, BMW, Pfizer, Shell International and Maytag International.

ADVANTAGES AND DISADVANTAGES OF WEB-BASED DSS

Web-based DSS have reduced technological barriers and made it easier and less costly to make decision-relevant information available to managers and staff users in geographically distributed locations. Because of the World Wide Web infrastructure, enterprise-wide DSS can now be implemented at a relatively low cost in geographically dispersed companies to dispersed stakeholders, including suppliers and customers. Using Web-based DSS, organizations can provide DSS capability to managers over an intranet, to customers and suppliers over an extranet, or to any stakeholder over the global Internet.

The Web has increased access to DSS, and it should increase the use of a well-designed DSS in a company. Using a Web infrastructure for building DSS improves the rapid dissemination of "best practices" analysis and decision-making frameworks, and it should promote more consistent decision making on repetitive decision tasks across a geographically distributed organization. The Web also provides a way to manage a company's knowledge repository and to

Web also provides a way to manage a company's knowledge repository and to bring knowledge resources into the decision-making process. One can hope that Web-based delivery of DSS capabilities will promote and encourage ongoing improvements in decision making processes.

Also, the Web can reduce some of the problems associated with the competing "thick client" enterprise-wide DSS architecture where special software needs to be installed on a manager's computer. It becomes much easier to add new users and initial training needs are often minimal. Web-based DSS reduce costs of operations, administration, support and maintenance as well as end user training costs. Web-based DSS also facilitate centralized management and maintenance of information technology resources.

With many Web-based, data-driven DSS products, managers with a browser have the same type of ad hoc reporting and interactive data analysis capability as that provided by "thick client" tools. Web technology is and will continue to change the way organizations deliver all types of documents and data.

What are the potential problems with Web-based DSS? First, user expectations may be unrealistic; especially in terms of how much information they want to be able to access from the Web. Second, there may be technical implementation problems, especially in terms of peak demand and load problems. Third, it is costly to train decision support content providers and to provide them with the necessary tools and technical assistance. Fourth, the continuing "browser wars" between Microsoft and Netscape that make some applications unreadable on one or the other browser are also a potential problem. Fifth, Web-based DSS create additional security concerns. Finally, using the Web for decision support may result in the accumulation of obsolete materials, especially management reports and documents or alternatively require hiring someone to monitor the currency of decision information.

CONCLUSIONS AND COMMENTARY

The World Wide Web has created a major opportunity to deliver more quantitative and qualitative information to decision makers. Web architectures and networks permit Information Systems professionals to centralize and control information and yet easily distribute it in a timely manner to managers who need it. Also, intranets are providing many opportunities for securely delivering information from data warehouses and external databases to a manager's desktop in a format that permits and encourages frequent use and follow-on analysis.

The Web has not resolved all problems associated with building, developing and delivering enterprise-wide DSS, and many questions about Web-based DSS remain controversial. The following questions are still being debated, but at this point the associated responses seem like reasonable answers. Can a Web-based DSS provide a company with a competitive advantage? *Sometimes*, especially in knowledge-oriented businesses. Does a Web-based DSS have significant cost advantages compared to other competing DSS technologies? *Usually*, especially in large-scale implementations where companies have multiple, geographically dispersed sites. Sometimes it is more cost advantageous to Web-enable a legacy

DSS for Internet access. Will a Web-based DSS speed application deployment and increase access to both structured and unstructured data? *Yes*, in most situations.

Will a Web-based DSS improve decision making? *Perhaps;* the optimists think so. Will Web-based DSS provide a broader knowledge base for decision making? *Yes,* in most cases, once the "knowledge" is on-line. Does Web access increase the value of a data warehouse? *Yes,* if the data is meaningfully displayed and drill-down is available to decision makers.

Does a Web-based DSS provide timely, user-friendly, and secure distribution of business information? *Yes,* if a good development product is selected and if the implementation is successful. Can a Web-based Decision Support System be managed and maintained? *Yes;* the tools for managing the Web server and Web content are maturing. Will information on a Company Web site expand in an uncontrolled manner? *No*, assuming a person manages the knowledge base. Will managers be able to locate what they need when they need it? *Probably;* staff need to organize information in meaningful ways, and search engines need to be available for unexpected information queries.

Does a Web-based DSS help mobile managers, sales staff, and customer support staff? *Yes*; information access and analysis is much easier and more widely available. Does a Web-based, interorganizational DSS help customers and suppliers? *Yes;* customers and suppliers can make better choices. Are Web-based agents and alerts useful and practical? *Yes,* if one understands what agents are and how to use them. An alert or agent can help a busy manager stay informed about more key performance indicators.

The Web makes it possible to deploy a global enterprise-wide DSS. Will Web-based DSS facilitate corporate growth? Improve productivity? Improve profitability? *Yes;* appropriately designed DSS can impact the corporate bottom-line.

Along with the Web-based opportunities for building innovative DSS come new challenges. Managers must choose which Web technologies to use and decide how to deploy these new technologies. Also, managers must learn how to use Web and Internet technologies to really gain a competitive advantage. This means that to implement Web-based and interorganizational DSS, it is essential to develop appropriate strategies and organizational structures, redesign business processes, integrate the technologies and associated information into decision-making processes, evaluate costs and benefits, and manage new types of business relationships.

The Web is the platform of choice and the new frontier for innovative DSS. All of the Web DSS development environments have strengths and weaknesses, but the capabilities are increasing rapidly, and the Web DSS user interfaces are impressive compared to those of only a few years ago. DSS built using Web technologies will take on a new importance as accessible and useful tools for improving business decisions (cf., Power, 2000).

Chapter 12

Evaluating Decision Support System Projects

INTRODUCTION

Information technologies support a more global society, and many companies now compete in markets all around the world. To compete effectively, companies must integrate transaction processing and decision support systems. New systems are needed to support managers working in this new market environment. Telecommunications, shared databases, groupware, and data-driven and model-driven DSS must be integrated and coordinated. Many barriers, including language, differing regulations, and technology issues, must be overcome to make global transaction processing and decision support integration a reality. Integration in a company will not likely occur as part of one large-scale project; rather, it will most likely occur incrementally through the implementation of many smaller projects.

Most observers agree that new technologies have created many opportunities to implement innovative Decision Support Systems. This is the good news. The bad news is that many projects will not meet expectations, and some will be spectacular failures. To increase the success rate, it is essential to carefully evaluate proposed DSS projects.

Many managers and MIS professionals are involved in evaluating proposed DSS projects. The technical managers who need to focus on evaluating DSS projects include the chief information officer, corporate Information Technology (IT) professionals, database administrators, and network administrators. The business managers who evaluate innovative DSS projects include senior managers, strategic planners, business development managers, competitive intelligence analysts, and market researchers.

During a project proposal evaluation, one must be skeptical and must ask probing questions. Also, it is important to understand and use evaluation tools and techniques. For a DSS project, it is very important to examine technological risks. But, organizational culture and international issues may be equally important when evaluating some DSS projects.

Common evaluation questions include: What is the return on investment for the proposed DSS project? What is the payback period? What is the opportunity cost? What are the anticipated benefits? What can be done with the proposed system that cannot be done with the current information systems? Do competitors have a data warehouse or On-Line Analytical Processing (OLAP) or an Executive Information Service (EIS)? Managers should ask these questions about a proposed or even an in-process DSS project, but it may be difficult to provide satisfactory answers. Almost everyone agrees that evaluating and justifying a DSS project can be difficult and challenging.

This chapter focuses on the process of evaluating proposed DSS projects, especially Web-based projects; evaluation tools; evaluation criteria; international DSS issues, ethics and privacy issues, and finally, conclusions about evaluating DSS projects.

DSS PROJECT EVALUATION PROCESS

Managers evaluate many types of projects, but those involving information technologies are often considered challenging. Evaluating DSS projects is especially difficult and yet it must be an ongoing process for large-scale DSS projects. Evaluation activities should be commensurate or proportionate to the scope, complexity, and cost of a proposed DSS project. Project scope refers to the number of potential users, the size of the project staff, the potential impacts on existing systems, and the amount of programming or development effort that will be required. Also, project sponsors and project managers must decide what amount and type of evaluation is appropriate and necessary in their company's IT management environment. A very bureaucratic or political environment may necessitate additional evaluation activities.

A discussion of the process of evaluating DSS projects generates many questions. For example, when should DSS projects be evaluated? Should in-house capabilities be examined? When does vendor evaluation occur? What is the role of the project team in DSS project evaluation? Who should do the evaluation? Is a feasibility analysis always needed? How many "go-no go" opportunities do managers have? Most managers can add to this list. The next few paragraphs offer some suggestions about commonly asked questions.

Figure 12.1 portrays the evaluation process as a multi-stage cycle of development and evaluation. The scale of the project and the development approach determines what activities will actually occur and in what sequence. Evaluation should be performed periodically from the initial idea stage to the final post-implementation project evaluation. A DSS project can be revised or even canceled at any stage. The resources that have been expended on a project are "sunk" costs. One should not continue a bad project solely because money and resources have already been expended on it. Managers need to know when to cut their losses and divert funds to more feasible projects. Managers also need to know when, despite setbacks or unanticipated costs, that it is desirable to continue an important project.

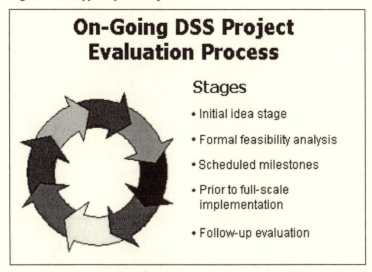

On-Going DSS Project Evaluation Process

Stages

• Initial idea stage

• Formal feasibility analysis

• Scheduled milestones

• Prior to full-scale implementation

• Follow-up evaluation

Figure 12.1   On-Going DSS Project Evaluation Process

First, there are several possible times and ways to evaluate a DSS project. At different times in the development of a DSS, a different type of evaluation may be needed. An initial DSS idea often needs nurturing. So at the initial idea stage, it is often appropriate to have a positive, developmental evaluation. At some point in the design stage for a DSS project, a feasibility study needs to be completed. Even small-scale end user-built DSS projects need to be evaluated. Often a feasibility study actually improves the understanding of a proposed DSS. The extent of the feasibility study should be a function of the size or scope and type of proposed DSS. A feasibility study for a Web-based, data-driven DSS should be much more extensive than a study for a small-scale model-driven DSS on a single personal computer.

Managers should conduct some type of evaluation of a large-scale DSS project at each step in the systems development life cycle or after each major change in a prototype. Prior to implementation, an enterprise-wide or interorganizational DSS must be carefully evaluated. Managers should not hesitate to delay implementation if problems are encountered. A DSS project will fail dramatically if problems are encountered doing the initial roll-out for the DSS. A DSS is usually best introduced in stages. The initial user group is critical to the overall long-term success of the project. After implementation, DSS should be regularly reviewed and evaluated. Technologies and user needs change, and a process should be in place to ensure that an obsolete DSS is not hurting decision making rather than enhancing it.

In-house capabilities should always be examined when evaluating DSS projects. In general, DSS projects should be implemented by in-house Information Systems (IS) staff. Innovative DSS projects enhance expertise of company IS/IT employees and involve staff in improving business decision making. DSS applications should be treated as important business capabilities and not as candidates for outsourcing.

Since DSS are built using software development tools, vendor evaluation will be part of many innovative and large-scale DSS. When does vendor evaluation occur? Usually vendors are selected once a feasibility analysis is completed. Vendor capabilities and software should be considered in a feasibility study.

The DSS project team should have the major role in evaluating a proposed DSS project. The team should do the feasibility study and should evaluate the project regularly. A feasibility study is needed, but it may be very limited in the topics addressed (see Chapter 4). Canceling a project is always difficult, but managers can avoid this by actively managing DSS projects and by carefully evaluating the feasibility of proposed projects.

Large-scale DSS projects can be expensive. A data warehouse project can cost from $1 to $2 million and take from 1 to 3 years to complete. Business benefits can, however, be extensive. An International Data Corporation study (1996) of 62 firms found an average 3-year return on investment (ROI) of 401 percent, and the payback period can be very short.

A DSS can be a strategic system for a company; and project evaluation helps increase the chances of success and cost-effective implementation. Every DSS project has the same broad goal of providing some managers with the right information, in the right format, at the right time and at the right cost. So let's examine some tools that can help in the evaluation of this goal for a proposed DSS project.

EVALUATION TOOLS AND TECHNIQUES

For many years, business professors have been discussing the issues surrounding financial evaluation of capital expenditure projects. The argument continues. Typical evaluation tools recommended are ROI, Net Present Value (NPV), and discounted cash flow. These tools are closely tied to the capital budgeting process and are intended to provide a rational allocation of capital. This is a laudable goal.

Because managers are asked to spend funds on a DSS project, anticipated results and benefits should be quantified so that the requested expenditure can be evaluated in comparable units. But it is difficult to quantify the results and benefits of a DSS Project. DSS analysts are basically making estimates and guesses. A financial analysis is especially difficult because the costs are uncertain and many of the benefits are qualitative and intangible.

A number of alternative tools are available for evaluating DSS projects. Incremental value analysis is an evaluation of "soft" benefits, such as improving staff productivity, improving the speed of strategic actions, enhancing a company's competitive advantage, or improving access to data. Another alternative, the scoring approach, considers intangible benefits and other considerations that are not considered credible by analysts who only focus on financial criteria. A third alternative, the qualitative benefits scenario approach, attempts to estimate what decision making will be like when a proposed DSS is in place and hence speculates on how the company will benefit. All of these qualitative approaches have pluses and minuses, but each can be improved by understanding the up-side and down-side of a DSS project. Table 12.1 lists six different evaluation tools and techniques.

Evaluation Tools and Techniques
1. Cost-Benefit Analysis
2. Cost-Effectiveness Analysis
3. Incremental Value Analysis
4. Qualitative Benefits Scenario Approach
5. Research and Development Options Approach
6. Scoring Approach

Table 12.1   Summary of Evaluation Tools and Techniques

When choosing an evaluation method, many questions should be considered, including: Which tools work best? What technique should be used for this specific DSS project? Should different techniques be used for a data-driven than a model-driven DSS project? Does the cost of the project (amount of dollars to be spent) influence the best technique to be used?   The   next   few paragraphs assist in answering these questions and provide more details on the evaluation tools.

Cost-Benefit Analysis

The primary benefit of a DSS should be improved decisions. This intangible benefit presumes that managers will change their decision processes and actually use a new DSS. In a Sentry Market survey, 30 percent of respondents identified "access to data" as the biggest benefit of a data warehouse. Other important benefits of DSS and data warehouses include: improved data accuracy; better control of data; better data consistency; decentralization of data; cost savings; and less reliance on legacy systems. Few managers think that data warehouses will result in cost savings.

Typical measures in cost-benefit analysis (CBA) are ROI, NPV, and discounted cash flow. CBA is grounded in finance and accounting and closely tied to the budget process. This analysis addresses the allocation of capital and provides the appearance of accuracy and precision. CBA is useful for evaluating cost-savings projects and automation of current processes. CBA is difficult to use for decision support, infrastructure, and strategic projects. For example, cost models for data warehouses are not available. Benefits are tough to measure. Benefits are not quantifiable or easily converted to dollars.

Examples of DSS cost factors include direct hardware and software costs, project personnel costs, support services (vendors or consultants), process change costs (people, material), and incremental infrastructure costs. Examples of DSS benefit factors include improved access to data, improved accuracy and consistency of data used in decision making, faster access to decision support, and cost savings from process improvements.

Both tangible and intangible costs and benefits can be identified. A cost or benefit is tangible if the consequences can be quantified. Intangible costs and benefits are difficult, and sometimes impossible to quantify. Intangible results need to be considered in an evaluation, but too many intangibles limit the validity of a CBA.

CBA is a systematic, quantitative method for assessing the life cycle costs and benefits of competing alternatives. It involves explicitly stating assumptions, disregarding sunk costs and prior results, estimating direct and indirect costs and benefits, discounting costs and benefits, and performing sensitivity analysis. Discounting involves calculating how much a dollar of costs or benefits is worth today, even though it will be realized in the future. Discounting calculates the time value of money.

A CBA commonly follows six steps:

1.   Define alternatives for the proposed project.
2.   Collect cost and benefit data.
3.   Document assumptions.
4.   Estimate costs and benefits (direct, indirect, tangible, intangible).
5.   Establish measurement criteria (especially for benefits).
6.   Evaluate all alternatives using NPV, benefit/cost ratio or payback.

The DSS Project Evaluator Decision Aid (see Figure 12.2), available at DSSResources.COM, may be useful in determining whether or not to implement a DSS. The program uses the annual operating cost, development cost, benefits, the number of users, and the discount rate to determine the long-term return, payback, benefit/cost ratio, and several other values important to consider when developing a DSS. The cost per user ratio is useful for determining how expensive the DSS is per person using the DSS. The benefit/cost ratio can be used to determine whether the total discounted benefits of the project are greater than the total discounted costs. Discounted means that they are adjusted for a fixed rate of inflation, the discount rate. If it is less than one, the total benefits are less than the total costs. The payback tells how many years it will take until overall benefits exceed overall costs. The LT (Long Term) return is the overall value of the DSS, excluding costs to develop the DSS.

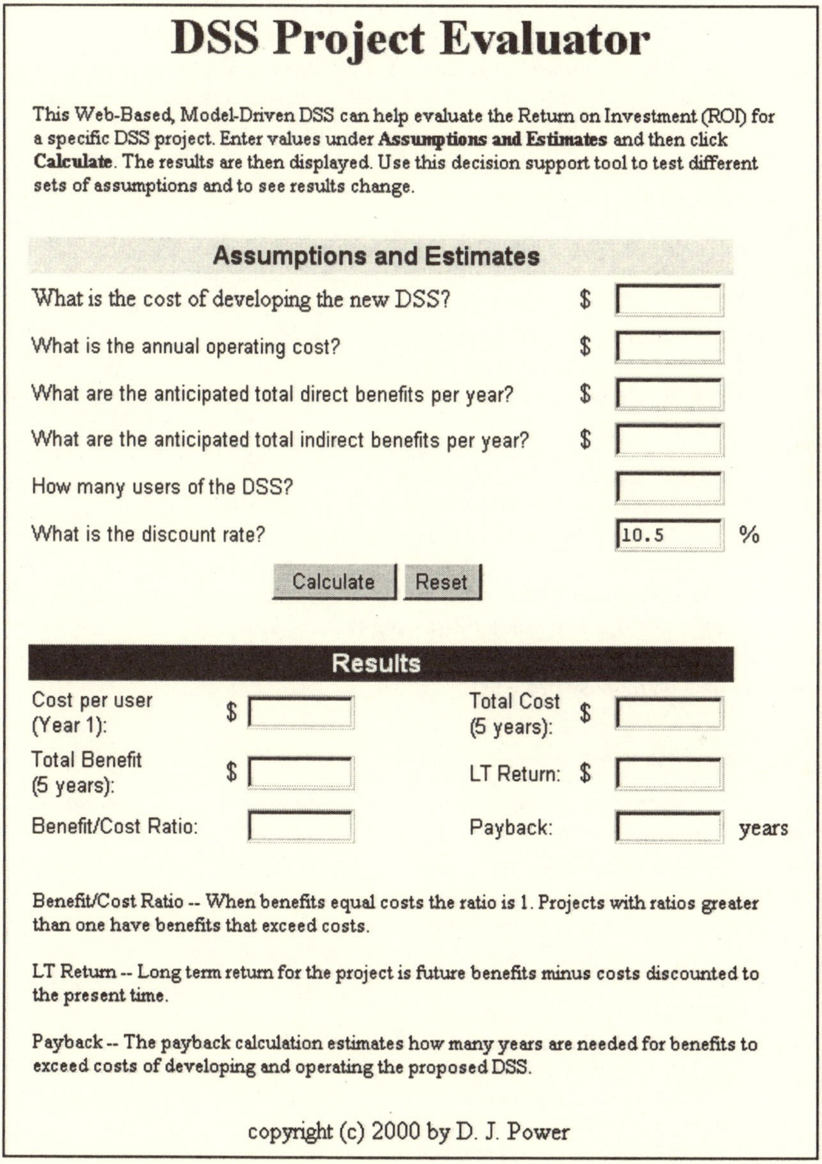

DSS Project Evaluator

This Web-Based, Model-Driven DSS can help evaluate the Return on Investment (ROI) for a specific DSS project. Enter values under **Assumptions and Estimates** and then click **Calculate**. The results are then displayed. Use this decision support tool to test different sets of assumptions and to see results change.

Assumptions and Estimates

What is the cost of developing the new DSS? $ [   ]

What is the annual operating cost? $ [   ]

What are the anticipated total direct benefits per year? $ [   ]

What are the anticipated total indirect benefits per year? $ [   ]

How many users of the DSS?   [   ]

What is the discount rate?   [10.5   ] %

[Calculate] [Reset]

Results

Cost per user (Year 1):	$ [ ]	Total Cost (5 years):	$ [ ]
Total Benefit (5 years):	$ [ ]	LT Return:	$ [ ]
Benefit/Cost Ratio:	[ ]	Payback:	[ ] years

Benefit/Cost Ratio -- When benefits equal costs the ratio is 1. Projects with ratios greater than one have benefits that exceed costs.

LT Return -- Long term return for the project is future benefits minus costs discounted to the present time.

Payback -- The payback calculation estimates how many years are needed for benefits to exceed costs of developing and operating the proposed DSS.

copyright (c) 2000 by D. J. Power

Figure 12.2   DSS Project Evaluator Decision Aid

Cost-Effectiveness Analysis

A cost-effectiveness analysis is a simplified CBA where one assumes that all of the alternatives have either the same benefits or the same costs. The analysis is simplified because only benefits or costs need to be calculated, not both. In this analysis, the best alternative is the one with the greatest benefits or the lowest cost. This type of analysis is sometimes more feasible when costs or benefits are hard, or would be expensive to measure.

Incremental Value Analysis

Peter Keen (1981) proposed a tool that is appropriate with rapid prototyping. This tool examines alternatives, stimulates new ideas, and asks, "what if?" The process is based on value, rather than emphasizing costs. The incremental value analysis process involves five steps:

1. Establish the operational list of benefits that the DSS must achieve to be acceptable.
2. Establish the maximum cost that one is willing to pay to achieve the benefits.
3. Build and assess prototype Version 0.
4. Establish cost and determine benefit threshold for Version 1.
5. Build Version 1; monitor benefits and costs and evolve to Version N.

The main advantages of the value analysis approach are that it is simple and easy to understand. The method attempts to reduce risk by requiring prototyping. Prototyping or staging can be very difficult for some DSS projects, especially data warehouse projects.

Qualitative Benefits Scenario Approach

Paul Schoemaker (1995), in "Scenario Planning: A Tool for Strategic Thinking," discusses a qualitative tool for evaluating information systems projects. This analysis tool helps executives imagine possible futures. Scenario planning is not "day dreaming," but rather, a rigorous process for assessing and preparing for the future. It helps executives estimate what decision making may be like when a proposed DSS is implemented. The steps include:

1. Identifying basic trends and uncertainties.
2. Constructing scenario themes.
3. Conducting quantitative research.
4. Developing decision scenarios.
5. Envisioning the DSS Project implemented.
6. Describing the use of the proposed DSS.
7. Discussing benefits that result from the new DSS.
8. Checking the scenario for consistency and plausibility.
9. Discussing risks and uncertainties.
10. Estimating the upper and lower bounds on costs and the development schedule.

A quantitative CBA is part of the qualitative benefits scenario approach, but the evaluation decision does not narrowly focus on only costs and benefits.

Research and Development Options Approach

In an article, "Uncovering the Hidden Value in High Risk Investments," David Sharp (1991) proposes a more complex "options" approach.

Options are valuable; they provide the ability to take advantage of certain opportunities at a later time. In real estate terminology, an option is a right purchased for a fee to buy or sell property within a specified time and at a specified price. The value of an option may actually increase with uncertainty and project duration. Options analysis should consider expenditures for both incremental DSS development and maintaining flexibility to build a future DSS. The research and development options approach has three steps:

1. Identify the options embedded in a given investment. What is done now incrementally to create future DSS opportunities?
2. Evaluate the environment and circumstances in which each might be exercised. Under what circumstances should more be invested in the proposed DSS?
3. Evaluate whether the total value of the options outweighs any shortfall in cash flow value from the expenditures; "How much would we be willing to pay now for this future flexibility and opportunity?"

This approach can be difficult to explain to managers and MIS staff. The key issue is expanding DSS opportunities. This method evaluates the proposed DSS as a research and development effort rather than as a capital investment.

Scoring Approach

Parker, Trainor, and Benson (1989) describe a method for evaluating IS projects called information economics that can be considered more generally as a decision analysis scoring approach. It considers intangible benefits and other considerations that are not considered credible by analysts who only focus on financial criteria. This approach uses the firm's business and IS strategic plans as part of an IS project evaluation. The process involves weighting factors to reflect how well the project satisfies a given factor. Points are assigned to each impact criterion. The scores are summarized; projects are ranked.

The process involves selecting a rating system to make numerical comparisons. Multiple raters evaluate each alternative on benefit and cost factors. Raters also weight the benefit and cost factors in terms of importance. Finally, an analyst calculates a weighted score for each alternative. Business justification of economic impact involves assessing strategic alignment, competitive advantage, management information support, competitive response to the project, and strategic or organizational risk. Technical viability involves examining the strategic systems architecture, technical uncertainty, and system infrastructure risk. A multi-factor evaluator decision aid is available at DSSResources.COM.

DSS PROJECT EVALUATION CRITERIA AND RISK FACTORS

Whitten, Bentley, and Barlow (1994) define four evaluation "tests" for IS projects:

Economic Test — a measure of the cost-effectiveness of a project or solution. This is often called a cost-benefit analysis. This test was discussed extensively in the prior section.

Operational Test — a measure of how well the solution of problems or a specific solution will work in the organization. It is also a measure of how people feel about the DSS proposal.

Schedule Test — a measure of the reasonableness of the project timetable. Can deadlines be met? Are milestones appropriate?

Technical Test — a measure of the practicality of a specific technical solution and the availability of technical resources and expertise. In some DSS proposals technical issues are the major risk concern.

Which of the criteria should be the focus at various project evaluation stages? The initial evaluation should focus on the project need and the anticipated benefits. The focus should be on the operational test. As the project evaluation continues, more feasibility issues need to be evaluated, and the benefits need to be assessed more carefully to insure that project advocates are not inflating benefits and minimizing problems. The economic test may be revisited a number of times, but it should be a major part of a feasibility analysis.

As noted in Chapter 2, DSS projects have various levels of risk associated with them. When DSS projects have ambiguous objectives and low structure, the projects have higher levels of risk because the costs and scope of work of the project are hard to define. The schedule and technical tests are very important for such high-risk projects. Also, because the objectives of the project are ambiguous, it can be difficult to assess the return on the investment. When returns are hard to assess, more qualitative economic analyses are used.

DSS projects with a higher degree of structure and more clearly defined objectives generally are lower risk. More detailed planning is possible for projects with specific objectives. The size or scope of a DSS project in terms of the number of users served and the size of databases developed also has an impact on the risk of the assessed projects. Small DSS projects in terms of scope or cost tend to be of lower risk than large projects. Finally, the sophistication of the technology and the experience of the developers using the technology influence the overall project risk. The ultimate decision to invest in a DSS project should not be based solely on project risk. As noted in the discussion of gaining competitive advantage with innovative DSS projects, the project that is most likely to result in a competitive advantage is sometimes the riskiest project.

In general, evaluation activities and the application of the economic, operational, schedule and technical tests should be proportionate to the size/scope, complexity, and cost of a proposed DSS project. In narrow-scope DSS projects that impact few users and are highly structured, the amount of analysis and evaluation should often be limited, but as the project size and scope increases and the project becomes less structured, project risk increases, and, hence, more frequent and more elaborate evaluation is needed. For large scope, low structure DSS projects, multiple detailed evaluations are probably needed and justified.

In all project evaluations, one needs to consider the longer term affects of short-term decisions that have been based solely upon short-horizon cost savings. DSS may reduce some costs, but that is not usually the motivating factor for a new system. No DSS project decision should be made in isolation. Even small projects can sometimes have million dollar impacts. It is important to broadly examine DSS project impacts. Once a DSS project is completed, managers need to follow up and periodically evaluate what is working well with the system and why, as well as assess problems that are being encountered.

INTERNATIONAL AND CULTURAL ISSUES

As companies expand into the global marketplace, DSS must assist managers of users from many nations. There are many issues and obstacles that need to be evaluated in considering such projects. Some of the obstacles to using technology to support decision making in global corporations include: accounting and currency issues, different regulations and import/export restrictions, lack of spontaneous or informal communication among individuals when using communications-driven DSS, the impersonality of electronic communications, cultural differences including languages and different work-hours, a multiplicity of technology standards, the possible lack of a telecommunications infrastructure, different interpretations of screen displays and terminology, and time zone differences. It may also be difficult to build trust and commitment among individuals who are primarily using electronic communications. The following section explores these issues in more detail.

Accounting and Currency Issues

Accounting and other business practices differ from country to country. This difference in standards makes getting accurate financial reports difficult. Currency conversion and fluctuations are another source of challenge in designing some DSS.

Culture

The purpose of a DSS is to inform decision makers, and ignoring cultural issues may create misinformation or misinterpretation. For example, not all cultures have the same assumptions about group decision making and hence the use of a Group DSS may be more effective in some settings than others. In some cultures, the norm is that all should have an equal voice in decision making. Some cultures encourage an open and collaborative problem-solving atmosphere. Some cultural norms support detailed meeting notes and a very structured decision-making process. The project team needs to consider such cultural issues.

Impersonality of Electronic Communication

In a global corporation, managers use information and communication technologies to overcome time and distance barriers. In the future, there will be fewer "real" face-to-face meetings and probably more interactive video face-to-face meetings. Bulletin boards will proliferate and email will be the dominant form of electronic communication. This change may isolate managers in different parts of a company. To keep from getting out of touch, managers need to work harder to communicate feelings and develop trust relationships. Communications-driven DSS should probably include pictures of participants and background materials.

Lack of Spontaneous or Informal Communication

When using a communications-driven DSS in a global corporation, much of the information sharing will probably involve e-mail, bulletin boards and other non-real-time methods of communication. Also, most of the communication will be written, and not face-to-face. This behavioral change means that there will be less spontaneous and informal communication in the company. This possibility and its consequences must be anticipated.

Language

English is the unofficial language of business and technology. The problem with accepting this conclusion about language usage when constructing a specific DSS is that it may create a communication barrier between managers. Knowledge of English varies widely, and American and British business English differs in terminology. Some countries, such as China, require that a certain percent of business documents be written in the native language. France requires that all public documents be written in French. DSS may need to be available in multiple languages, and definitions of key terms should be provided.

Regulations and Import/Export Restrictions

Some laws and regulations insist that a certain percentage of data collected in a country must be processed there. Also, some countries have data import/export restrictions. This makes it harder to aggregate all data assembled throughout the world. These restrictions can have a major impact on the design of data-driven DSS.

Screen Displays

Culture affects evaluations of DSS screen layout and design. Language can cause confusion in screen displays. Also, colors and icons may have different emotional and political meanings in different countries. For example, a red, octagonal sign is not universally interpreted to mean "stop."

Telecommunications Infrastructure

Telecommunications access, reliability, and standards differ from country to country. In many countries, the government owns or controls the communication industry and it may be difficult to install communication lines. Costs are also a factor. Costs for telecommunications in Europe may be 10 to 12 times more than in the United States. Some possible solutions to this are Virtual Private Networks and satellite systems. Technological infrastructure in different countries varies and constrains DSS implementation.

Time Zone Differences

There are 25 different time zones throughout the world. This makes it harder for companies to have real-time meetings and to have standard working hours for all of their employees. A dispersion of managers also means DSS need to be available at all times. Overcoming time zone impacts on decision making is difficult. In some ways, global managers need to never sleep, or at least function on short naps most of the time. Communications-driven DSS may reduce some of these impacts, but it cannot completely remove the problems.

One possible solution to many of the above issues is Information Systems Internationalization. Internationalization is the process of planning and implementing IS products and services so that they can easily be adapted to specific local languages and cultures. The internationalization process is sometimes called translation or localization. Localizing a DSS can include: allowing space in user interfaces for translation of text into languages that require more characters; developing DSS with products like Web editors or authoring tools that can support international character sets (Unicode); creating graphic images so that text labels can be translated inexpensively; creating flexible user interface designs; and using examples in help systems and software documentation that have a universal or global meaning. At a minimum, the above issues must be addressed in the evaluation of a proposed DSS that will have a global reach.

ETHICS AND PRIVACY ISSUES

Projects can fail for many reasons. A systematic evaluation process, and the appropriate use of evaluation tools can reduce project failures. One set of issues that can create problems is easy to minimize or overlook. These issues relate to the ethics of using a specific DSS or privacy issues raised by using specific data in a DSS. Both managers and MIS professionals need to be sensitive to ethics and privacy issues.

One might think that a DSS is ethically neutral and that project proposals shouldn't raise any moral or value issues. This view ignores the important role that principles and values play in making decisions. When model-driven or knowledge-driven DSS are constructed, developers make assumptions that can have ethical impacts on choices. For example, establishing a criterion or weight in a model may exclude inappropriately certain alternatives. Also, some decisions are considered so value-laden that many people would be uncomfortable with developing a DSS to assist a decision maker. For example, a decision to commit suicide or have an abortion would involve serious moral or ethical issues. One cannot specify all of the ethical issues that might be relevant to a specific DSS proposal, but once a proposal reaches the feasibility stage, the project sponsor needs to specifically address the ethical issues associated with the project.

Privacy concerns are also easy to ignore during the evaluation of a DSS proposal. In many societies people expect that certain personal and behavioral information about them will be kept private. For example, in the United States, many people assume that religious donations and hospital records will be kept private. This information belongs to the person and doesn't belong to a company, the public, or the government. Managers need to insure that data used in DSS does not infringe on the privacy rights of individuals. The exact extent of privacy rights for employees, customers, and other data providers is not always clearly defined. In general, unless there is a clearly compelling reason to risk violating an individual's privacy, the "fence" to protect privacy of data should be higher and larger than minimum requirements.

CONCLUSIONS AND COMMENTARY

The World Wide Web has created a major opportunity to deliver more quantitative and qualitative information to decision makers. To exploit these opportunities and successfully implement innovative DSS, managers need to redesign business processes, integrate information technologies and associated information into decision-making processes, evaluate costs and benefits, and manage new types of business relationships. DSS projects must be evaluated in this broad context of corporate "readiness" (see Appendix II).

Learning enough to understand and evaluate an innovative DSS project is expensive. Managers and IS/IT staff need to do more than read a book. IS/IT staff should actually work with development tools prior to beginning a development project. The MIS unit may want to hire a consultant; staff should attend seminars, training sessions, and talk to vendors. The process of learning about innovative DSS opportunities will be time consuming and costly. Companies may need to spend a few hundred thousand dollars on a prototype or a departmental data mart. In firms with multi-million dollar IS/IT budgets, DSS prototype and data mart projects are needed and they should be viewed as "a learning experience". General managers need to spend enough money on DSS projects so that IS/IT managers and business managers can learn about the different types of DSS and can evaluate the costs and benefits and decide what is the most appropriate direction for their company (cf., Power, 1998).

In general, a detailed qualitative analysis of a proposed DSS at its initiation stage is the most that managers can reasonably expect. Although in some situations financial analysis tools can be useful, their use in evaluating a major DSS project provides only the appearance of accuracy and precision. When making a DSS project decision, managers should generally ask, "What are the expected results and benefits?" rather than "What is the anticipated ROI?"

Justifying DSS projects with ROI and NPV calculations is possible, but such an analysis does not accurately reflect the value of most DSS (cf., Baatz, 1996). Costs and benefits of DSS have an impact on many parts of an organization. In many ways the real benefits are created more by changes in the organization, than by the DSS itself. Managers should not necessarily demand a positive ROI from a Decision Support System project, but they *must* demand positive results. Today, investigating innovative DSS projects is a business necessity. DSS can create competitive advantage and improve the operation and management of a company. Building DSS is an investment in improving the performance of a company, and such projects are excellent employee and corporate development experiences.

Appendix I: Decision Support Readiness Audit

The following questions can help assess a company's readiness and sophistication in developing, evaluating and using Decision Support Systems (DSS). The questions should be answered "Yes" or "No," but each response should be evaluated individually to identify deficiencies or opportunities to improve a company's capabilities. Where each "Yes" answer counts for one point, a score greater than 32 indicates a very positive company environment for developing innovative DSS.

1. Does your firm actively manage decision-relevant information?

Yes ☐ No ☐

2. Has your firm implemented any computerized systems to support decision making?

Yes ☐ No ☐

3. Does your firm have any Strategic Information Systems?

Yes ☐ No ☐

4. Is Information System and Information Technology (IS/IT) planning and strategy focused on strategic questions?

Yes ☐ No ☐

5. Are business processes designed to support use of Information Technology?

Yes ☐   No ☐

6. Has your company's corporate culture had a positive impact on the IS/IT strategy your firm is implementing?

Yes ☐   No ☐

7. Has your firm examined its business processes from both a customer service and an information technology perspective?

Yes ☐   No ☐

8. Has a problem with a specific decision or decision process led managers to consider developing or improving a DSS?

Yes ☐   No ☐

9. Have the key decision processes in the company been identified?

Yes ☐   No ☐

10. Is your company using rapid prototyping to develop small-scale DSS?

Yes ☐   No ☐

11. Does your company use a structured systems development process for all large-scale projects?

Yes ☐   No ☐

12. Are DSS software development products used in your company?

Yes ☐   No ☐

13. Does your company have user interface guidelines for DSS?

Yes ☐   No ☐

14. Does your company involve potential users in the design and development of new DSS applications?

Yes ☐   No ☐

15. Are users satisfied with the user interfaces of current DSS?

Yes ☐   No ☐

16. Will your firm's IS/IT architecture and organization of IT resources support additional decision support capabilities?

Yes ☐   No ☐

17. Does your company have a network and high-speed Internet access?

Yes ☐   No ☐

18. Does your company have a DSS security policy?

Yes ☐   No ☐

19. Does your company use groupware or Group DSS?

Yes ☐   No ☐

20. Does your company have an intranet based on Web technologies?

Yes ☐   No ☐

21. Does your company have a computer-supported meeting room or a video conferencing facility?

Yes ☐   No ☐

22. Are any computerized tools used to support team projects?

Yes ☐   No ☐

23. Is one major relational database product used in your company?

Yes ☐   No ☐

24. Does your company have a data warehouse or a data mart?

Yes ☐   No ☐

25. Does your company have any data-driven DSS?   Yes   No

26. Does your company have any document-driven DSS?   Yes   No

27. Are users satisfied with the quality of data captured and stored at your company?   Yes   No

28. Does your company have an Executive Information System (EIS)?   Yes   No

29. Are any model-driven DSS used in your company?   Yes   No

30. Do decision-makers develop and maintain some model-driven DSS?   Yes   No

31. Has your company implemented any knowledge-driven DSS?   Yes   No

32. Does your company use data mining for analysis of business data?   Yes   No

33. Does the MIS group have any knowledge-driven DSS or data mining development projects underway?   Yes   No

34. Has your firm deployed any Web-based DSS?   Yes   No

35. Does the MIS group support Web technologies and Web applications development?

Yes ☐   No ☐

36. Does your firm have any plans for Web-based DSS?

Yes ☐   No ☐

37. Does your company create budgets for major DSS projects?

Yes ☐   No ☐

38. Are managers involved in evaluating proposed DSS projects?

Yes ☐   No ☐

39. Are cultural and international issues considered in evaluating DSS projects?

Yes ☐   No ☐

40. Is a DSS project evaluation checklist used?

Yes ☐   No ☐

Appendix II: DSS User-Centered Design Checklist

EASY TO UNDERSTAND

1. Does the DSS user interface design focus on the decision task, e.g., approving loan applications, monitoring key results metrics, allocating resources?
2. Does the interface style reflect the user's point of view and conception of what is being done, rather than the designer's point of view?
3. Does the DSS user interface present only information relevant to the user's decision task(s)?
4. Do system capabilities enhance user task accomplishment? For example, is color or blinking text used appropriately?
5. Are abbreviations, mnemonics, codes, and acronyms based on normal language usage, specific job related terminology, or a known logic?
6. Does the DSS design take advantage of what the user already knows?
7. Is terminology for labeling, commands, messages, and prompts consistent with the user's frame of reference? A term should mean what a user thinks it means.
8. Do icons directly represent the associated object or action?
9. Is the DSS designed to do what the user would naturally or naively guess it should do?
10. Does the DSS design maintain visual consistency as well as action consistency?
11. Does the DSS design maintain consistency in the display, labeling terminology, system control, and abbreviations?
12. Is the DSS designed so the user is able to easily predict how it will respond to actions?

EASY ORIENTATION AND NAVIGATION

1. Is the DSS designed so the user knows where she is, what she can do there, and how she can leave a page or the system?
2. Does each screen and window have a descriptive title, placed in a consistent location?
3. Does the DSS design provide cues to identify the currently displayed page and the total number of pages in a multipage display?
4. Are applicable menus and control options available to the user at all times?
5. Does the DSS design provide the user a means to log-off a DSS by a single action (e.g., menu option, command input)?
6. Does the DSS design require a confirmation to exit without saving changes?

ENHANCE PRODUCTIVITY

1. Does the DSS design and specific features take job requirements and decision tasks into consideration and support job accomplishment?
2. Does the DSS design avoid the use of acronyms and abbreviations?
3. Does the DSS design require recognition rather than recall memory where possible?
4. Does the DSS design use units of measurement familiar to the user? Do not require the user to transform units of measurement.
5. Does the DSS design keep screen density as low as possible (for warning and emergency messages, preferably less than 25 percent of the screen space)?
6. Does the DSS design maintain consistent display formatting within the system?
7. Does the DSS design use colors for coding and emphasis?
8. Does the DSS design display only task-related information and place all data related to one task on a single screen?
9. Does the DSS design highlight data, a message, a menu item, an icon, or other display structure as feedback to acknowledge that the user has selected the item?
10. Does the DSS design provide users with information about the current system status as it affects their work (for example, printing delays, inoperable peripherals, and processing delays due to system load)?
11. When the completion of a command results in a consequence that is not visible to the user, does the DSS design provide a feedback message that describes the actions resulting from the command in simple, direct, positive language?

MAINTAIN INTEGRITY OF THE DSS

1. Does the DSS design maintain the integrity of DSS data?
2. Does the DSS design build protection around dangerous operations and permit the user to undo things that have been done?

3. Does the DSS design require users to confirm that they want to perform a critical, potentially hazardous, or potentially destructive command before execution?
4. Does the DSS design provide on-line Help with summary information initially, and with more detailed explanations available on request?
5. Does the DSS design permit the user to enter Help at any point and use a simple, standard action for the user to request Help?
6. Does the DSS design provide an easy means of returning to the task after accessing Help?

PROVIDE CONTROL TO USERS

1. Does the DSS design help the user feel in control of a decision support session?
2. Does the DSS design give the user multiple means for doing things and let the user, not the computer, set the pace?
3. Does the DSS design provide for simple command language control of a DSS by advanced users?
4. Does the DSS design require the user to enter any particular data only once and then have the system access that data if needed?
5. Does the DSS design permit the user to request a more detailed explanation of feedback?
6. Does the DSS design use neutral wording in feedback messages?
7. Is the DSS designed so users are unlikely to make "errors"?

The above checklist is based on a document prepared at NASA called HCI Guidelines and the guidelines and factors identified by Shneiderman (1992) and Larson (1982).

Appendix III: Key Decision Support System Terms

A

Ad Hoc Query – Any spontaneous or unplanned question or query. An ad hoc query is often developed with an Ad Hoc Query and Reporting tool and Structured Query Language (SQL).

Ad Hoc Query Tool – An end-user tool that accepts an English-like or point-and-click request for data and constructs a query to retrieve the desired data from a database. See *report and query tools*.

Aggregate Data or Aggregated Data – Data that results from applying a process to combine data elements. These terms refer to data that is summarized.

Analytical Hierarchy Process (AHP) – An approach to decision making that involves structuring multiple choice criteria into a hierarchy, assessing the relative importance of these criteria, comparing alternatives for each criterion, and determining an overall ranking of the alternatives.

Analytical Information System – A descriptor for a broad set of information systems that assist managers in performing analyses based on tools like dimensional analysis, on-line analytical processing, simulation, optimization, quantitative models, and statistics.

Artificial Intelligence (AI) – A branch of computer science that studies how computer software can imitate the cognitive activities of people. AI software, including expert system software, is used in building knowledge-driven DSS. See *expert system*.

B

Business Data – Data about people, places, things, business rules, and events used to operate a business. See *data*.

Business Intelligence (BI) – Business Intelligence is a popularized, umbrella term introduced by Howard Dresner of the Gartner Group in 1989 to describe a set of concepts and methods to improve business decision making by extracting and analyzing data from databases. The term is sometimes used interchangeably with briefing books and executive information systems. Data-driven DSS provide Business Intelligence. The most commonly marketed BI software is query and reporting software.

Business Process – A "collection of activities that takes one or more kinds of input and creates an output that is of value to the customer" (Hammer and Champy, 1993). Business processes usually include one or more decision processes. See *decision process*.

Business Process Reengineering (BPR) – The rethinking and redesign of business processes to achieve major improvements in performance. Hammer and Champy (1993) argue BPR should involve fundamental changes and radical improvements in performance or "starting over." This concept is sometimes referred to as business process redesign, business reengineering or reengineering.

Business Transaction – A work task recorded by a data capture system that creates, modifies, or deletes business data. Each transaction represents a fact describing a single business event. Examples of transactions include a purchase made at a grocery store or a loan application entered at a bank.

C

Client/server Architecture – A network architecture in which computers on a network act as a server, managing files and network services, or as a client where users run applications and access servers. Clients are computers that rely on servers for resources like Web pages, data, files, and printing.

Cognitive Overload – A psychological phenomenon characterized by an overload of information for a decision maker. Overload occurs when the amount of information exceeds a person's cognitive capacity.

Communications-Driven DSS – A DSS that uses network and communications technologies to facilitate collaboration and communication. Communications technologies are central to supporting decision making and provide the dominant decision support functionality. Related concepts include *groupware, video conferencing*, and *GDSS*.

Competitive Advantage – A skill, resource, or capability of an organization that is a strength, that is unique or proprietary, and that is sustainable for at least three years. It is something important that an organization does much better than its competitors.

Cost/Benefit Analysis (CBA) – This analysis addresses the allocation of capital. CBA is a systematic, quantitative method for assessing the life cycle costs and benefits of competing alternatives. Typical measures in CBA are return on investment (ROI), net present value (NPV), and discounted cash flow.

Critical Success Factors (CSF) – Key areas of business activity in which favorable results are necessary for a company to reach its goals. Key performance indicators (KPIs) are often linked to CSF and monitored in Data-driven DSS targeted for senior executives.

Cycle Time – The elapsed time from when a decision or business process is initiated to when it is completed.

D

Data – Binary representations of atomic facts, text, graphics, bit-mapped images, sound, analog or digital video segments. Data is the raw material of any information system. Data producers supply data and it is used by information consumers to create information. See *business data.*

Data Dictionary – A database about data elements and database structures. A data dictionary is a catalog of all data elements that contains their names, structures, and information about their usage. It is a central location for metadata. Normally, data dictionaries are designed to store a limited set of available metadata, concentrating on the information relating to the data elements, databases, files, and programs of implemented systems.

Data-Driven DSS – This type of DSS derives its functionality from access to and manipulation of a very large time-series of internal company data and, sometimes, external data. Data-driven DSS help analyze, display and manipulate large structured data sets that contain numeric and short character strings. Databases accessed by ad-hoc query tools provide the most elementary level of functionality. Data warehouse systems that support the analysis of data provide additional functionality. Data-driven DSS with OLAP and Spatial DSS provide the highest level of functionality and decision support that is linked to analysis of large collections of historical data. See *Spatial DSS.*

Data Flow Diagram (DFD) – A modeling method used for process modeling that graphically depicts business processes and the logical flow of data through a process.

Data Mining – A class of analytical applications that search for patterns in a database. Data mining is the process of sifting through large amounts of data to produce data content relationships. Data mining tools use a variety of techniques including case-based reasoning, data visualization, fuzzy query and analysis, and neural networks.

Data Modeling – A process that organizes a database designer's thinking about the appropriate structure for the decision support data store. A conceptual data model shows the overall logical structure of a database. In general, a data model is any method for visualizing the information needs of a system.

Data Quality – High-quality data is accurate, timely, meaningful, and complete. Data-driven DSS must have high-quality data; low-quality data can result in bad decisions. Assessing or measuring data quality is a preliminary task associated with evaluating the feasibility of a data-driven DSS project.

Data Visualization – This term refers to presenting data and summary information using graphics, animation, 3-D displays, and other multimedia DSS tools.

Data Warehouse – A database designed to support decision making in organizations. It is batch updated and structured for rapid online queries and managerial summaries. Data warehouses contain large amounts of data. Bill Inmon (1995) defines a data warehouse as a subject-oriented, integrated, time-variant, nonvolatile collection of data in support of management's decision-making process. According to Ralph Kimball (1996), "A data warehouse is a copy of transaction data specifically structured for query and analysis."

Decision – The choice of one alternative solution from among a number of alternatives; a statement indicating a commitment to a specific course of action. Three types of decisions include selection of an alternative including a yes or no decision, evaluation of one or more alternatives, and design and construction of a solution.

Decision Analysis (DA) Tools – DA tools help decision makers decompose and structure problems. The aim of these tools is to help a user apply models like decision trees, multi-attribute utility models, Bayesian models, or Analytical Hierarchy Process (AHP).

Decision-Oriented DSS Design – An approach to building DSS that involves predesign description and diagnosis of decision making (cf., Stabell 1983) and then either rapid prototyping, structured systems development (SDLC) or end-user development.

Decision Process – The steps or analyses that lead to a decision. Decision processes are often part of larger business processes. See *business process*.

Decision Process Audit – An activity that can be included as part of a decision-oriented diagnosis to review operational and managerial decision processes. The audit typically includes five steps and it may focus narrowly on a single process or more broadly on decision process in a unit or an entire organization.

Decision Room – A physical arrangement for a communications-driven or group DSS in which individual workstations are available to each participant in a meeting room.

Decision Support Analyst – A support staff user of Decision Support Systems who prepares special studies for middle-level and senior managers. These analysts may use a Data-Driven DSS to conduct an ad hoc query that is then analyzed with a statistical package, Excel or a desktop OLAP tool. They may build small Model-Driven DSS and write-up the results of the analysis. See *DSS analyst*.

Decision Support Readiness Audit – A checklist of questions that can help assess a company's capabilities and readiness to develop innovative and successful DSS.

Decision Support Systems (DSS) – A class of information system that supports decision-making activities (cf. Sprague and Carlson, 1982). Interactive computer-based systems intended to help decision makers use data, documents, knowledge and models to identify and solve problems and make decisions. Five more specific types include: *communications-driven, data-driven, document-driven, knowledge-driven* and *model-driven DSS*.

Decision System – A computer-based program intended to monitor and control processes and make routine decisions.

Decision Variables – In a model-driven DSS, a decision variable is a factor or parameter that is chosen or determined by a decision maker. A decision variable is sometimes called a controllable or independent variable and its range of values constrains the choices of a decision maker.

Descriptive Model – Physical, conceptual, or mathematical model that describes a situation as it is or as it appears.

Deterministic Model – A mathematical model that is constructed for a condition of assumed certainty. The model builder assumes there is only one possible result for each alternative course of action.

Development Environment – A development environment is used by a DSS designer or builder and typically includes software for creating and maintaining a DSS. This term is often used with expert system technologies. See *DSS generator.*

Dialog System – The hardware and software that create and implement a user interface for a DSS. A DSS dialog system creates the human-computer interface. See *user interface.*

Document-Driven DSS – A document-driven DSS integrates a variety of storage and processing technologies to provide document retrieval and analysis. An organized collection of documents provides the functionality for a document-driven DSS. Document-driven DSS help analyze, display and manipulate text including logical units of text called documents. Examples of documents that might be accessed by a document-based DSS are policies and procedures, product specifications, catalogs, and corporate historical documents, including minutes of meetings, corporate records, and important correspondence. A search engine is a powerful decision-aiding tool associated with a document-driven DSS (cf., Fedorowicz, 1993, pp. 125–136).

Domain Expert – A person who has expertise in the domain in which a specific knowledge-driven DSS is being developed. A domain expert works closely with a knowledge engineer to capture an expert's knowledge in a computer readable representation often called a knowledge base.

Drill Down/Up – An analytical technique that lets a data-driven DSS user navigate among levels of data ranging from the most summarized (up) to the most detailed (down).

DSS Analyst – An intermediary or liaison between users and DSS developers. He/she may work as a member of a DSS application support team. A DSS analyst often works gathering requirements, analyzing solutions, writing specifications, maintaining product information as well as assisting in training and documentation support. A DSS Analyst often works with users to define and document system requirements for Decision Support Systems. A DSS analyst may help redesign business processes to better use a computerized Decision Support System. Some DSS analysts manage a specific DSS or ensure data integrity in a focused data mart like a customer data mart. See *decision support analyst.*

DSS Architecture – It includes the IS/IT architecture components relevant to the DSS. A DSS may be a subsystem of a larger information system and a specific DSS may have multiple types of decision support subsystems. See *system*.

DSS Development Tools – Software components (such as editors, code libraries, specific objects, visual interfaces) that facilitate the development of a specific DSS.

DSS Generator – A computer software package that provides tools and capabilities that help a developer build a specific DSS (cf., Sprague and Carlson, 1982, p. 11). Microsoft Excel is an example of a DSS generator for creating small-scale data and model-driven DSS. See *development environment*.

E

e-Business – Electronic business is a broad term for using Internet and Web technologies to provide, deliver and enable transaction processing and decision support on intranets and extranets for a wide array of stakeholders and customers.

e-Meeting – A term for a meeting supported by full-motion video, audio, and Web meeting tools. One or more participants in the meeting are participating remotely. It is possible that all participants are in different physical locations. An e-meeting can involve the use of communications-driven DSS.

Enterprise-Wide DSS – A specific DSS that supports a large group of managers across the various units and levels of a business enterprise or organization. A synonymous term is *organizational DSS*.

Evolutionary Design Process – A systematic process for systems development that is recommended for use in creating model-driven DSS. A portion of the DSS is quickly constructed, then tested, improved, and enlarged in systematic steps. This methodology is similar to prototyping and iterative design. See *prototyping*.

Exception Reporting – A reporting philosophy and approach that supports "Management by Exception". Reports should be designed to display significant exceptions in results and data. The idea is to "flag" important information and bring it quickly to the attention of managerial users of the report. Exception reporting can be implemented in any type of DSS, but it is particularly useful in data-driven DSS and EIS.

Executive Information Systems (EIS) – EIS are data-driven DSS intended to provide current and appropriate information to support decision making for senior executives. The emphasis of EIS is on graphical displays and an easy-to-use interface that presents information from a corporate-wide database. EIS provide reports or briefing books to top-level executives and offer strong reporting and drill-down capabilities. Executives can use an EIS to monitor key performance indicators and critical success factors. See *critical success factors*.

Expert System – It is an Artificial Intelligence system with specialized problem-solving expertise. The "expertise" consists of knowledge about a particular domain, understanding of problems within that domain, and "skill" at resolving a specific problem. Expert system technologies are commonly used to build knowledge-driven DSS.

Extranet – An intranet that is accessible to authorized external stakeholders. An extranet provides various levels of access and decision support. A username and password determine what parts of an extranet one can view and use. See *intranet* and *portal*.

F

Facilitator – A person who manages the use of a group Decision Support System in a decision room from initial planning of a meeting through actual operation of the GDSS.

Feasibility Study – A study of the technical and economic prospects for developing a specific DSS that is completed prior to actually committing resources to developing a proposed DSS.

Firewall – Hardware and software, or a combination of both, that evaluates incoming and outgoing data. If a data packet does not meet certain criteria, it is denied access. A firewall is designed to prevent unauthorized access to or from a private network.

Function-Specific DSS – A decision support system for decisions about some function an organization performs. For example, a DSS may support a marketing function like advertising or a production function like resource planning.

G

Geographic Information System (GIS) – A category of software and systems that represents data using maps. It helps people access, display, and analyze data with geographic content and meaning. GIS software is used to build spatial DSS.

Goal-Seeking – The capability of asking the computer software what values certain variables must have in order to attain desired goals. It is a tool that uses iterative calculations to find the value required in one cell (variable) in order to achieve a desired value in another cell.

Graphical User Interface (GUI) – A GUI is a program interface that uses a computer's graphics capabilities to make the program easier to use. Graphical interfaces use a pointing device to select objects, including icons, menus, text boxes, etc. A GUI includes standard formats for representing text and graphics. See *user interface*.

Group Decision Support System (GDSS) – An interactive, computer-based system that facilitates solution of unstructured problems by a set of decision makers working together as a group. It aids groups, especially groups of managers, in analyzing problem situations and in performing group decision-making tasks like brainstorming. A GDSS is a hybrid DSS that emphasizes both the use of communications and qualitative decision heuristics. See *communications-driven DSS*.

Groupware – Software designed to support more than one person working on a shared task. Groupware helps users coordinate and keep track of ongoing projects and tasks. It helps people work together through computer-supported communication, collaboration, and coordination. Groupware applications include email, video, scheduling, bulletin boards, chat, and collaborative writing and drawing systems. See *communications-driven DSS*.

H

Heuristics – The informal, judgmental knowledge of an application area that provides procedures or the "rules of good judgment" in the field. Heuristics also encompass the knowledge of how to solve problems efficiently and effectively.

Hypertext – An approach for handling text and other information by allowing the user to jump from a given topic to related topics.

Hypertext Markup Language (HTML) – An authoring language used to create documents on the World Wide Web. HTML uses markup tags to define the structure and layout of a Web document. One important tag, an anchor tag, is used to specify hypertext links. Extensible Markup Language (XML) is a related markup language for describing data elements in a web page.

I

Icon – A visual, graphic representation of an object, word, or concept.

Independent Variables - Variables in a model that are controlled by the decision maker or the environment and that influence the results of a decision (also called input variables or parameters). See *decision variables*.

Industry-Specific DSS – A computer-based system that helps a manager accomplish a specific task in a specific industry environment like banking or hospitals.

Inference – Inference is the process of drawing a conclusion from given evidence. It means to reach a decision by reasoning.

Inference Engine – That part of an expert system or knowledge-driven DSS that actually performs the reasoning function and knowledge processing.

Information – Data that has been processed to add or create meaning and, ideally, knowledge for the person who receives it. Information is an output of information systems including DSS.

Information Economics – This term refers to evaluating DSS/IS projects using a scoring approach that assesses technical and company tangible and intangible benefits and costs (see Parker, Trainor and Benson, 1989).

Information Systems Architecture – A formal definition of the elements or parts of an information system including decision support systems. The architecture defines business processes and rules, the system structure, technical framework, and product technologies for an information system. The architecture also defines the structures and controls that define how the platform can be used, and the categories of applications that can be created on the platform. It includes the hardware and software used to manage information and communication; the tools used to access, package, deliver, and communicate information; the standards, models, and control frameworks; and the overall configuration that integrates the various components (cf., Applegate et al., 1996).

Interdependent Decisions – A series of interrelated decisions. A sequential set of decisions are usually interdependent.

Internet – The Internet (capitalized) refers specifically to the DARPA Internet and the Transmission Control Protocol/Internet Protocol (TCP/IP) that it uses. The Internet is a collection of packet-switching networks and routers that uses the TCP/IP protocol suite and functions as a single, cooperative virtual network. It is a global Web connecting more than ten million computers. Visit The World Wide Web Consortium (http://www.w3.org/) for more information about the Internet.

Interorganizational DSS – An interorganizational DSS is a DSS that serves a company's stakeholders including customers or suppliers. An interorganizational DSS provides stakeholders with access to a company's intranet and authority or privileges to use specific DSS capabilities. Companies can make a data-driven DSS available to suppliers or a model-driven DSS available to customers to design a product or choose a product.

Intranet – An internal organizational network using TCP/IP with at least one Web server that is only accessible by an organization's members or others who have specific authorization. A firewall and password protection limit access to the network. The intranet is used to share corporate information, including DSS capabilities.

J

Java – An object-oriented programming language developed by Sun Microsystems. A Java applet running on a Web page provides more user interaction and dynamic information updating. Java is platform independent.

JavaScript – A programming language that is highly integrated with Web browser objects. JavaScript is downloaded as part of an HTML page and it is processed by the Web browser as it is received. JavaScripts consist of functions that are called as a result of Web browser events.

K

Knowledge – Knowledge refers to what one knows and understands. Knowledge is sometimes categorized as unstructured, structured, explicit, or implicit. What we know we know is called explicit knowledge. Knowledge that is unstructured and understood, but not clearly expressed, is called implicit knowledge. If the knowledge is organized and easy to share, then it is called structured knowledge. To convert implicit knowledge into explicit knowledge, the knowledge must be extracted and formatted.

Knowledge Acquisition – The extraction and formulation of knowledge derived from various sources, especially from experts.

Knowledge Base – A collection of facts, rules, and procedures organized into schemas. A knowledge base is the assembly of all the information and knowledge of a specific field of interest.

Knowledge-Driven DSS – Knowledge-driven DSS can suggest or recommend actions to managers. These DSS are person-computer systems with specialized problem-solving expertise. The "expertise" consists of knowledge about a particular domain, understanding of problems within that domain, and "skill" at solving some of these problems. Tools used for building knowledge-driven DSS are sometimes called Intelligent Decision Support methods (cf., Dhar and Stein, 1997). Data mining tools can be used to create knowledge-driven DSS. See *data mining*.

Knowledge Engineer – An AI specialist responsible for the technical side of developing an expert system. The knowledge engineer works closely with the domain expert to capture the expert's knowledge in a knowledge base.

Knowledge Management (KM) – KM is the distribution, access, and retrieval of unstructured information about "human experiences" between interdependent individuals or among members of a workgroup. Knowledge management involves identifying a group of people who have a need to share knowledge, developing technological support that enables knowledge sharing, and creating a process for transferring and disseminating knowledge. Document-driven DSS can support KM.

Knowledge Management Software (KMS) – KMS can store and manage unstructured information in a variety of electronic formats. The software may assist in knowledge capture, categorization, deployment, inquiry, discovery, or communication. Knowledge management software is an important delivery component for document-driven DSS. See *document-driven DSS*.

L

Linear Programming – A mathematical model for optimal solution of resource allocation problems.

Local Area Network (LAN) – A networking technology that connects computers in a small area like a building or an office. It may involve premise wiring or radio or infrared technology (a wireless LAN).

M

Management Information System (MIS) – It is a broad umbrella term for any information system that provides managers with on-line access to information. Historically, an MIS is "an integrated, man/machine system for providing information to support the operations, management, and decision-making functions in an organization. The systems utilize computer hardware and software, manual procedures, management and decision models, and a database"

(Davis, 1974, p. 5). The term is sometimes used narrowly for an information system that provides management reports.

Metadata or Meta Data – Data about the data in a data warehouse or database. Metadata provides a directory to help locate data; it is a guide to mapping data as it is transformed from the operational environment to a data warehouse environment; and it serves as a guide to the algorithms used for summarization of current detailed data. Metadata is semantic information associated with a given variable. Metadata must include business definitions of the data and clear, accurate descriptions of data types, potential values, original source system, data formats, and other characteristics. Metadata includes the name, length, valid values, and description of a data element.

Methodology – A system of principles, practices, and procedures applied to a specific branch of knowledge.

Middleware – A communications layer that allows applications to interact across hardware and network environments.

Model Base – A collection of preprogrammed quantitative models (e.g., statistical, financial, optimization) organized as a single unit.

Model-Driven DSS – This type of DSS emphasizes access to and manipulation of a model. The decision support functionality comes from the ability to manipulate the model for "What if?" or sensitivity analysis. Simple statistical and analytical tools provide the most elementary level of functionality. Some OLAP systems that allow complex analysis of data may be classified as hybrid DSS systems providing both modeling and data retrieval and data summarization functionality. In general, model-driven DSS use complex financial, simulation, and optimization models to provide decision support. Model-driven DSS use data and parameters provided by decision makers to aid decision makers in analyzing a situation, but they are not usually data intensive, that is, very large databases are usually not needed for model-driven DSS.

Modeling Tools – Software programs that help developers build mathematical models. Spreadsheet functions and planning languages like IFPS are modeling tools.

Multidimensional Database (MDB) – A database that lets users analyze large amounts of data. An MDB captures and presents data as arrays that can be arranged in multiple dimensions. Multi-dimensional databases can have multiple outcome or performance variables, with a common set of dimensions. A multidimensional view of data is especially important for data-driven DSS.

Multiparticipant DSS – A decision support system that supports multiple participants engaged in a decision-making task (or functions as one of the participants). See *Group DSS*.

N

Normalization – The process of reducing a complex data structure into its simplest, most stable structure. In general, the process entails the removal of redundant attributes, keys, and relationships from a conceptual data model.

O

On-Line Analytical Processing (OLAP) – Software for manipulating multidimensional data from a variety of sources. The software can create various views and representations of the data. OLAP software provides fast, consistent, interactive access to shared, multidimensional data.

Operational or Transaction Database – The database of a transaction processing system. An operational database is often the source of data for a data warehouse. It contains detailed data used for the day-to-day operations of the business. The data continually changes as updates are made and reflects the last transaction.

Optimize – The decision strategy of choosing the alternative that gives the best or optimal overall value.

Organizational DSS - A multiparticipant DSS is designed to support a decision maker in a setting that has a more elaborate infrastructure than a group. For example, participants have specialized roles, restricted communication patterns, and differing authority levels. See *enterprise-wide DSS* and *interorganizational DSS*.

P

Pivot – Changing the dimensional orientation of a display or report. It means to rotate or turn. In a pivot table one changes the variables on the vertical or horizontal axes.

Portal – A portal provides users with an integrated, personalized, and secure Web-based interface to business content including information, application, and collaboration services. A portal may be accessed from an intranet or the Internet. A DSS portal emphasizes accessing decision support applications.

Project Scope – A measure of the number of potential users, the size of the project staff, the potential impacts on existing systems, and the amount of programming or development effort that will be required.

Prototyping – A strategy in system development in which a scaled-down system, or portion of a system, is constructed in a short time, tested, and improved in several iterations. A prototype is an initial version of a system that is quickly developed to test the effectiveness of the overall design being used to solve a particular problem. Prototyping is similar to the Evolutionary (Iterative) Design Process. It is sometimes termed rapid prototyping and is similar to rapid application development (RAD). See *rapid application development*.

Q

Query – Generically, "query" means "question." Usually, it refers to a complex Structured Query Language statement used for decision support. See *Ad Hoc Query* or *Structured Query Language*.

R

Rapid Application Development (RAD) – A systems development methodology that specifies incremental iterative development with constant feedback from potential users. The point is to keep projects focused on delivering value and to keep clear and open lines of communication. See *prototyping*.

Rational Decision Behavior – Rational decision behavior is goal-oriented in reaching a decision. Behavior is guided by the consequences likely to result from the selection of a given alternative. A decision maker believes based upon analysis that a chosen alternative will result in achieving one or more desired objectives. Rational decision behavior can be supported by DSS.

Record – A group of data elements, consisting of one value for each of a prescribed set of relational fields.

Report and Query Tools – These tools produce a tabular list of information from data stored in a relational database. The most common Business Intelligence tool is a report and query tool. Report and Query tools provide limited functionality for building data-driven DSS. See *ad hoc query tool*.

Representation – The formulation or view of a problem. Developed so the problem will be easier to solve. Also, in the ROMC approach to DSS design a representation is a way of visualizing or presenting information like a chart or a table. See *ROMC design approach*.

Result Variables – In a model-driven DSS, a result variable shows the consequences or outcomes of changing decision variables. Result variables are also referred to as dependent variables. See *decision variables*.

ROMC Design Approach – A systematic approach for developing large-scale DSS, especially user interfaces. *ROMC* stands for *R*epresentations, *O*perations, *M*emory Aids, and *C*ontrol Aids. It is user-oriented approach for stating system performance requirements (cf., Sprague and Carlson, 1982).

Rule – A rule is a formal way of specifying a recommendation, directive, or strategy, expressed as IF (premise) THEN (conclusion). Rules are the primary building blocks of rule-based, knowledge-driven DSS.

S

Scalability – The ability to scale hardware and software to support larger or smaller volumes of data and more or fewer users. It also refers to the ability to increase or decrease size or capability in cost-effective increments with minimal impact on the unit cost of business and the procurement of additional services.

Semistructured Decisions – Decisions in which some aspects of the problem are structured and others are unstructured. See *structured decisions* and *unstructured decisions*.

Sensitivity Analysis – A sensitivity analysis involves running a decision model several times with different inputs so a modeler or decision maker can analyze alternative results. One examines the outcomes from a model-driven

DSS over the range of one or more input parameters to determine if they are sensitive to small changes in inputs. See *"What If" analysis*.

Simulation – Simulation is a modeling technique for conducting one or more experiments that tests various outcomes resulting from a specific quantitative model of a system. There are two distinct types of simulation models: Monte Carlo simulation and systems simulation.

Spatial DSS – It is a sub-category of data-driven DSS. A Spatial DSS uses Geographic Information Systems (GIS) technologies to support managers in analyzing data with a geographic or spatial component.

Special Decision Study – An analysis prepared to support decision-making in situations that are especially important and novel. Situations that are very unstructured, involve negotiation or bargaining or that are political are also likely candidates for special decision studies. Existing data-driven DSS may be used for ad-hoc queries or models may be built in such studies, but it is usually not appropriate to build new DSS in these situations.

Specific DSS – A computer-based system that helps a person accomplish a specific decision task. "Specific DSS are the hardware/software that allow a specific decision maker or group of them to deal with specific sets of related problems" (cf., Sprague and Carlson, 1982, p. 10).

Spreadsheet – It is a computer program that has a collection of cells whose values can be displayed on a computer screen. A spreadsheet summarizes information and presents the information in a format to help a decision maker. Decision support systems built using spreadsheet software are called Spreadsheet DSS.

Star Schema – A relational database structure organized around a central fact table joined to a few smaller dimension tables using foreign key references. The fact table contains numeric items that represent relevant business facts like price, discount values, number of units sold, and dollar value. The facts are typically retrieved using dimensions. Information is classified into two groups: facts and dimensions. The name "star schema" comes from the pattern formed when the fact and dimension tables are represented as an entity-relationship diagram (E/RD).

Strategic Information System (SIS) – A SIS is any information system that changes organizational goals, products, services, or environmental relationships of an organization and provides a competitive advantage. DSS can be strategic information systems, but every DSS is not a SIS and some DSS are basic business systems needed to compete in an industry.

Structured Decisions – Refers to standardized or repetitive decisions situations for which solution techniques are already available. Structured decisions are sometimes called routine or programmed decisions. The structural elements in such situations include alternatives, criteria, goals, and environmental conditions. All of these elements are known, defined, and understood for structured decisions. A decision system can sometimes be developed to automate structured decisions. See *decision system*.

Structured Query Language (SQL) – It is a set of commands used to process and retrieve data in a relational database. Some major database management systems (DBMSs) that support SQL are DB2, Oracle and Sybase. See *ad hoc query tool* and *report and query tools*.

Suggestion DSS – It is another name for a knowledge-driven DSS used by Alter (1980). It uses artificial intelligence technologies like rules and frames to draw inferences and make suggestions and recommendations to managers and other decision-makers. See *knowledge-driven DSS*.

System – An interrelated set of components including people, activities, technology and procedures that are designed or intended to achieve a predefined purpose. A system is usually decomposable into subsystems.

Systems Development Life Cycle (SDLC) – SDLC is a process by which systems analysts, software engineers, programmers, and end-users build systems. It is a project management tool, used to plan, execute, and control systems development projects. Typical steps in the cycle include: 1) Determine user requirements; 2) Systems analysis; 3) Overall system design; 4) Detailed system design; 5) Programming; 6) Testing; and 7) Implementation. Developing a written document that must be reviewed and approved concludes each step in the SDLC. It is sometimes called the "Waterfall" approach or model.

T

Table – A term used in relational database management systems to identify a collection of related attributes or fields. A table can be viewed as a collection of data rows that share the same column attributes. A table has a primary key that uniquely identifies each row in a table. A table can also contain primary keys from another table called foreign keys.

Transaction Processing System (TPS) – A computerized system designed to expedite and automate transaction processing, record keeping, and simple reporting of business transactions. See the terms *business transaction* and *operational or transaction database*.

U - V

Unstructured Decisions – A complex decision where no standard solutions exist for resolving the situation. Some or all of the structural elements of the decision are undefined, poorly defined, or unknown. For example, goals may be poorly defined, alternatives may be incomplete or non-comparable, and choice criteria may be hard to measure or difficult to link to goals.

User Friendly – An evaluative term for a DSS's user interface. The phrase indicates users judge a user interface as to easy to learn, understand, and use.

User Interface – The component of a computerized support system that allows bi-directional communication between a system and its user. This component is also called the dialogue component or human-computer interface of a DSS. An interface is a set of commands or menus through which a user communicates with a program. See *graphical user interface*.

Video Conferencing – Real-time, two-way communications with full motion video images. Video conferencing is audio-video telecommunication support of simultaneous interactions among participants.

Virtual Organization – An organization that uses e-mail, Web-based DSS and other technology tools to facilitate communication, coordination, collaboration and control and that operates without regard to time and place constraints. The term also refers to an organization made up of independent contractors and small companies that work together using information technologies.

W - X - Y - Z

Web-based DSS – A computerized system that delivers decision support information or decision support tools to a manager or business analyst using a "thin-client" Web browser like Netscape Navigator or Internet Explorer. The computer server that is hosting the DSS application is linked to the user's computer by a network with the TCP/IP protocol. In many companies, a Web-based DSS is synonymous with an enterprise-wide DSS. Web-based DSS can be communications-driven, data-driven, document-driven, knowledge-driven, model-driven, or a hybrid.

"What If" Analysis – Changing the value of an input variable to determine what will change in the output of a model. The capability of "asking" a model-driven DSS, what happens if I change this value? See *sensitivity analysis*.

References

Aberdeen Group, Inc. (1995, July 7). Data Warehouse Query Tools: Evolving to Relational OLAP. *Viewpoint 8* (8).

Aldag, R.J. & Power, D.J. (1986). An Empirical Assessment of Computer-Assisted Decision Analysis. *Decision Sciences 17* (4), 572–588.

Alexis, M., & Wilson, C.Z. (1967). *Organizational Decision Making.* Englewood Cliffs, N.J.: Prentice-Hall.

Allen, B.P. (1994, March). Case-based Reasoning: Business Applications. *Communication of the ACM 37* (3), 40.

Alter, S.L. (1977). A Taxonomy of Decision Support Systems. *Sloan Management Review 19* (1), 39–56.

Alter, S.L. (1980). *Decision Support Systems: Current Practice and Continuing Challenge.* Reading, MA: Addison-Wesley.

Anthony, R.N. (1965). *Planning and Control Systems: A Framework for Analysis.* Cambridge, MA: Harvard University Press.

Applegate, L., McFarlan, F. W., & McKenney, J. L. (1996). *Corporate Information Systems Management.* Chicago, IL: Irwin.

Applegate, L. & Pearlson, K. (1994). Mrs. Fields, Inc., 1977–1987. Cambridge, MA: Harvard Business School case 194–064.

Applegate, L. (1994). Frito-Lay, Inc.: A Strategic Transition (1980–1986). Cambridge, MA: Harvard Business School case 194–107.

Baatz, E.B. (1996, October 1). Digesting the ROI Paradox. *CIO Online.* <http://www.cio.com>.

Barrow, C. (1990, Spring). Implementing an Executive Information System: Seven Steps for Success. *Journal of Information Systems Management,* 41–46.

Bennett, J.L. (Ed.). (1983). *Building Decision Support Systems.* Reading, MA: Addison Wesley.

Berry, M.J. & Linoff, G. (1997). *Data Mining Techniques for Marketing, Sales, and Customer Support.* New York: Wiley Computer Publishing.

Bonczek, R.H., Holsapple, C.W. & Whinston, A.B. (1981). *Foundations of Decision Support System,* New York: Academic Press.

Bulkeley, W.M. (1992, January 28). "Computerizing" Dull Meeting Is Touted as an Antidote to the Mouth that Bored. *Wall Street Journal 73,* B1, B8.

Callon, J. (1996). *Competitive Advantage Through Information Technology.* New York: McGraw-Hill.

Carlson, E. (1979, Winter). An Approach for Designing Decision Support Systems. *Data Base.*

Clemons, E.K. & Weber, B.W. (1990). Strategic Information Technology Investments: Guidelines for Decision Making. *Journal of Management Information Systems 7*(2), 9–28.

Codd, E.F., Codd, S.B., & Salley, C.T. (1993). Providing OLAP (On-line Analytical Processing) to User-Analysts: An IT Mandate. E. F. Codd & Associates at <www.arborsoft.com>.

Connolly, T., Jessup, L.M., & Valacich, J.S. (1990, June). Effects of Anonymity and Evaluative Tone on Idea Generation in Computer-Mediated Groups. *Management Science 36* (6), 689–703.

Crossland, M.D., Wynne, B., and Perkins, W.C. (1995). Spatial Decision Support Systems: An Overview of Technology and a Test of Efficacy. *Decision Support Systems 14,* 219–235.

Daft, R.L. & Lengel, R.H. (1986). Organizational Information Requirements, Media Richness, and Structural Design. *Management Science 32,* 554-571.

Darling, C. & Semich, J. (1996, November). Wal-Mart's IT Secret: Extreme Integration. *Datamation.*

Datamation White Paper. (1997). The Evolution of Data Warehousing. *Datamation.* <http://www.datamation.com>.

Data Warehousing Institute. Ten Mistakes to Avoid. <http://www.dw-institute.com/papers/10mistks.htm>.

Davis, G. (1974). *Management Information Systems: Conceptual Foundations, Structure, and Development.* New York: McGraw-Hill.

Davis, J.L. (1999, March 1). United Overhaul Brings Decision-making Down to Earth. *InfoWorld.*

Dearden, J. (1966, May-June). Myth of Real-time Management Information. *Harvard Business Review,* 123–132.

Delbecq, A.L., Van de Ven, A.H. & Gustafson, D.H. (1975). *Group Techniques for Program Planning.* Glenview, IL: Scott, Foresman.

Dennis, A.R., Nunamaker, J.F., & Vogel, D.R. (1990-1991, Winter). A Comparison of Laboratory and Field Research in the Study of Electronic Meeting Systems. *Journal of Management Information Systems 7*(3), 107–135.

Dennis, A.R., Quek, F., and Pother, S. K. (1996). Using the Internet to Implement Support for Distributed Decision Making. In P. Humphreys, L. Bannon, A. McCosh, P. Migliarese, & J. C. Pomerol (Eds.), *Implementing Systems for Supporting Management Decisions: Concepts, Methods and Experiences.* London: Chapman & Hall.

DeSanctis, G. & Gallupe, R.B. (1985, Winter). Group Decision Support Systems: A New Frontier. *DATABASE.*

DeSanctis, G. & Galuppe, R.B. (1987, May). A Foundation for the Study of Group Decision Support Systems. *Management Science 33* (5).

Dhar, V. & Stein, R. (1997). *Intelligent Decision Support Methods: The Science of Knowledge.* Upper Saddle River, NJ: Prentice-Hall.

Donovan, J.J. & Madnick, S.E. (1977). Institutional and Ad Hoc DSS and Their Effective Use. *Data Base 8* (3).

Drucker, P.F. (1988, January-February).   The Coming of the New Organization. *Harvard Business Review 66* (1).

Drucker, P.F. (1998, August 24). The Next Information Revolution. *Forbes.* <http://www.forbes.com/>.

Duncan, R. (1974). Characteristics of Organizational Environments and Perceived Environmental Uncertainty. *Administrative Science Quarterly 17,* 313–327.

Eliot, L. (1997, December/January). Using Simulation as a Real Tool. *Decision Line,* 13–14.

Eom, S., Lee, S.M., Somarajan, C. & Kim, E.B. (1997, April-June). Decision Support Systems Applications Research: A Bibliography (1988-1994). *OR Insight 10* (2), 18–32.

Evans, P. B. & Wurster, T. S. (1997, September-October). Strategy and the New Economics of Information. *Harvard Business Review.*

Fedorowicz, J. (1993). A Technology Infrastructure for Document-Based Decision Support Systems. In R. Sprague & H. J. Watson, *Decision Support Systems: Putting Theory into Practice* (3rd ed.), 125-136. Englewood Cliffs, NJ: Prentice-Hall.

Feeny, D.F. & Ives, B. (1990). In Search of Sustainability: Reaping Long-term Advantage from Investments in Information Technology. *Journal of Management Information Systems 7*(1), 27–46.

Freeman, E. (1997, July).   Data Mining Unearths Dollars from Data. *Datamation* <http://www.datamation.com>.

Frisch, A. (1995). *Essential System Administration.* Sebastopol, CA: O'Reilly & Associates, Inc.

Galitz, W.O. (1985).   *Handbook of Screen Format Design* (2nd ed.). Wellesley, MA: QED Information Sciences, Inc., 1985.

Galal, H., Stoddard, D., Nolan, R. and Kao, J. (1996). VeriFone: The Transaction Automation Company. Harvard Business School   Case 195-088, 1994. In   L. Applegate, F. W. McFarlan, & J. L. McKenney. *Corporate Information Systems Management: Text and Cases* (4th ed.). Chicago: Irwin.

Gates, W., with N. Myhrvold and P. Rinearson. (1995). *The Road Ahead.* New York: Viking Penguin USA.

Gerber, C. (1996, May 1).   Excavate Your Data.   *Datamation* <http://www.datamation.com/PlugIn/issues/1996/may1/05asoft3.html >.

Gerrity, T.P., Jr. (1971, Winter). The Design of Man-Machine Decision Systems. *Sloan Management Review 12* (2), 59–75.

Gill, T.G. (1995). Early Expert Systems: Where Are They Now? *MIS Quarterly 19* (1), 51-81.

Golden, B., Hevner, A., & Power, D.J. (1986). Decision Insight Systems: A Critical Evaluation. *Computers and Operations Research 13* (2/3), 287–300.

Golub, A.L. (1997). *Decision Analysis: An Integrated Approach*. New York: Wiley.

Gray, P. & Nunamaker, J.F. (1996). Group Decision Support Systems. In R. Sprague and H.J. Watson (Eds.). *Decision Support for Management*. Upper Saddle River, NJ: Prentice Hall.

Gray, P. & Watson, H.J. (1998). *Decision Support in the Data Warehouse*. Upper Saddle River, NJ: Prentice-Hall.

Greenfield, L. (2000). Data Mining. LGI Systems, Inc. <http://www.dwinfocenter.org/datamine.html >.

Gulliksen, J., Lantz, A., & Boivie, I. (1999, January). User Centered Design in Practice—Problems and Possibilities. Centre for User Oriented IT Design. <http://www.nada.kth.se/cid/pdf/cid_40.pdf>.

Hackathorn, R. D. & Keen, P.G.W. (1981, September). Organizational Strategies for Personal Computing in Decision Support Systems. *MIS Quarterly 5* (3), pp. 21–27.

Hammer, M. (1990, July–August). Reengineering Work: Don't Automate, Obliterate. *Harvard Business Review*.

Hammer, M. & Champy, J. (1993). *Reengineering the Corporation*. New York: Harper Collins.

Handy, C. (1995, May-June). Trust and the Virtual Organization. *Harvard Business Review*.

Hollingshead, A. B., McGrath, J. E., & O'Connor, K.M. (1993, August). Group Task Performance and Communication Technology: A Longitudinal Study of Computer-Mediated Versus Face-to-Face Work Groups. *Small Group Research*, 307-333.

Holsapple, C.W. & Whinston, A.B. (1996). *Decision Support Systems: A Knowledge-based Approach*. Minneapolis, MN: West Publishing Co.

Hogue, J.T. & Watson, H.J. (1985, April). Current Practices in the Development of Decision Support Systems. *Information and Management*, 205–212.

Houdeshel, G. & Watson, H. (1987, March). The Management Information and Decision Support (MIDS) System at Lockheed-Georgia. *MIS Quarterly 11* (1). (Rev. 1992).

Huber, G.P. (1984, September). Issues in the Design of Group Decision Support Systems. *MIS Quarterly 8* (3), 195–204.

Huber, G.P. (1990). A Theory of the Effects of Advanced Information Technologies on Organizational Design, Intelligence, and Decision Making. *Academy of Management Review 15* (1), 47–71.

Humphreys, P., Ayestaren, S., McCosh, A., & Mayon-White, B. (Eds.). (1997). *Decision Support in Organizational Transformation*. London: Chapman & Hall.

Hunt, C. (1992). *TCP/IP Network Administration*. Sebastopol, CA: O'Reilly & Associates, Inc., 1992.

IBM. (1998). Data Mining: Extending the Information Warehouse Framework. <http://www.almaden.ibm.com/cs/quest/papers/whitepaper.html>.

Inmon, W.H. (1993). *Building the Data Warehouse*. New York: John Wiley & Sons.

Inmon, W.H. (1995). What Is a Data Warehouse? *PRISM 1* (1), <http://www.cait.wustl.edu/cait/papers/prism/vol1_no1/>.

International Data Corporation. (1996). The Foundations of Wisdom: A Study of the Financial Impact of Data Warehousing. Toronto, Canada.

Janis, I.L. & Mann, L. (1977). *Decision Making: A Psychological Analysis of Conflict, Choice and Commitment.* New York: The Free Press.

Jessup, L.M. & Valacich, J.S. (Eds.). (1993). *Group Support Systems: New Perspectives.* New York: Macmillan.

Jones, D. (1997-1999). A University Course on Systems Administration. Department Math and Computing, Central Queensland University. The Study Guide. <http://www.infocom.cqu.edu.au>.

Keen, P.G.W. (1981, March). Value Analysis: Justifying Decision Support Systems. *MIS Quarterly*, 1–15.

Keen, P.G.W. (1991). *Shaping the Future: Business Design Through Information Technology.* Boston, MA: Harvard Business School Press.

Keen, P.G.W. and Scott Morton, M. S. (1978). *Decision Support Systems: An Organizational Perspective.* Reading, MA: Addison-Wesley.

Keenan, P. (1997). Using a GIS as a DSS Generator. Working Paper MIS 95/9, Department of MIS, Graduate School of Business, University College Dublin. <http://mis.ucd.ie>.

Kirkner, B., Ladd, E., O'Donnell, J. et al. (1996). *Running a Perfect Netscape Site.* Indianapolis, IN: Que.

Kelly, F. (1997). Implementing an EIS. *CEOReview.com.* <http://www.ceoreview.com>.

Kettinger, W., Grover, V., Guha, S., & Segars, A. (1994). Strategic Information Systems Revisited. *MIS Quarterly,* 31–55.

Kimball, R. (1996). *The Data Warehouse Toolkit: Practical Techniques for Building Dimensional Data Warehouses.* New York: John Wiley & Sons.

Lambert, R. (1996, March). Data Warehousing Fundamentals: What You Need to Know to Succeed. *Data Management Review.* <http://www.data-warehouse.com/resource/articles/lamb8.htm>.

Larson, J. (1982). *End User Facilities in the Nineteen Eighties.* Los Alamitos, CA: IEEE Computer Society.

Lee, S. M., Moore, L. J. & Taylor, B.W., III. (1985). *Management Science* (2nd ed.). Dubuque, IA: Wm. C. Brown Publishers, 431–434.

Little, J.D.C. (1970, April). Models and Managers: The Concept of a Decision Calculus. *Management Science 16* (8), B466–485.

Little, J.D.C. (1975). Brandaid, an On-Line Marketing Mix Model, Part 2: Implementation, Calibration and Case Study. *Operations Research 23* (4), 656-673.

Mallach, E. (1994). *Understanding Decision Support Systems and Expert Systems.* Burr Ridge, IL: Irwin.

Makridakis, S. & Wheelwright, S.C. (1982). *The Handbook of Forecasting: A Manager's Guide.* New York: Wiley.

Marakas, G. (1999). *Decision Support Technology for the 21st Century.* Englewood Cliffs, NJ: Prentice-Hall.

Martin, E., DeHayes, D., Hofer, J., & Perkins, W. (1994). *Managing Information Technology: What Managers Need to Know*. New York: Macmillan Publishing Co.

McDermmot, J. (1984). Building Expert Systems. In W. Reitman (Ed.), *Artificial Intelligence Applications for Business*. Norwood, NJ: Ablex.

McFarlan, F.W., McKenney, J.L., & Pyburn, P. (1983, January/February). The Information Archipelago – Plotting a Course. *Harvard Business Review*.

McGoff, C., Hunt, A., Vogel D., & Nunamaker, J. (1990, November-December). IBM's Experiences with GroupSystems. *Interfaces*, 39–50.

Methlie, L.B. & Sprague, R.H. (Eds.). (1985). *Knowledge Representation for Decision Support Systems*. Amsterdam: North-Holland.

Michaelsen, R. & Michie, D. (1983, November).   Expert Systems in Business. *Datamation*, 240–246.

Mintzberg, H. (1973). *The Nature of Managerial Work*. New York: Harper and Row.

Mintzberg, H., Raisinghani, D., & Theoret, A. (1976, June). The Structure of "Unstructured" Decision Processes. *Administrative Science Quarterly 21*, 246–275.

Nakayama, Y. & Mizutani, H. (1990). Model-Based Automatic Programming for Plant Control. Proceedings of the 6th Conference on Artificial Intelligence Applications.

Nemeth, E., Snyder, G., Seebass, S., & Hein, T. (1995). *UNIX System Administration Handbook* (2nd ed.). Upper Saddle River, NJ: Prentice-Hall.

Neumann, S. (1994). *Strategic Information Systems: Competition Through Information Technologies*. New York: Macmillan.

Nolan, R.L. (1983, Winter).   Building the Company's Computer Architecture Strategic Plan. *Stage by Stage* (Nolan, Norton & Company) 2: 1-7.

O'Neil, B., Schrader, M., Dakin, J. and others. (1997). *Oracle Data Warehousing*. Indianapolis, IN: SAMS Publishing, 1997.

Parker, M.M. (1996).   *Strategic Transformation and Information Technology*. Upper Saddle River, NJ: Prentice Hall.

Parker, M.M., Trainor, H.E., & Benson, R. J. (1989). *Information Strategy and Economics*. Upper Saddle River, NJ: Prentice Hall.

Pendse, N. (1998, January 11).   What Is OLAP? *The OLAP Report*, <http://www.olapreport.html/FASMI.HTM>.

Pendse, N. (1999, November 4). The Origins of Today's OLAP Products. *The OLAP Report*. <http://www.olapreport.com/origins.htm>.

Phusitasai, S. (1998, June). "Virtual Organization": Management Trend in the Future. *IAVO On-line Journal*.

Porter, M.E. (1979, March-April). How Competitive Forces Shape Strategy. *Harvard Business Review*.

Porter, M.E. & Millar, V.E. (1985, July-August). How Information Gives You Competitive Advantage. *Harvard Business Review*.

Porter, R. (1994). The Data Warehouse: 2 Years Later Lessons Learned. *CAUSE Conference*. ID Number: CNC9446.

Powell, R. (2001, February). DM Review: A 10 Year Journey. *DM Review*. <http://www.dmreview.com>.

Power, D.J. (1983, September). The Impact of Information Management on the Organization: Two Scenarios. *MIS Quarterly 7*(3), 13–20.

Power, D.J. (1985). Using the Symptoms, Problems and Treatment Framework to Structure Knowledge for Management Expert Systems. In L. Methlie, L. & R. Sprague (Ed.), *Knowledge Representation for Decision Support Systems*, 245–254. New York: North-Holland Publishing Co.

Power, D.J. (1988, June). Anticipating Organization Structures. In J. Hage (Ed.), *Futures of Organizations*, 67–79. New York: Lexington Books.

Power, D.J., Meyeraan, S., & Aldag, R. (1994). Impacts of Problem Structure and Computerized Decision Aids on Decision Attitudes and Behaviors. *Information and Management 26*, 281–294.

Power, D.J. (1997, October 21). What Is a DSS? *DSStar 1* (3). <http://dssresources.com/papers/whatisadss>.

Power, D.J. (1998). Finding DSS Resources on the World Wide Web. *Journal of Decision Systems 7*, 7–20.

Power, D. J. (1998, August 18, 25). Web-Based Decision Support Systems. Part I and II. *DSStar 1* (33/34).

Power, D.J. (2000, October). A History of Microcomputer Spreadsheets. *Communications of the Association for Information Systems 4,* Article 9.

Power, D.J. (1998, February 3, 10). Justifying a Data Warehouse Project. Part I and II. *DSStar 2* (5/6).

Power, D.J. (2001, June). Supporting Decision-Makers: An Expanded Framework. *Informing Science eBook*.

Power, D.J. (2000, August). Web-Based and Model-Driven Decision Support Systems: Concepts and Issues. Proceeding of Americas Conference on Information Systems, Long Beach, CA.

Power, D. J. & Hevner, A.R. (1985, April). Executive Workstations: Issues and Requirements. *Information and Management 8*, 213–220.

Pritsker, A.B. and Sigal, C.E. (1983). *Management Decision Making: A Network Simulation Approach*. Englewood Cliffs, NJ: Prentice-Hall.

Quinn, P., Andrews, B., and Parsons, H. (1991, January-February). Allocating Telecommunications Resources at L.L. Bean, Inc. *Management Science 21*(1), 75–91.

Raden, N. (1995, October 30). Data, Data Everywhere. *Information Week*.

Raiffa, H. (1968). *Decision Analysis*. New York: Random House.

Rakshit, A., Krishnamurthy, N. and Yu, G. (1996, March-April). System Operations Advisor: A Real-Time Decision Support System for Managing Airline Operations at United Airlines. *Interfaces 26* (2).

Render, B. & Stair, R.M., Jr. (1988). *Quantitative Analysis for Management* (3rd ed.). Needham Heights, MA: Allyn and Bacon.

Rob, P. and Coronell, C. (1997). *Database Systems: Design, Implementation, and Management*. Cambridge, MA: Course Technology.

Rockart, J.F. (1979, March/April). Chief Executives Define Their Own Data Needs. *Harvard Business Review*.

Saaty, T.L. (1980). *The Analytic Hierarchy Process*. New York: McGraw-Hill.

Saaty, T.L. (1990). How to Make a Decision: The Analytic Hierarchy Process. *European Journal of Operations Research 48,* 9–26.

Sauter, V. (1997). *Decision Support Systems.* New York: John Wiley & Sons.

Schoemaker, P. (1995, Winter). Scenario Planning: A Tool for Strategic Thinking. *Sloan Management Review,* 25–40.

Scott Morton, M.S. (1971). *Management Decision Systems: Computer-based Support for Decision Making.* Boston, MA: Division of Research, Graduate School of Business Administration, Harvard University.

Sharp, D. J. (1991, Summer). Uncovering the Hidden Value in High Risk Investments. *Sloan Management Review,* 69–74.

Shneiderman, B. (1992). *Designing the User Interface: Strategies for Effective Human-Computer Interaction* (2nd ed.). Reading, MA: Addison-Wesley.

Silver, M.S. (1991, March). Decisional Guidance for Computer-based Decision Support. *MIS Quarterly 15* (1), 105–122.

Silver, M.S. (1991). *Systems that Support Decision Makers: Description and Analysis.* Chichester, UK: John Wiley & Sons.

Simon, H.A. (1965). The New Science of Management Decision. *The Shape of Automation for Men and Management.* New York: Harper Torch Books.

Smith, B.C., Leimkuhler, J. F., & Darrow, R. M. (1992). Yield Management at American Airlines. *Interfaces,* 8–31.

Sprague, R.H., Jr.. (1980, December). A Framework for the Development of Decision Support System. *MIS Quarterly 4* (4).

Sprague, R.H. & Carlson, E.D. (1982). *Building Effective Decision Support Systems.* Englewood Cliffs, NJ: Prentice-Hall.

Sprague, R.H. & Watson, H.J. (Eds.). (1996). *Decision Support for Management.* Englewood Cliffs, NJ: Prentice-Hall: 1996.

Stabell, C.B. (1983). A Decision-Oriented Approach to Building DSS. Chapter 10 in Bennett, J. L., *Building Decision Support Systems.* Reading, MA: Addison-Wesley, 1983.

Starfield. A.M., Smith, K. A. Bleloch., A. L. (1990). *How to Model It: Problem Solving for the Computer Age.* New York: McGraw-Hill.

Sullivan, D. (2001). *Document Warehousing and Text Mining.* New York: Wiley Computer Publishing.

Swain, J. J. (1997, October). Simulation Goes Mainstream. *OR/MS Today.*

Swanson, E.B. & M.J. Culnan. (1978, December). Document-Based Systems for Management Planning and Control: A Classification, Survey, and Assessment. *MIS Quarterly.*

Tauhert, C. (1998, March). For Underwriting, NC Blue Turns to an Expert. *Insurance & Technology Magazine.*

Tapscott, D. (1998, November 17). How Are Internet Technologies Changing Industries? *USA TODAY.* <http://www.usatoday.com>.

Taylor, W. (1995, November). At Verifone It's a Dog's Life (And They Love It!). Fast Company. <http://www.fastcompany.com>.

Taylor, L. (Ed.). (1998). Client/Server Frequently Asked Questions. <http://www.abs.net/~lloyd/csfaq.txt>.

Thearling, K. (1998). Data Mining and Advanced DSS Technology, an On-Line Data Mining Tutorial. <http://www3.shore.net>.

Thierauf, R.J. (1982). *Decision Support for Effective Planning and Control: A Case Study Approach.* Englewood Cliffs, NJ: Prentice Hall.

Thomsen, E. (1997). *OLAP Solutions: Building Multidimensional Information Systems.* New York: John Wiley.

Trull, S. G. (1966, February). Some Factors Involved in Determining Total Decision Success. *Management Science*, B-270–B-280.

Turban, E. (1995). *Decision Support and Expert Systems: Management Support Systems* (4th ed.). Englewood Cliffs, NJ: Prentice Hall.

Turban, E. & Aronson, J. (1998). *Decision Support Systems and Intelligent Systems* (5th ed.). Englewood Cliffs, NJ: Prentice-Hall.

Tyo, J. (1996, July 8, 15). OLAP Tools. *Information Week.* <http://techweb.cmp.com>.

Udo, G.J. & Guimares, T. (1994, July) Empirically Assessing Factors Related to DSS Benefit. *European Journal of Information Systems.*

Vickers, G. (1967). *Towards a Sociology of Management.* New York: Basic Books.

Vine, D. (1995, May). Bending Space and Time: The Virtual Organization. *Internet World.*

Vroom, V. & Yetton, P. (1973). *Leadership and Decision-Making,* Pittsburgh: University of Pittsburgh Press.

Watson, S.R. & Buede, D.M. (1987). *Decision Synthesis: The Principles and Practice of Decision Analysis.* Cambridge: Cambridge University Press.

Watson, H.J., Rainer, R.K., & Houdeshel, G. (1992). *Executive Information Systems: Emergence, Development, Impact.* New York: John Wiley & Sons.

Waterman, D.A. (1986). *A Guide to Expert Systems.* Reading, MA: Addison-Wesley.

Webster, J. (2000, October 30). Shared Knowledge Builds Partnerships. *InternetWeek Online.*

Whitten, J.L., Bentley, L.D., & Barlow, V. M. (1994). *Systems Analysis and Design Methods* (3rd ed.). Burr Ridge, IL: Irwin.

Yoon, Y., Guimaraes, T., & O'Neal, Q. (1995, March). Exploring the Factors Associated with Expert Systems Success. *MIS Quarterly 19* (1), 83-106.

Index

About the Author

DANIEL J. POWER is Professor of Information Systems and Management at the College of Business Administration, University of Northern Iowa, Cedar Falls. He holds a doctorate in Business Administration from the University of Wisconsin–Madison, has developed decision support software and systems, and in his research studies has examined impacts of DSS on managers. Dr. Power has published numerous book chapters and proceedings papers and has authored more than 20 articles for the important journals of his field. He also serves as editor of DSSResources.COM, the knowledge repository about computerized systems that support decision making.